Praise for *The State of the Univ*

"Positioning himself against Yale Universit
defense of Liberal Education as a crucial source for 'the preservation of individual freedom,' Stanley Hauerwas asks the obvious but uncomfortable question, freedom for what? If students pass through the courses in the curriculum as consumers and sightseers, they will replicate and extend the modern malaise of a life lived without reference to anything that makes its moments intelligible. If the university is to be more than a reflection of an atomized society, those who live in it, says Hauerwas, must ask two questions academics either avoid (here I am one of his examples) or answer with empty pieties: what is a university for and whom does it serve? It is the great merit of Hauerwas' book that it refuses to back away from these questions, even as it acknowledges the difficulty of giving a full and satisfying answer to them. A witty, learned, and very human meditation on the relationship between the factories of knowledge and the knowledge of God."

Stanley Fish, Florida International University

"With characteristic conversational energy, Hauerwas asks his readers to take seriously the difference that those who confess the God of the gospel can bring to institutions of learning. The book grows out of the free, generous, and lively wisdom of faith, and deserves to be widely debated."

John Webster, King's College, Aberdeen

"This book by an eminent Christian theologian is provocative for thinking fruitfully about our troubled times. Hauerwas has a subtle, learned, and compassionate mind, which he brings to bear on the secular state in which we live and on the secular knowledge produced in our universities to serve it. Non-Christians like myself will find reading this book a mind-widening experience."

Talal Asad, CUNY

"Whether one agrees or disagrees with some of the positions Hauerwas stakes out, reading his work is always a bracing intellectual experience – and a deeply Christian one. *The State of the University* proves no exception. With characteristic theological craftsmanship, humor, and passion, Hauerwas turns his sights on the contemporary university, in all its dignity, wrongheadedness, goodness, and confusion. Anyone interested in the fate of theological knowledge in contemporary society, anyone interested in serious education (or lack thereof) in liberal democracies, anyone who cares for the mission of the church in the twenty-first century will profit considerably from reading and rereading this book."

Thomas Albert Howard, Gordon College, University of Oxford

Illuminations: Theory and Religion

Series editors: Catherine Pickstock, John Milbank, and Graham Ward

Religion has a growing visibility in the world at large. Throughout the humanities there is a mounting realization that religion and culture lie so closely together that religion is an unavoidable and fundamental human reality. Consequently, the examination of religion and theology now stands at the centre of any questioning of our western identity, including the question of whether there is such a thing as "truth."

ILLUMINATIONS aims both to reflect the diverse elements of these developments and, from them, to produce creative new syntheses. It is unique in exploring the new interaction between theology, philosophy, religious studies, political theory, and cultural studies. Despite the theoretical convergence of certain trends they often in practice do not come together. The aim of ILLUMINATIONS is to make this happen, and advance contemporary theoretical discussion.

Published:
Sacrifice and Community: Jewish Offering and Christian Eucharist
Matthew Levering

The Other Calling: Theology, Intellectual Vocation and Truth
Andrew Shanks

The State of the University: Academic Knowledges and the Knowledge of God
Stanley Hauerwas

Forthcoming:
The End of Work: Theological Critiques of Capitalism
John Hughes

The State of the University

Academic Knowledges and the Knowledge of God

Stanley Hauerwas

Blackwell Publishing

BLACKWELL PUBLISHING
350 Main Street, Malden, MA 02148-5020, USA
9600 Garsington Road, Oxford OX4 2DQ, UK
550 Swanston Street, Carlton, Victoria 3053, Australia

First published 2007 by Blackwell Publishing Ltd

3 2008

Library of Congress Cataloging-in-Publication Data

Hauerwas, Stanley, 1940–
The state of the university : academic knowledges and the knowledge of God / by Stanley Hauerwas.
p. cm.—(Illuminations : theory and religion)
Includes bibliographical references and index.
ISBN 978-1-4051-6247-0 (hardcover : alk. paper) — ISBN 978-1-4051-6248-7 (pbk. : alk. paper)
1. God (Christianity)—Study and teaching. 2. Knowledge, Theory of (Religion) 3. Christian education. 4. Church and education. I. Title.

BT108.H38 2007
230.071′1—dc22

2006034808

A catalogue record for this title is available from the British Library.

Set in 10.5/12pt Sabon
by SPi Publisher Services, Pondicherry, India
Printed and bound in Singapore
by Markono Print Media Pte Ltd

The publisher's policy is to use permanent paper from mills that operate a sustainable forestry policy, and which has been manufactured from pulp processed using acid-free and elementary chlorine-free practices. Furthermore, the publisher ensures that the text paper and cover board used have met acceptable environmental accreditation standards.

For further information on
Blackwell Publishing, visit our website:
www.blackwellpublishing.com

To

Sylvester Evans
Donald Fogg
Savannah Hall
Joanna Hauerwas
Dawn Haughton
Paula Hunter
Greg Jones
Willie Torain
Adrianne Wesley

Contents

Contents

Preface

Greg Jones told me to write a book like this. So he is to be held accountable for whatever is good in the book as well as whatever is not so good. Greg is not only a good friend, but he is also my Dean. The amount of work he must do to sustain the work of the Divinity School I suspect few of us appreciate. It, therefore, gives me great pleasure to include him among those to whom this book is dedicated.

I get up at five every morning and I get to work by six. But Sylvester, Donald, Savannah, Dawn, Adrianne, Paula, and Willie have already long been at work readying the Divinity School for another day. The amount of work they must do to sustain the work of the Divinity School I suspect few of us appreciate. It, therefore, gives me great pleasure to dedicate this book to them.

Joanna Hauerwas, my mother, lived a life that was a life of work. She came from hard-scrabble Mississippi only to marry a Texas bricklayer. Mother died on May 2, 2006 at the age of 92. The amount of work she had to do to sustain my life I suspect I have never fully appreciated. It, therefore, gives me great pleasure to include her among those to whom this book is dedicated.

Carole Baker, my assistant, has done the work necessary to bring this book to print. But more importantly she has read and helped me say better what I have often not said well. Sheila McCarthy read and criticized these essays and in general helped me think about the form this book should take. Without Paula Gilbert my life, and the work necessary for writing books like this, would not be possible. She also works hard, but her love has taught me how to rest.

Introduction

I am a creature of two distinct but interrelated worlds – the university and the church. It is not clear to me which of those worlds has had the most determinative shaping for my life. I have, therefore, often reflected as well as written on the relation between the church and the university no doubt with a view of trying to make sense of my life. This book, however, is my first sustained attempt to explore systematically how Christians might understand our participation in the work of the university as well as the difference Christian practice might make for how the work of the university is understood.[1]

But *The State of the University: Academic Knowledges and the Knowledge of God* is not another book about the relation of the church and the university. I have read and learned much from George Marsden and James Burtchaell, but this book is not primarily about what has been or should be the relation between the church and the university. Rather this book is my attempt to explore and test the way I have been taught and continue to try to teach myself how to do Christian theology. Accordingly *The State of the University* develops the suggestions I made in the

[1] One of the first articles I published tried to address the turmoil surrounding the university occasioned by the civil rights movement and the anti-Vietnam protest. I wrote it during my second year of teaching at Augustana College in Rock Island, Illinois. It was published with the title, "Problematics of a 'Christian College' " in the Lutheran magazine, *The Cresset*, 34, 4 (May, 1971), pp. 6–8. I am pleased to note that *The Cresset* has begun to publish essays from the past and one of the essays chosen was "Problematics of a 'Christian College' " which appeared in *The Cresset*, 66, 5 (June, 2003), pp. 54–7. For anyone interested in my past reflections on the university there are two chapters on the relation of the university to the church in *Christian Existence Today: Essays on Church, World, and Living In Between* (Grand Rapids: Brazos Press, 1995), pp. 199–237. *Christian Existence Today* was originally published in 1988. The chapters are entitled "Truth and Honor: The University and the Church in a Democratic Age" and "How Christian Universities Contribute to the Corruption of the Youth". *After Christendom?* (Nashville: Abingdon Press, 1999) has a chapter entitled "The Politics of Witness: How We Educate Christians in a Liberal Society," pp. 133–52. The new Preface in this second edition might be of interest to those following Stout's criticisms of me. "Christians in the Hands of Flaccid Secularists: Theology and 'Moral Inquiry' in the Modern University" is in *Sanctify Them in the Truth: Holiness Exemplified* (Edinburgh: T & T Clark, 1998), pp. 201–18.

last chapter of *With the Grain of the Universe: The Church's Witness and Natural Theology*.[2] I begin to explore there the difference my Barthian account of "natural theology" might make for the knowledges characteristic of the modern university as well as how those knowledges might be theologically disciplined.

I ended *With the Grain of the Universe* with a discussion of the university in imitation of Alasdair MacIntyre who tested his argument in the Gifford Lectures, *Three Rival Versions of Moral Enquiry: Encyclopedia, Genealogy, and Tradition*, by providing an account of the implications for the organization of the modern university.[3] In a similar fashion I thought it useful to provide an analysis of the university's role in the formation of knowledges that often make it difficult for Christians to make rational sense of what we believe both for ourselves as well as for those who do not share the practices of our faith. Indeed I fear too often university curriculums make it impossible for anyone, Christian and non-Christian alike, to make sense of the world in which we find ourselves.

Of course some think the way I have done theology makes it impossible for Christians to make sense of or participate in the world. I have not written *The State of the University* to counter such judgments, but I hope some of the chapters of this book will at least "puzzle" those who accuse me of recommending that Christians withdraw from the world. Indeed I hope that readers may find a "humanism" represented in this book that challenges those who think anyone with my Christological and ecclesial convictions cannot be in conversation with those who do not share my convictions. Bruce Marshall, in an article on George Lindbeck's work, says what I take to be the case; that is,

> if Christian identity is forged by the God who has accepted our flesh and death for the life of the world (and not just of the church), then the church's engagement with the world will intensify precisely as her concentration on her identity in Christ intensifies, and will diminish as the church loses a sense of her own distinctive identity. In this case the church's vivid sense of her mission to a world made to receive Christ, and the church's commitment to her own identity-constituting doctrines, will tend to vary in direct, not inverse, proportion. There is no logical connection between sociological resistance to cultural assimilation and theologically sectarian withdrawal from the world.[4]

[2] Stanley Hauerwas, *With the Grain of the Universe: The Church's Witness and Natural Theology* (Grand Rapids: Brazos Press, 2001), pp. 231–41.

[3] Alasdair MacIntyre, *Three Rival Versions of Moral Enquiry: Encyclopedia, Genealogy, and Tradition* (Notre Dame: University of Notre Dame Press, 1990), pp. 216–36.

[4] Bruce Marshall, "Lindbeck Abroad," *Pro Ecclesia*, 15, 2 (Spring, 2006), p. 232.

Marshall observes, moreover, that Lindbeck's insistence on the tight connection between practice and belief for understanding what it means for Christians to claim what we believe is true does not mean Lindbeck disavows intrasystematic "truth." Rather it means, at least in my terms, that the truthfulness of Christian convictions depends on the witness of truthful lives. An appeal to the necessity of such witness may suggest to some that to which the witness witnesses does not involve cognitive claims. The burden of the argument in this book, indeed of everything I have written, is to challenge that presumption by suggesting that theology is a knowledge that should rightly be represented in the curriculums of a secular or church-sponsored university.

In her book, *Revelation and Theopolitics: Barth, Rosenzweig, and the Politics of Praise*, Randi Rashkover argues that Barth and Rosenzweig represent a "theology of testimony." By a theology of testimony Rashkover means "a theology that is based on the notion that knowledge of God is possible only in the context of the ethical labor of the elect individual who seeks through her moral endeavor to testify to the loving act of the transcendent God."[5] Rashkover argues such a testimony or witness is an obedient response to a loving and commanding God, but neither Barth nor Rosenzweig reduce the religious life to blind obedience. "Rather, for Rosenzweig, theological witness is expressed and related to the world through a testimony of pragmatic verification. For Barth, witness takes place through the church's self-critical effort to articulate the Word of God in the world prior to the kingdom of God."[6] For both Barth and Rosenzweig, therefore, witness is a practical deed.[7]

Rashkover's account of a "theology of testimony" is similar to my emphasis on "witness" as the necessary condition for any consideration of the truthfulness of Christian convictions.[8] Witness, moreover, is a characteristic exemplified not only in lives but also in the knowledges that such lives exhibit and produce. Universities are one of the locations for the articulation as well as the testing of our knowledges. By focusing on the university, therefore, I hope to explore what it means for Christians to claim that what we believe reveals as well as is in accordance with the grain of the universe.

5 Randi Rashkover, *Revelation and Theopolitics: Barth, Rosenzweig, and the Politics of Praise* (London: T & T Clark, 2005), p. 3.

6 Rashkover, *Revelation and Theopolitics*, p. 5.

7 Thus my presentation of Barth's theology in *With the Grain of the Universe* as an exemplification of James's understanding of verification in *The Will to Believe*, that is, that the truth of much that we believe depends on our having the virtues required in order to know the way things are (*With the Grain of the Universe*, pp. 50–61).

8 Rashkover's identification of the individual does not, I think, mean she assumes such an individual exists separate from the community that makes them individual. Nor does her appeal to "transcendence" assume that transcendence is a predication of God more determinative than God's covenant with Israel. I mention these issues only because some may think they suggest that Rashkover's understanding of testimony is quite different than my understanding of witness. I do not think that to be the case.

That project is the reason several of the essays in this book are not directly about the university. For example, Chapter 2, "Leaving Ruins: The Gospel and Cultural Formations" is my attempt to show that Yoder's critique of "Constantinianism" does not entail the presumption that Christians have no stake in the production of a material culture. Indeed the exact opposite is the case if, as Yoder also argues, the alternative to Constantinianism is not to be anti-Constantinian, but rather to develop local forms of life that can sustain the necessary visibility of the church as an alternative to the world. "Leaving Ruins," therefore, is my attempt to show how memory must have material form if the church is to be capable of producing knowledges sufficient to resist those disciplines characteristic of the modern university that would make the church invisible.

This last comment may suggest to some that *The State of the University* continues my alleged "anti-modernist" polemic. I hope, however, that the analysis I provide in this book will suggest I have no idea what it would mean to reject in general something called "modernity." I am quite well aware that there are many "modernities," just as there are many "liberalisms" and "secularisms," but I also think it to be the case that there is a link between the politics that would relegate the church to the private and the knowledges of the university that legitimate the subordination of the church to the state in the name of peace. In several of the chapters in this book, but particularly in "The End of 'Religious Pluralism'," I argue that the very descriptions that are assumed as givens in many university subjects, descriptions such as "religions" and/or "pluralism," legitimate a politics and correlative knowledge that Christians must challenge if we are to serve the "modern" world.[9]

The arrangement of the chapters in this book might have been different, but I hope the reader will find the way I have ordered the chapters to be helpful. The chapters are not in the order in which I wrote them. The first chapter, "Theological Knowledge and the Knowledges of the University: Beginning Explorations," I wrote after I had written "How Risky is *The Risk of Education*," and "Pro Ecclesia, Pro Texana." I put "Theological Knowledge and the Knowledges of the University" at the beginning, however, because I think that essay provides an overview in which the subsequent chapters can best be read. I hope the reader will take seriously the subtitle, "Beginning Explorations." I certainly do not think I have answered the question, "What kind of knowledge is theology?" in this book. Nor have I adequately begun to show how the knowledge of God compares with other knowledges.

I hope this book is a good beginning toward addressing those questions, but it is just that – a beginning. Hans Frei's essay, "The Case of Berlin, 1810" in his *Types of Christian Theology* is the necessary place anyone must begin who wishes to wrestle with the question of theological

9 Peter Ochs rightly reminds me that our task is never to "reject" but to "repair" the wounds of modernity – wounds too often inflicted by Christian unfaithfulness.

knowledge.[10] Frei focuses on the University of Berlin because he takes it to be as close as one can get in reality to the ideal type of a *Wissenschaft* university. According to Frei the University of Berlin was founded on the presumption that all specific fields should meet the test of being an "inquiry into the universal, rational principles" so that the subjects that constituted the university would be internally and mutually coherent.[11]

Frei observes that this understanding of the university was secular not only in the sense of being religiously neutral, but also because it prohibited any allegiance from inhibiting the free exercise of critical reason. Christian theology, as Kant had argued in his "The Conflict of the Faculties," was exactly the kind of allegiance that could not pass the test of critical reason.[12] Under such a regime theology could only be a university subject by being transformed into a historical discipline. Theology proper could be included in a university, according to Kant, only if it was understood to be a knowledge necessary for the professional training of ministers who were to be trained as civil servants in service to the state.

Frei's analysis of the fate of theology as determined by the University of Berlin is the necessary background for the argument of *The State of the University*. For I try to show, that in spite of the quite different presumptions about the nature of the university in America, the implications for theology as a knowledge worthy of inclusion in the modern university have been very similar to those Frei describes in his essay on

10 Hans Frei, *Types of Christian Theology*, edited by George Hunsinger and William Placher (New Haven: Yale University Press, 1992), pp. 95–115.

11 Frei, *Types of Christian Theology*, p. 98. *The State of the University* was written before Thomas Albert Howard's book, *Protestant Theology and the Making of the Modern German University* (Oxford: Oxford University Press, 2006), was published. Howard's book confirms Frei's account of the transformation of theology necessary for theology to become a university subject. Howard notes, however, that Schleiermacher, while conceding the state's interest in the university and theology, feared the state "would 'gradually appropriate and absorb them into itself so that subsequently one can no longer decide whether they have arisen freely and for their own purposes or by administrative fiat.' "(p. 170) Yet Howard's account makes clear that is exactly what happened in the name of developing a "theological science" exemplified most fully in Harnack. Howard ends his book with an account of the Harnack/Barth exchange from 1923 suggesting that their "debate's polarizing points and counterpoints, its echoes of past and anticipation of future conflicts, and the far reaching institutional, intellectual, and deeply personal stakes involved, remains today a rich and relevant heritage, and a profoundly conflicted one. We remain, perhaps, between the times." (p. 418) A lovely conclusion if I am right that the knowledges constitutive of the modern university are designed to deny that we live "between the times." I recommend Howard's book as crucial for anyone interested in the issues raised in *The State of the University*.

12 Emmanuel Kant, *The Conflict of the Faculties* in *Religion and Rational Theology*, translated and edited by Allen Wood and George DiGiovanni (Cambridge: Cambridge University Press, 1996). For a detailed account of the role of Kant for the transformation of the university see Randall Collins, *The Sociology of Philosophies: A Global Theory of Intellectual Change* (Cambridge: Harvard University Press, 1998), pp. 618–87.

the University of Berlin. The American universities were, of course, anything but the exemplification of one ideal type. American universities were, and often still are, strange combinations of the German research university, joined to the English university tradition in which the university is assumed to be the place where the moral character of students is determined, yet trying, as French universities do, to train "young, middle-class men to be officials of the state and servants of society."[13] Given the complex character of American universities, particularly given the support of many American universities by various churches, one would think theology might have been recognized as a knowledge crucial to the work of the university. But in fact theology as a knowledge in general has fared no better in American universities than it did at the University of Berlin.

The title, *The State of the University*, is not meant, therefore, to suggest that I am trying to provide an assessment of the current state of the university though there is some of that kind of work done in this book. Rather the title is meant to indicate that universities as we know them, public or private, secular or religious, produce and reproduce knowledges that both reflect and serve the state. The university is the great institution of legitimation in modernity whose task is to convince us that the way things are is the way things have to be. The specialization, what some would describe as fragmentation, of the knowledges that constitute the curriculums of the modern university is crucial for the formation of people to be faithful servants of the status quo and, in particular, the modern nation state.

It is tempting to justify the inclusion of theology in the university as one more specialized form of knowledge. But the attempt to make theology a subject among other subjects cannot help but make theology something it is not.[14] Theology properly understood as knowledge of

13 Steven Marcus, "Humanities from Classics to Cultural Studies: Notes Toward the History of an Idea," *Daedalus*, 135, 2 (Spring, 2006), p. 15. Marcus's account of the various influences on the development of American higher education is an oversimplification, but such generalizations are quite helpful. The argument of *The State of the University* turns Kant on his head. Kant argued medicine, law, and theology could be included in the university because they served the state. The "lower" faculty was to be independent of government because it is concerned only with truth discovered by reason. I argue that most subjects in the contemporary university Kant associated with "reason" now primarily serve the state and that theology is one of the few disciplines that has a chance to be free and rational.

14 Paul Griffiths makes this point in his reply to James Stoner's, "Theology as Knowledge: A Symposium" in *First Things*, 163 (May, 2006), pp. 24–6. Griffiths quite rightly argues that the object of theology is God, making theology a quite different discipline than those that deal with politics, birds, or the cosmos. Griffiths observes God, properly considered, cannot be part of the metaphysical furniture of the universe. Accordingly Griffiths argues that God's essence cannot be known by reason because this would make God not God. Which means that theology is different from any other university subject. I am not convinced, however, that this means, as Griffiths argues, that theology is a knowledge that has no place in the *Wissenschaft* university. Griffiths does observe that the philosophical presuppositions of the modern university may themselves be deeply confused.

God means theology cannot be restricted to one "field." Therefore in *The State of the University* I try to suggest the difference theology might make for the production of knowledges in universities who owe their existence to the church. Of course I am happily not alone in this endeavor. Many Christian academics are beginning to explore the difference their faith might make for how they pursue their subject.[15] The kind of questions that need to be explored, however, goes well beyond questions about what difference it might make for how someone understands their work in a field as a Christian. I think if we are to have our knowledges shaped by the radical character of the Gospel, Christians may well find that the disciplines they represent may be quite different than those shaped in universities that do not serve the church.[16]

Please note I am not trying to argue for something called the Christian University. Sam Wells has pointed out to me when "Christian" is used as an adjective you can be confident that you are reproducing the habits of Constantinianism. Rather I am pressing the question of the difference church practices might make for the very shape of knowledges in the university. Given, for example, the Gospel imperative that we are to forgive enemies; what difference might that make for the practice of the law? Given that we believe that all creation glorifies God, how should we think about the attempt to reduce creation to "nature" in the name of mechanistic explanations? These are not questions I think should or could only be asked at universities shaped by the church, but hopefully such questions should be on the agenda of any university that deserves the name university.

15 See, for example, the recent anthologies: *Christianity and the Soul of the University: Faith as a Foundation for Intellectual Community*, edited by Douglas Henry and Michael Beaty (Grand Rapids: Baker, 2006) and *Scholarship and Christian Faith: Enlarging the Conversation*, edited by Douglas Jacobsen and Rhonda Hustedt Jacobsen (Oxford: Oxford University Press, 2004).

16 I certainly admire, however, those that press questions about the methodological constraints of a field that prevent strong religious convictions from being considered. See, for example, Scott Thomas's recent challenge to the field of international relations in his *The Global Resurgence of Religion and the Transformation of International Relations: The Struggle for the Soul of the Twenty-First Century* (New York: Palgrave, 2005). I am also quite impressed by efforts to do the kind of interdisciplinary work represented by Wentzel van Huyssteen in his *Alone in the World: Human Uniqueness in Science and Theology* (Grand Rapids: Eerdmans, 2006). I am sure he is right to suggest that given the multidimensional nature of human rationality we theologians should be able to, indeed we must, enter into "a pluralist interdisciplinary conversation" (p. 17). I confess I am less sure than van Huyssteen that we know what we are talking about when we talk of human uniqueness, but I take the question of human uniqueness to be a fruitful agenda. Like van Huyssteen I too am critical of speculative accounts of the Imago Dei, but my concerns are shaped more by Christological issues than his – i.e., I believe the main reason we have to think the human plays a particular role in the economy of salvation is that the Second Person of the Trinity was conceived in Mary. Finally, van Huyssteen is admirably clear that his account cannot "prove" God but rather at the most suggests that intrinsic to the human is a religious dimension and experience. That may be so, but even if it is I am not clear what theological significance such a dimension does or should have.

I cannot nor do I wish to deny that the position I develop in this book is ambiguous. For example, some may wonder, given my critique of the secular university, whether I want Christians to continue to support as well as teach at those universities. Or do I want Christians to establish new universities determined by curriculums shaped by Christian practices? I do not know how to answer these questions. I certainly do not want Christians to abandon the secular university. Those universities are not secular through and through any more than universities that claim to be Christian are Christian through and through. I am not even sure I think any university is a university through and through. I assume, therefore, if a "secular" university is open to the challenge Christians should represent then no Christian should turn down that opportunity. Indeed I assume we are in an in-between time in which secular universities may be more hospitable to Christian knowledges than many universities that are allegedly Christian.

Of course, as I suggest in *The State of the University*, the question is not whether a university might be open to a knowledge shaped by the practice of the church, but rather whether a church exists to produce a knowledge that is formed by the Gospel. In this book I try to identify some of the pathologies that have stilled the Christian imagination and intellect. In particular I argue that Wendell Berry has rightly challenged the penchant for abstraction so characteristic of the contemporary university. Nothing is more abstract or abstractive than money and money unfortunately too often makes it unnecessary for universities to be articulate about why the knowledges they legitimate should be university subjects or whom such knowledges serve. The modernist presumption that knowledge is an end in itself is just the kind of justification one would expect to be given by universities in a capitalist market. Unfortunately that presumption has been one that has tempted Christians to confuse what it means to be catholic with the abstractions that characterize the false universalisms of modernity.

Interestingly enough if locality is the alternative to Constantinianism it is also the alternative to the abstractions created by as well as to justify the knowledges that legitimate the liberal state. The chapters in the second half of *The State of the University* are attempts to provide exemplifications of how locality and the liturgical time of the church has the potential to provide some resistance to the abstractions that dominate the discourse of the allegedly "global" universities.[17] In particular "Pro Ecclesia, Pro Texana" challenges the presumption that the teaching of ethics is sufficient to insure that graduates are virtuous.[18]

[17] For the development of this understanding of liturgy, time, and politics see *Liturgy, Time and the Politics of Redemption*, edited by C.C. Pecknold and Randi Rashkover (Grand Rapids: Eerdmans, 2006).

[18] I wrote "Pro Ecclesia, Pro Texana" before the publication of Harry R. Lewis's *Excellence Without a Soul: How a Great University Forgot Education* (New York: Public Affairs, 2006). I think, however, his book not only confirms my analysis of the contemporary university but also exemplifies why there is no constructive response

I believe, for example, that the US invasion of Iraq is a crucial test case for the work of the university. Even though many people associated with universities in America are critics of the war in Iraq, that war was conceived, prosecuted, and continues to be justified by those whose understanding of the world was shaped by the university.[19] I have included the chapter on "Christians and the So-Called State (We Are In)" to suggest the difference a Christian perspective should make if we are to attain a critical distance from the rhetoric of war after September 11, 2001, but also because in that essay I suggest how abstraction can lead to war. If the universities of America had been training graduates to exercise the word care, which should be a characteristic of an educated person, at least some doubt might have been raised in response to the claim after September 11, 2001 that "We are at war."[20]

I have included "Democratic Time" not only because it sets the stage for the argument of "The State of the Secular," but also because by responding to Stout's challenge in *Democracy and Tradition* I indicate that a recovery of theological knowledge will also entail a distinct politics. I am not anti-democratic, but I fear too often appeals to democracy underwrite accounts of time that seduce Christians to forget that we believe we live in a quite different time constituted by the worship of God. The knowledges characteristic of the modern university, allegedly produced to serve democratic processes, betray the presumption we do not have the time to do the hard, slow work of peace. I believe, as I argue in "The State of the Secular," that universities shaped by prayer at least have the possibility to produce knowledges that embody the patience that is an alternative to the world's impatience. Moreover I am convinced that any

on strictly secular grounds. Lewis quite rightly argues that "the university has lost, indeed has willingly surrendered, its moral authority to shape the soul of its students" (p. 159–60), but he fails to see that his appeal to "the Enlightenment ideal of human liberty" (p. 62) is the reason no such authority can exist. Lewis sees quite clearly that moral education has withered in the face of the market, but he fails to see how the knowledges represented in the curriculum have created the world he now thinks problematic.

19 Andrew Bacevich has written the definitive study that documents the intellectual developments that have shaped American foreign policy, which has seemed to make war and, in particular, the war in Iraq inevitable. See his *The New American Militarism: How Americans Are Seduced by War* (New York: Oxford University Press, 2005). For an analysis that supports Bacevich's claims see Donald Kennedy, "The Wages of a Mercenary Army: Issues of Civilian and Military Relations," *Bulletin of the American Academy*, LIX, 3 (Spring, 2006), pp. 12–16.

20 The kind of radical rethinking I am trying to suggest required for the production of knowledges that should be characteristic of universities is exemplified in Enda McDonagh's and my "Appeal to Abolish War". See, for example, my essay "Reflections on the 'Appeal to Abolish War'," in *Between Poetry and Politics: Essays in Honor of Enda McDonagh*, edited by Linda Hogan and Barbara Fitzgerald (Dublin: Columba Press, 2003), pp. 135–47 and Stanley Hauerwas, Linda Hogan, Enda McDonagh, "The Case for the Abolition of War in the Twenty-First Century," *Journal of the Society of Christian Ethics*, 25, 2 (Fall/Winter, 2005), pp. 17–36.

democracy worthy of that name requires that people exist who have been shaped by such patience-determined knowledge.[21]

Universities are elite institutions, but I do not think that necessarily makes them anti-democratic particularly if democracy is understood as the politics that refuses to silence the voice of the poor. Christianity is the faith of the poor. The chapter, "To Love God, the Poor, and Learning," is my attempt to suggest what it might look like for the educative task of the church to be disciplined by the love of the poor. The work of the university to produce through research new knowledge is often justified by claiming that such knowledge will give us the power to eradicate poverty and/or eliminate disease. Christians in contrast, at least according to Gregory of Nazianzus, must learn to love the poor. Such a love does not mean we should not work to lessen the plight of the poor, but it does mean such work cannot help but be destructive if we have not learned first to love the poor. Such a love surely must make a difference in the university, for what and how we know what we know as well as how we learn and teach.

I have included the pieces in the Appendices because I like them and they have some relevance to the subject of this book. The first, "The Good of This Place," was written for a panel that was organized as part of the celebration surrounding the inauguration of Richard Brodhead in 2004. I hope this "little speech" suggests I have tried to be a good servant of the university that has graciously given me a place to work and teach for many years. I hope it also expresses my admiration for Richard Brodhead. Universities are obligated to develop elegant speech. Duke is fortunate to have as our president someone who believes in and exemplifies such speech.[22] "Seminaries are in Trouble" at least suggests I am not "picking on" universities unfairly. Seminaries, institutions directly responsible to the church, manifest all the problems I associate with the universities. Therefore I found it fitting to end the book with a

21 I hope soon to explore this understanding of democracy with my colleague and friend Romand Coles. He is already well ahead of me in thinking through what such a democratic practice might look like. See his *Beyond Gated Politics: Reflections for the Possibility of Democracy* (Minneapolis: University of Minnesota Press, 2005). Coles argues that the future of democracy depends on moving beyond dominant forms of liberal democracy by "focusing on cultivating *specific* traditions; communities of deliberation; social, economic, and political practice; virtues; visions of the good or of God" (p. xvii). In doing so Coles thinks local politics provides the crucial training ground for developing the habits necessary for generously listening to one another that is the only alternative we have to avoid bureaucratic professionalization (p. xxviii).

22 Duke, of course, has recently become famous for the horrific behavior of one of our athletic teams. I am often asked why I have not said more about the event. My answer is this book. What happened is not peculiar to Duke, of course, but I worry that the placelessness that threatens Duke is part of the problem. How such an event could happen in the South suggests a forgetfulness indicating that something is deeply problematic about the intellectual formation we give students – and note, the intellectual formation is not nor should it be distinguished from their moral formation.

commencement address I gave at Virginia Theological Seminary that deals with time and involves questions concerning seminary training. Moreover ending this book with a tribute to Rowan Williams I thought particularly appropriate. For one of the ways to ask what universities should be about is to ask: What do universities need to do to in order to produce as well as sustain people like Rowan Williams?

Calling attention to Rowan Williams, moreover, makes explicit the character of the essays that make up this book. I have made no attempt to hide from the reader that these essays were written for particular contexts and tasks. Ireland, Australia, Waco, Texas, and even a country called America, matter for the argument I am making. Bruce Kaye, Luigi Giussani, David Burrell, Stanley Fish, Wendell Berry, Fred Norris, Gregory of Nazianzus, and John Howard Yoder must exist – or at least have existed – to make sense of the argument I have tried to develop. I realize readers may not know these people as I do, but I nonetheless hope something of their life and work is exhibited in the chapters their lives have made possible.

I do not want, however, to give the impression that this is just a random series of essays put together to look like a book. I am aware that some may think that describes all my books. It is true that most of what I write I do so because I have been asked to address this or that subject or audience. But I almost always have in mind the next subject I need to take up if I am to develop arguments that I hope are destined to be a book. To be sure I had no idea when I was asked to write on Gregory of Nazianzus to honor Fred Norris I would discover the argument I developed in that essay. Contingency is everything creating connections otherwise not discoverable. I hope the reader will enjoy being surprised as much as I have been.

Anticipating surprise, however, makes me wonder whether I should have written this "Introduction." I hope that readers will not think by reading the "Introduction" they have a summary of the book. Indeed I hope after having read *The State of the University* readers will find the "Introduction" failed to adequately prepare them for the complex interrelation of the chapters in the book. Of course it is finally not for me to tell those kind enough to read *The State of the University* what they are reading, rather I simply hope they will enjoy the book as much as I have enjoyed writing it. Even more I hope what I have tried to do in this book will be an invitation for others to join in the work of theology.

1

Theological Knowledge and the Knowledges of the University: Beginning Explorations

1. BEGINNING EXPLORATIONS

It is no secret that theology is no longer considered a necessary subject in the modern university. I am getting old, but I have given myself the task before I die to understand better why this is the case and what, if anything, might be said that could help those that assume that theology is not to be part of modern university curriculums to think again. Yet I have to admit that I am unsure how to pursue this subject, beset as it is by historical, political, and intellectual developments not easily separated. So the subtitle of this chapter, "Beginning Explorations," not only is an attempt to be truthful about the status of the claims I make in this chapter, but also is a call for help. I would and will welcome those who can help me ask the right questions or even know where to begin thinking about where to begin.

That it is assumed that theology is not a proper subject in the modern university is a given. But it is not clear why it is assumed that the kind of knowledge theology represents is in some fashion deficient when compared to other academic subjects. Of course some may object that theology can be taught in the modern university as long as you assume that theology names no more than a report on what was once believed or is still believed by Christians. Such a view, however, makes the issue far too easy. Theology proper may involve such reports, but theology as a discipline is a constructive and normative mode of reflection on how and what Christians believe about the way things are in the light of our conviction that the way things are has been created by God.[1]

[1] I do not think theology is an activity peculiar to Christians. It is quite clear that many Jewish thinkers are theologians. I am sure Islamic thinkers often "do" theology. I identify theology with Christianity, because that is the theology I know. My hunch, however, is that the need for theology may be different for Jews, Muslims, and Christians. That is clearly a topic for another day and for someone far more learned than myself. David Burrell, C.S.C., has done the best work so far on this subject. See his *Freedom and Creation* (Notre Dame: University of Notre Dame Press, 1993).

It is my conviction that until we can make some headway on these issues, all the talk about how the Christian university might be different than other universities is just that: it is merely talk or, put more negatively, such talk is ideological. Yet given the complex reality of the contemporary university, Christian or non-Christian, it is not easy to know how the question or questions involving why or how theological knowledge may or may not be a legitimate subject in the university can be pursued. If, for example, most academics think there is no problem for departments of economics and schools of business to presume the normative status of the capitalist order, that is, capitalism can be advocated between consenting adults, why is there such a problem with theology? I assume the answers to the question why theology is excluded from the university differ from one institution to another. But in order to make the question concrete, I think a speech by the President of Yale, Richard Levin, nicely exemplifies some of the major reasons why theology is thought to be at best not necessary for educating students and at worst a subject that cannot pass the epistemological standards necessary to be an academic subject.

2. AN EXHIBIT OF THE PROBLEM

Soon after becoming President of Yale, Richard Levin addressed the incoming class of 1993. Since this was the first address Levin made as President, much thought obviously went into what he had to say. The address was entitled, "The Capacity for Independent Thought" and was reprinted in the *Yale University Magazine*. Levin begins by noting it is important to make clear what those newly entering Yale as well as their parents are "buying for all that money."[2] According to Levin they are buying a liberal education that is different from a professional education or vocational training.

Some, he notes, define liberal education in terms of a curriculum associated with great works of literature, philosophy, and history. Others, following Cardinal Newman, argue that liberal education is an end in itself directed to no purpose other than the free exercise of the mind. Levin observes, however, that these views need not be in conflict and in fact a report by the Yale College faculty in 1827, underwritten by the then President of Yale, Jeremiah Day, argued that the development of qualities of mind and mastery of certain specific content were inseparable. According to Levin, the faculty recognized that the corpus of knowledge appropriate to liberal education was not immutable. "As knowledge varies, education should vary with it."[3]

[2] I will not be able to give the page numbers of quotes from Levin's speech because they were cut off by the Xerox machine. The address, however, covered only three pages in the *Yale Magazine*.

[3] Levin seems unaware that what the Yale Report of 1827 meant by "quality of mind" was quite different than what it meant by the turn of the century. In his

Levin claims that as observers and forecasters of the development of the liberal curriculum in America the authors of the 1827 Yale report were quite accurate. The curriculum has changed but the university is still committed to providing a liberal education. In particular Levin observes "We no longer consider rhetoric and theology, for example, to be indispensable subjects." Such subjects cannot be at the heart of a liberal education according to Levin because the essence of such an education is "to develop the freedom to think critically and independently, to cultivate one's mind to its fullest potential, to liberate oneself from prejudice, superstition, and dogma."

Science and mathematics are, therefore, crucial for the development of such a mind. In pure mathematics and theoretical physics, for example, one learns how to reason deductively from clearly defined premises. In the experimental sciences one learns the method of induction, how to make proper inferences from evidence. Similarly, the great works of western philosophy provide examples of how the mind liberates itself from prejudice by the rigorous application of reason to questions of how we know and how we act.

Levin argues what is read does matter, but less attention should be paid to race, ethnicity, and gender of the authors read, and more to how they confront what it means to be human.

Yet whatever the content of the curriculum might be, Levin argues that it is not the role of the university to teach these freshmen what to think but rather how to think. In order to drive this point home, Levin quotes Thomas Jefferson's advice to his nephew Peter Carr in 1787: "Fix reason firmly in her seat, and call to her tribunal every fact, every opinion. ... Lay aside all prejudice on both sides, and neither believe nor reject anything, because any other persons ... have rejected it or believed it. Your own reason is the only oracle given you by heaven, and you are answerable, not for the rightness, but uprightness of the decision." Levin comments that such an endorsement of reason and independent critical thinking has not lost its importance. "The university remains committed to these values of the Enlightenment."

Levin observes that the argument he has made against "useful" knowledge allies him with Cardinal Newman, who rejected utilitarian arguments for support of higher education. But Levin also notes that Newman "with some irony" noted that an education aimed solely at

---

The Emergence of the American University (Chicago: University of Chicago Press, 1965), Laurence Veysey notes that people like Noah Porter of Yale thought the task of the university was to discipline the mental and moral faculties by forcing the student to work hard in abstract subjects. Veysey quotes Frederick Jackson Turner of Wisconsin to illustrate this view: "The student who has acquired the habit of never letting go of a puzzling problem – say a rare Greek verb – until he has analyzed its every element, and understands every point in its etymology, has the habit of mind which will enable him to follow out a legal subtlety with the same accuracy." Levin does note that in contrast to the nineteenth century the Yale faculty no longer considers the mandatory study of Greek and Latin to be necessary.

developing the capacity to reason can be defended on utilitarian grounds because it produces good citizens. Such an education does so because a man so trained has a clear and conscious view of his own opinions and judgments, "a truth in developing them, an eloquence in expressing them, and a force in expressing them. It teaches him to see things as they are, to go right to the point, to disentangle a skein of thought, to detect what is sophistical, and discard what is irrelevant. It prepares him to fill any post with credit, and to master any subject with facility."

According to Levin, liberal education is, therefore, a crucial source for "the preservation of individual freedom and democracy." Democracies depend on citizens who have been liberally educated, that is, who have the capacity for reason, reflection, and critical judgment. Citizens so educated are the most reliable source of resistance to forces of prejudice and intolerance that always threaten to undermine free inquiry and free expression.

I have taken the time to present President Levin's account of liberal education not because I think it peculiarly perverse, but because it so nicely articulates the general assumptions that are assumed as a given in American education. Of course we may wonder how anyone could become president of a major American institution who assumes that Thomas Jefferson and Cardinal Newman can be in agreement about anything. But perhaps President Levin should not be held accountable. He is an economist. But surely his speechwriter should have known better.

3. THE INCOHERENCE OF THE UNIVERSITY

More troubling than the sources Levin uses to support his views, however, is how his speech belies the university he administers. I am not suggesting Levin is consciously duplicitous in his advocacy of a liberal education. Rather I am suggesting that quite understandably he is unable to give a coherent account of the diverse reality that is the modern university which I assume Yale represents. For Yale University, like almost any large university in America, is constituted by utilitarian and research endeavors that are not consistent with Levin's advocacy of a liberal education. The freshmen, moreover, will discover in their first week of classes that Levin's speech has little to do with the reality of Yale.

In his extraordinary account of the crucial period from 1865 to 1910 of the American university, Laurence Veysey helps us understand how the universities we now inhabit came to be. Veysey notes that the early justification of the universities – committed to defend what Protestants understood as orthodoxy – as the place where the mental and moral faculties of the students were disciplined by rigorous study of ancient languages was soon defeated. The defeat of this mode of education was not the result of a clear alternative educational theory or practice, but rather was more a response to the need for the university to justify itself to a quite different social order than the one that gave birth to early Harvard and Yale.

According to Veysey, after the Civil War almost every significant change in higher education lay "in the direction of concessions to the utilitarian type of demand for reform."[4] Students were to be educated for "real life," which meant they were to be made citizens of a democratic nation by being trained in the university with the skills befitting their vocational ambitions. Veysey notes that the appeal to democracy was as ubiquitous as it was vague,[5] but such an appeal served to justify the acceptance by universities of subjects that had once been excluded. The founding of Cornell gave institutional form to this kind of university, but the appeal to democracy was also shaping developments at Harvard under President Eliot.[6]

The development of the "serviceable university" resulted in a transformation of the curriculum by the beginning of a variety of new departments of learning. Departments of education, domestic science, business administration, sanitary science, physical education, and engineering became part of the accepted curriculum of the university. David Starr Jordan, the President of Cornell, Indiana, and Stanford, declared in 1899 that "it is not for the university to decide on the relative values of knowledge. Each man makes his own market, controlled by his own standards. It is for the university to see that all standards are honest, that all work is genuine."[7]

At the same time as utilitarian justifications were shaping the university, the influence of German universities in their stress on research was also having an effect on the American university. Though often associated with the founding of Johns Hopkins University, Veysey argues, the ideal of the "pure scientist" became widespread throughout American institutions. The emphasis on science for science's sake in an interesting way resulted in an increasing specialization of knowledge shared with the movement toward practicality.[8] In fact, however, the assumptions of the "intense seeker after new knowledge" took on the characteristics once associated with religion. Veysey even suggests these determined

4 Veysey, p. 60.

5 Veysey identifies at least seven different meanings of democracy as applied to the university: (i) equality of all fields of learning no matter how technical or novel; (ii) equality of treatment of all students attending the university; (iii) all those attending the university meant that all qualified should be admitted to the university; (iv) those prepared by the university were well positioned for individual success; (v) the desire for a wide diffusion of knowledge throughout society; (vi) the idea that the university should receive its direction directly from the non-academic mass of citizens; and (vii) setting a high standard of individual morality (pp. 63–5).

6 Veysey reports that Eliot responded to a paper by President Hadley of Yale on the organization of the thirteenth-century university with his customary audacity: "The American university has nothing to learn from medieval universities, nor yet from those still in the medieval period" (p. 94).

7 Veysey, p. 114.

8 Veysey, p. 142.

researchers were the new monks in service to an ideal of the university that was increasingly seen as an alternative to the religious past.[9]

Yet the influence of Germany was to be balanced by the continuing appeal of Oxford and Cambridge. So for many the university was still considered the crucial institution for the liberalizing of culture through the training of gentlemen.[10] It was assumed that the training of the cultured personality was to be done primarily through what we now call the humanities.[11] The commitment to the humanities in the name of educating the "well-rounded individual" was often associated with colleges, but was also very influential at Yale and Princeton. However, this commitment to scholarship as a formation of an elite (which meant it was sometimes seen to be in tension with democracy) could be found in figures such as the Harvard philosopher, George Santayana. Santayana put the matter this way: "There are always a few men whose main interest is to note the aspects of things in an artistic or philosophical

9 Edward Shils observes that "In the allegedly practical and 'materialistic' American society of the period after the Civil War, there was still a deep piety that had ceased to be monopolized by the doctrines of ecclesiastical Christianity. The seriousness with which fundamental knowledge was pursued by universities aroused the admiration of those possessed by this enduring piety. By their concern with fundamental learning, the universities were able to become, in a sense, the heirs of the churches. More specialized, more practical institutions could claim neither that vital inheritance nor the consequent support of private patrons and state legislators" ("The Order of Learning in the United States: The Ascendancy of the University," in *The Organization of Knowledge in Modern America*, edited by Alexander Oleson and John Voss (Baltimore: Johns Hopkins Press, 1976), p. 31).

10 Charles Johnson, a professor at Trinity College in North Carolina, identified in 1892 five elements he thought crucial to the development of literary taste: (i) an instinctive appreciation of vowel and consonant "sound-sequence"; (ii) perception of a word to its meaning; (iii) the ability to recognize a thought system; (iv) the perception of the delicate revelations of the author's personality that make some books good in the highest sense; and (v) to be able to see the embodiment of a vital and congruous character in fiction (Veysey, pp. 184–5).

11 It is a mistake, however, to think the description "humanities" describes a unified subject. Veysey notes by the end of the 1880s the humanists had split into two different groups. One camp identified by the term "culture" resisted tendencies toward specialization and scientistic justification. The other camp, influenced by German scholarship, advocated advanced research that required increasing specialization necessary to justify the scholarship associated with the Ph.D. Veysey notes that the former espoused values associated with the elites of the college-trained, though they distanced their defense of their subjects from the past association with Christian orthodoxy (Laurence Veysey, "The Plural Organized Worlds of the Humanities," in *The Organization of Knowledge in Modern America*, edited by Alexander Oleson and John Voss (Baltimore: Johns Hopkins Press, 1976), pp. 35–6). In *The Emergence of the American University* Veysey observes the commitment to liberal learning often meant a downgrading of Christian theology. This did not mean that the proponents of culture were skeptics, but rather that religion was no longer a central focus for their academic outlook. He quotes John Bascom who announced in 1881 that "Religion is not so much the foundation of morals, as morals the foundation of religion" (p. 203).

way. They are rather useless individuals, but as I happen to belong to the class, I think them much superior to the rest of mankind."[12]

For anyone associated with the university it is not hard to see the continuing influence of these developments Veysey locates in the antebellum university in America. Yet as helpful as Veysey's description of these various emphases may be, I think even more important is his attention to the development of the institutionalization of the university from 1890 to 1910. By 1890 the university was assumed to be part of the American landscape. In short it had become a success.[13] The success meant that however the faculty may have understood the work of the university, the main character of the university was determined by the emerging bureaucratic structure. The university was now an institution identified by "the administration": characterized by a hierarchy composed of trustees, president, deans, department chairmen, and finally the faculty.[14] No matter what the faculty thought about educational alternatives, the administrator was bound to be a diplomat and politician if he was to serve the institution. Holders of such offices thrive on compromise, wanting all sorts of diverse people to go away pleased.[15]

Veysey observes:

> Here, then, was a major and controversial new force in American academic life. In response to what conditions had it appeared? The most important answer lies with the institution. Both intellectually and in terms of structure, the American university was becoming too diverse easily to define – or to control. The adherence of academic leaders to varying educational philosophies, the emergence of crystallized departments of learning, and the presence of larger numbers of students all contributed to this result. Often an undergraduate college basically English in conception was wedded, by loose financial ties, to a Germanic graduate school. To European eyes an American institution such as Harvard might seem "a chaos." No longer did any overall intellectual

12 Veysey, *The Emergence of the American University*, pp. 213–14.

13 Not to be missed, however, is the "success" of a university did not necessarily mean that the students in the universities shared the same commitments as their teachers. Veysey notes that few undergraduates desired to identify themselves with the work of the institution in any lasting sense. Undergraduates resembled a conscript army rather than a dedicated core of professionals. Veysey extends this metaphor by observing "from one point of view the university existed primarily to keep students in temporary custody amid surroundings which their parents approved" (*The Emergence*, p. 269). Veysey claims that few students took up learning for the sake of learning which also helps account for the "spectacular" rise of athletics, and in particular football, as an (if not the most) important aspect of college life for undergraduates.

14 Veysey, *The Emergence of the American University*, pp. 302–11. That Veysey does not mention "provosts" only indicates he wrote in 1965.

15 Veysey, *The Emergence of the American University*, p. 311.

> formula exist to counter (or to cloak) such fragmentation; neither the Christian religion in any of its varieties, nor positive science, nor humane culture proved *self-evidently* capable of making sense out of the entire range of knowledge and opinion. As long as argument in these terms was possible, the university could mean no one thing. Santayana despairingly commented: "Each man knows the value of his work ... but he feels also the relativity of this work and of its value without being able to survey the whole organism of human interests and adjust himself confidently to the universal life."[16]

I think that helps explain why President Levin's address is such an incoherent but interesting document. Levin at once privileges the sciences to supply both inductive and deductive forms of rationality in order to defend a liberal understanding of the purpose of the university. He seems to disavow all utilitarian justifications other than that training in the sciences and reading the great works of western philosophy will produce people capable of sustaining democracy. As I suggested above, however, such an account fails to do justice to the utilitarian justification of many of the disciplines, including Levin's discipline of economics, so characteristic of the modern university and no doubt true of Yale. It is equally the case that the sciences do not understand themselves to be "pure," but rather represent research agenda funded by the National Science Foundation (NSF) and National Institutes of Health (NIH) and justified by the promise of future developments.[17]

Perhaps even more troubling, Levin seems to have no understanding of the problematic character of his understanding of rationality. He seems to assume that the "prejudice, superstition, and dogma" from which we are to be liberated by reason has been decisively called into question by intellectual developments of the university.[18] From such a

[16] Veysey, *The Emergence of the American University*, p. 311.

[17] I have served eight years (to be sure at different times) on the Duke University Appointment, Promotion, and Tenure (APT) Committee. This is an advisory committee to the provost dealing with internal promotions to tenure as well as external appointments. It is surely an indication of the diverse character of the knowledges that constitute the contemporary university that those on the committee are not to judge "fields," but only the persons standing in their field. The "fields," moreover, become increasingly specialized in order to be able to claim that the person up for promotion or for external appointment is "the best in their field." It is quite common for chairmen of fields to come before the committee indicating they know quite little about a member of their department field.

[18] Alasdair MacIntyre's work stands as the most decisive critique of Levin's assumption that reason qua reason is not only possible but necessarily liberating. Indeed one of the important developments is the increasing recognition that the sciences are inadequately understood when they are divorced from their temporal and spatial contexts. For example, David Livingston has recently argued that there was a distinct regional pattern to the rise of scientific Europe which means it is appropriate to use geographical adjectives such as "English science," "French science," and "Russian

perspective his dismissal of theology, a dismissal no doubt he thinks justified by his assumptions about rationality, is quite simply arbitrary.[19] One suspects such dismissals of theology have more to do with the politics of liberal social orders than whether theology passes muster as a knowledge of the university. The determination of liberal societies to keep religious convictions private is one reason, if not the most important reason, theology is not thought to be appropriate in university curricula. Such curricula increasingly seem determined to avoid teaching any subject that is considered "controversial" because such subjects do not represent the kind of knowledge necessary to secure cooperation between individuals in liberal societies.

If I am right to describe Levin's address as a representative of the "incoherence" of the American university, one might think such an incoherence to be an opportunity for the reintroduction of theology as

---

science" (*Putting Science in its Place: Geographies of Scientific Knowledge* (Chicago: University of Chicago Press, 2003), p. 15). Livingston does not deny that the modern invention of the laboratory was an attempt to create a "placeless" science, but he argues that even laboratory knowledge turns out to be local: thus the difficulty in reproducing results from different laboratories. Livingston argues that there is good reason for suspecting that the term "science" is an "imaginary unity masking the disparate kinds of activity that trade under that label."

In his *An Examined Faith: The Grace of Self-Doubt* (Minneapolis: Fortress Press, 2004), James Gustafson provides a lovely account of the dissonance created by the diverse science and subjects an undergraduate might study and how that dissonance makes it difficult for such a student to maintain any strong theological convictions. Gustafson observes it is unfortunate that "undergraduate curricula seldom, if ever, provide an academic milieu in which students can deliberate about the dissonance even within the human sciences and humanities, not to mention theology, and weigh the alternatives to which they are exposed" (p. 32).

19 Whether an account of the diverse forms of reasoning in the diverse subjects of the university is possible is not clear to me. By serving on the APT committee I have learned that different disciplines use particular words to describe good work done in that discipline. For example, in physics the best work is described as "elegant" which seems to mean the implications of the work may not be understood or the work itself may not be understood, but the mathematics has an undeniable beauty. Work in mathematics is sometimes described as elegant, but mathematicians usually describe the best work as "deep." Deep mathematics usually indicates math not well understood in the community of mathematics. Once what was "deep" is generally understood, it becomes applied mathematics. Work in biology is usually described as "interesting" which means the work helps me understand or "see" what I had not understood. The primary words used in the social sciences are "robust," "powerful," "important," and "useful." "Robust" usually means work that helps the social scientist explain wider implications other than the ones the work was initially designed to accomplish. In the humanities the work is described as "influential" which seems to indicate that the work has changed the minds of other scholars who know something about that subject. In some fields in the humanities, such as philosophy, the work can be described as representing a powerful argument. I often reflect that the word that should best describe theology is "faithful" which may well make theology closer to mathematics and physics than the social sciences. At least in mathematics and physics it is still assumed that such work is committed to truth.

a subject in the modern university,[20] a subject that will probably be seen as one of the "methods" characteristic of religious studies departments. Of course, to have theology so located may not be an advantage, as few departments in the modern university are as controverted as "religious studies."[21] Indeed I think it is quite telling that departments of history and religious studies often are the last representatives of modernist presumptions about objectivity and rationality.

20 Some may well think "incoherence" an inappropriate description of the American university. After all, how many institutions in our society are "coherent"? "Incoherent" could equally be a description about most churches. By using the description "incoherent," I mean to do no more than suggest that no one has the authority or the intellectual resources to say what the university is for or whom it serves. I assume that one can and should give several responses to the question what the university is for, but it is by no means clear how those responses can be consistent with one another. That is why Veysey's account of the development of the modern university is so important. He helps us see that you do not need to be able to provide a coherent account of the activity that should characterize what universities are about as long as the university can be "administered." For a set of essays that on the whole assume that universities are beyond any possibility of their being a coherent account of their work see *The Postmodern University? Contested Visions of Higher Education and Society*, edited by Anthony Smith and Frank Webster (Philadelphia: Open University Press, 2002). In his essay, "The Postmodern University," Peter Scott observes the natural starting point to begin to think about the current university is what characteristics knowledge may have in the world in which we find ourselves. But he observes that "characteristics" suggest regularity and that is exactly what knowledge in our time does not possess (p. 36). In such a world Zygmunt Bauman suggests that the authority that now characterizes the intellectual is not the Cartesian *Cognito*, but rather, "I am talked about, therefore I am" (pp. 21–2).

21 One can cite a burgeoning literature about whether any coherence can be made for religious studies, but that is a subject for another time. However, for a particularly honest and revealing article that concerns how difficult it is to separate teaching "about" a religion without being an advocate, see Martin Jaffee, "Personal Self-Disclosure, Religious Studies Pedagogy, and the Skeptical Mission of the Public University," *Bulletin of the Council of Societies for the Study of Religion*, 33/2 (April 2004), 29–34. In his dissertation written at the University of Chicago, *Uses of Religion: The Dual Role of College Religion Departments at Mid-Century* (June, 2002), Robert Wilson-Black argues that the mid-century founders of religion programs were forced to create departments in the face of an inherent tension if not contradiction. "College administrators and many faculty and alumni leaders wanted religion courses to include Western moral and civic values. At the same time it was expected that, in such a department, students should come to identify religion as a viable academic subject outside of or in addition to advocacy for one particular religious perspective. The question for most of these founders eventually became this: How does one, or should one, extract oneself as a religion professor from the advocacy for a Christian religious life – which was expected to mediate the crises of Western civilization and higher education at that time – while establishing credibility among academic colleagues who looked askance at such advocacy? Establishing their programs from 1940 to 1951, many founders dealt with these contradictory demands by attempting to distinguish teaching a religion from other academic subjects like philosophy, from 'the church,' from 'sectarian theology,' from 'Christianity,' or from campus chapel programs. Their rhetoric, curricular reforms, and arguments for the uses of teaching religion encouraged a fragmented identity for religion departments, the residue of which remains to this day" (pp. 9–10).

John Milbank observes that the condition in which the modern university finds itself can provide what he characterizes as a cynical reason for theology in the university. That cynical reason is that:

> the utter incoherence and lack of ability to withstand the critical trial of reason does not matter so long as one can come up with cash and customers; in our postmodern era the "free, rational inquiry" of the Enlightenment which could reveal only formal truths as objectively real, thus handing over the whole realm of the substantive to the play of agnostic forces, has itself been inevitably invaded by such forces, since form feeds only on substantive, and never perfectly inhabits its own purity. Enlightenment, therefore, is bound to evolve into the postmodern mixture of the purest, most unbounded and therefore most rigorous logic, plus the most untrammeled sway of vanity and fashion. In many ways a "religious studies department" is well adapted to our era. But we should be warned: the point of fashion is to change, and religious constituencies may well yet further wither away, or more probably mutate and take their custom elsewhere, far away from universities (or what future will remain of them).[22]

4. THEOLOGY AND THE UNIVERSITY: CAN NEWMAN HELP?

I think Milbank is right to warn us against using the incoherence of the modern university to secure a place for theology. I have some sympathy, moreover, for his claim that at least one of the reasons that the university finds itself in disarray is because it has abandoned the theological task of studying that which is inimitably real. In his essay, "The Conflict of the Faculties: Theology and the Economy of the Sciences," with his customary audacity Milbank argues, contra Kant, that theology is now the only discipline capable of reclaiming the purpose of the university.[23] It is so

[22] John Milbank, "The Conflict of the Faculties: Theology and the Economy of the Sciences," in *Faithfulness and Fortitude: In Conversation with the Theological Ethics of Stanley Hauerwas*, edited by Mark Thiessen Nation and Samuel Wells (Edinburgh: T&T Clark, 2000), p. 40.

[23] Milbank obviously titled his essay to remind readers of Kant's famous essay, *The Conflict of the Faculties*. Milbank did so because he is, of course, arguing the exact opposite of Kant's position. In *The Conflict of the Faculties*, Kant distinguished between the higher and lower faculties noting that law, medicine, and divinity are called the higher faculties because they exist in the university only because they are useful to government. The lower faculties are not constituted by teaching that is adopted by order of a superior, but are determined by free, that is, autonomous, reason. Kant observes that most people are persuaded by the higher faculties because people want to be led, even duped. But Kant argues that for governments to place all authority in the higher faculties would invite anarchy. So government has a stake in the truths of the higher faculty being subject to the lower faculty in order to assure that any historical claims have a rational origin. Kant argued that Christianity is the most adequate form of rational religion, but the lower faculty must stand in judgment

because truth for theology is the adequation of knowledge with the real, but only God is the entirely real reality who is infinitely actual and infinitely knowing.[24] It is not, therefore, a question of the legitimacy of theology in the university, but rather unless all the "other disciplines are (at least implicitly) ordered to theology (assuming that this means participation in God's self-knowledge – as in the Augustinian tradition) they are objectively and demonstrably null and void, altogether lacking in truth, which to have any meaning must involve some sort of adequation (for mere 'coherence' can only concern the coherence of convention or appearances)."[25]

I confess I am tempted to side with Milbank if for no other reason than that his position is so offensive. Moreover, that such a position does not have a "snowball's chance in hell" of being realized in the university as we know it makes it all the more attractive. But we must still ask if Milbank's account of theology is true to the character of the church's understanding of the theological task. I wonder, for example, if Newman was alive today would he be saying something like Milbank? In order to answer that question I think it worth our while to look at Newman's understanding of theology and the role of theology in the university.

Newman's *The Idea of a University* has often been used as a defense of the "liberal arts college." No doubt Newman's insistence that the university is primarily about teaching not about creating new knowledge, though he was not against the pursuit of such knowledge elsewhere, is one of the reasons his book has been so appealing to those committed to passing on to future generations the "great texts."[26] I certainly do not mean to call into question many that have used Newman to defend "the tradition," but I think such readings can fail to do justice to the subtle account Newman gives of knowledge and, in particular, the knowledge of theology.

---

of exegesis. Kant also saw no reason to assume that the doctrine of the Trinity, "taken literally," should have any practical relevance. Kant is, therefore, led to the blunt claim – "it is superstition to hold that historical belief is a duty and essential to salvation" (Immanuel Kant, *The Conflict of the Faculties* in *Religion and Rational Theology*, translated and edited by Allen Wood and George DiGiovanni (Cambridge: Cambridge University Press, 1996), pp. 238–338; the last quote is from p. 285).

24 Milbank, p. 42. That theology is now done primarily in seminaries is part of the problem. Theology as the normative discipline of the church is rightly thought to be important for training people for the ministry, but theology is not a "professional discipline." If Milbank is right, and I think he is, theology must be part of the curriculum of any university that desires to have the purpose universities profess.

25 Milbank, pp. 45–6.

26 Newman makes the distinction between "discovery" and "teaching" in the "Preface" to *The Idea of a University*, edited, with Introduction and Notes, by Martin Svaglic (New York: Rinehart, 1960), p. XL. One always hesitates to disagree with Newman, but I think he was wrong to make this strict distinction between discovery and teaching. I am well aware that he simply assumed that this was a division of labor and no doubt sometimes it is, but I think all good teachers discover that teaching requires discovery. Aquinas certainly stands as an exemplification of why discovery and teaching cannot be separated.

For example, the claim with which Newman begins *The Idea of a University*, that is, that the university is "a place of teaching universal knowledge," is often interpreted in the modernist mode that makes Newman an advocate of knowledge as an end in itself.[27] It is certainly true that Newman argued that "liberal knowledge" is that which "stands on its own pretensions, which is independent of sequel, expects no complement, refuses to be informed (as it is called) by any end, or absorbed into any art, in order duly to present itself to our contemplation."[28] I do not think, however, that Newman is commending art for art's sake or knowledge as an end in itself; for the crucial word is "contemplation," and Newman being the good Augustinian that he was, knows that only God can be so contemplated.[29]

[27] I think the title, *The Idea of a University*, also often misleads people. They assume that "idea" means "ideal" or "essence," but as Ian Ker makes clear, Newman meant by idea that which grows gradually making possible our ability to see the connection between diverse aspects of a reality (Ian Ker, *John Henry Newman: A Biography* (Oxford: Oxford University Press, 1988), pp. 302–3). Newman, therefore, did not think *The Idea of a University* was recommending an idea that did not exist but he wished might exist. It is extremely important that the *a* in *The Idea of a University*, not be ignored. Newman knew the university had a history. That is why it is important to read Newman's *Rise and Progress of Universities and Benedictine Essays* (Notre Dame: University of Notre Dame Press, 2001) as a complementary text to *The Idea of a University*. The university exists for Newman even when there is no institution that bears that name. For example, he observes that in all times there have been universities and they have flourished because of the desire for learning and the need for teachers. If there has been a demand there has been a supply (*Rise and Progress of Universities*, p. 51). Though universities have often enjoyed the patronage of the rich, the teacher is strong just to the extent what he teaches has intrinsic value and attraction (pp. 164–5). For Newman the university is certainly an idea, but unless real people exist who teach and learn the idea is unfortunately just an "ideal." Moreover, a site must exist for the university to exist (p. 24). Which means Newman understood that the "idea" of the university would take quite different forms at different times and places.

[28] Newman, *The Idea of a University*, p. 81.

[29] L. Gregory Jones criticizes Newman for commending "knowledge for knowledge's sake," then observes that such a view of knowledge is defensible only when such a view is situated with the more comprehensive end constituted by our worship of God (in an unpublished paper, "Do Universities Still Care about Ideas? Newman's Proposal and its Implications for Christian Higher Education"). I am suggesting, and I think Jones is in agreement, that is exactly what Newman does. The problem occurs when some of Newman's bald statements are abstracted from his theological frame. Jones observes that Newman did not reject teaching courses on professional education, but Newman thinks such education is not the primary purpose of the university. However, Newman believes such an education is better taught in the university.

Even though I think Newman's view of knowledge for its own end can be defended, I think Newman was wrong to separate knowledge and virtue. He argues that philosophy, no matter how enlightened, gives no command over the passions, but surely that is to accept the view that philosophy is no more than a subject, the most important subject to be sure, in the curriculum. That said, however, I think Newman is right to say that "liberal education makes not the Christian, not the

Levin-like appeals to Newman in support of the liberal notion that the knowledges that constitute the university have no "use" fail to ask what Newman means by "universal knowledge." By "universal" Newman did not mean that the knowledges that constitute liberal learning cannot be justified by their utility, but rather that all knowledge was interconnected because the "universe in its length and breadth is so intimately knit together."[30] To be educated is not to be well read or to know a great deal about this or that subject. Rather, it is the

> only true enlargement of mind which is the power of viewing many things at once as one whole, of referring them severally to their true place in the universal system, or understanding their respective values, and determining their mutual dependence. Thus is that form of Universal Knowledge set up in the individual intellect, and constitutes its perfection. Possessed of this real illumination, the mind never views any part of the extended subject-matter of Knowledge without recollecting that it is but a part, or without the associations which spring from this recollection. It makes every thing in some sort lead to every thing else; it would communicate the image of the whole to every separate portion, till that whole becomes in imagination like a spirit, everywhere pervading and penetrating its component parts, and giving them one definite meaning.[31]

Philosophy, not theology, Newman believes to be the discipline that is distinct from all the sciences, that is, "in some sense" philosophy is "a science of sciences." Newman assumes that the university will be constituted by many subjects and no one person will be capable of pursuing

---

Catholic, but the gentleman." See *The Idea of a University*, p. 91. In his eloquent reexamination of Newman's *The Idea of the University*, Jaroslav Pelikan argues that the principle of knowledge as its own end "must be integrated with a larger and more comprehensive set of first principles, which can be summarized under the heading (likewise Aristotelian) of 'the intellectual virtues' " (*The Idea of the University: A Reexamination* (New Haven: Yale University Press, 1992), p. 43). Pelikan rightly calls attention to Aristotle which means, however, the intellectual virtues cannot be separated from the moral virtues. Ian Ker's paper at the University of Prince Edward Island conference (October 1–3, 2004), "Faith, Freedom, and the Academy: The Idea of the University in the 21st Century," quite persuasively argued that what Newman meant by a "gentleman" had little to do with class but rather Newman thought a gentleman is one with a well-educated mind. Ker also maintained that Newman thought such a person would or should be a Christian.

30 Newman, *The Idea of a University*, p. 38.

31 Newman, *The Idea of a University*, p. 103. In his *John Henry Newman: A Biography* (1988), particularly Chapters 9 and 10, Ian Ker stresses the importance of understanding what Newman meant by universal as the apprehension of the interconnectedness of the "whole."

them all.[32] A division of labor is necessary to insure the perfection of every art. Newman, for example, thinks attention should be given in the university to how wealth is produced. Therefore the study of political economy is to be expected.[33] But philosophy is that "habit of mind" in which "the comprehension of the bearings of one science on another, and the use of each to each, and the location and limitation and adjustment and due appreciation of them all" is undertaken. Gerard Loughlin notes that for Newman, philosophy "is not so much a body of knowledge distinct from the other sciences, as the cast of mind by which those sciences are apprehended and thus united. It is 'an intellectual... grasp of many things brought together in one.' It is not the unity of a general theory of everything, but of a community. Indeed, it is the university as such, in its universal scope and idea."[34]

32 Those that assume that Newman was a defender of a core curriculum constituted by the "liberal arts" often do not notice that he insisted that "Irish studies" be part of the disciplines taught in the Catholic University of Ireland. In her "Introduction" to Newman's *Rise and Progress of Universities and Benedictine Essays* (Notre Dame: University of Notre Dame, 2001), Katherine Tillman tells us that Newman "regularly attended" the lectures of Eugene O'Curry who held the Chair of Irish History and Archaeology (p. LXXIII). That Newman attended O'Curry's lectures is not surprising because Newman thought that in the sixth and seventh centuries Ireland saved Christianity. He observes "the Irish, whose brilliancy of genius has sometimes been considered, like the Greek, to augur fickleness and change, have managed to persevere to this day in the science of the saints, long after their ancient rivals have lost the gift of faith."

33 Newman, *The Idea of a University*, says, "Political economy is the science, I suppose of wealth – a science simply lawful and useful, for it is no sin to make money, any more than it is a sin to seek honour; a science at the same time dangerous and leading to the occasions of sin, as is the pursuit of honour too; and in consequence, if studied by itself, and apart from the control of Revealed Truth, sure to conduct a speculator to unchristian conclusions" (pp. 64–5). Later Newman observes that every art is improved by confining the professor of it to a single study, but though the art is advanced by such a concentration, the individual who pursues the discipline "goes back." According to Newman the advantage to the community is in inverse ratio to the person who commits himself to such a concentrated study (pp. 127–8).

34 Gerard Loughlin, "The University Without Question: John Henry Newman and Jacques Derrida on Faith in the University" (unpublished paper), pp. 18–19. The internal quotes come from *The Idea of a University*, 1852, Discourse V, pp. 423, 421, 428. Loughlin's reflections on Newman and Derrida were motivated by the closure of the Department of Religious Studies at the University of Newcastle. The Department of Philosophy had been closed some years earlier, occasioning Loughlin's question to the vice-chancellor whether you can have a university without a Department of Philosophy. Loughlin reports the vice-chancellor replied that you could have a university without a Department of Religious Studies and the vice-chancellor has made the theoretical possibility reality.

It would be quite instructive to compare Newman's understanding of the role of philosophy with Alasdair MacIntyre's account in his essay, "Aquinas's Critique of Education: Against His Own Age, Against Ours," in *Philosophers on Education: New Historical Perspectives*, edited by Amelie Oksenberg Rorty (London: Routledge, 1998), pp. 95–108. MacIntyre, like Newman, argues there is that of which theology can speak about which philosophy knows nothing and there are types of questions answers to which can only be given by philosophy. But there is also a range

The significance of philosophy for Newman is nowhere more evident than in his claim that "university teaching without theology is simply unphilosophical." Newman argues that theology, that science of God by which "the truths we know about God are put into a system, has at least as good a right to claim a place there as Astronomy."[35] Note he does not make a theological argument for the inclusion of theology in the university, but rather argues that given that the object of knowledge is truth, then theology – which is a knowledge – cannot be excluded from the university. Accordingly,

> if the various branches of knowledge, which are the matter of teaching in a University, so hang together, that none can be neglected without prejudice to the perfection of the rest, and if Theology be a branch of knowledge, of wide reception, of philosophical structure, of unutterable importance, and of supreme influence, to what conclusions are we brought from these two premises but this? that to withdraw Theology from the public schools is to impair the completeness and to invalidate the truthworthiness of all that is actually taught in them.[36]

The other sciences, therefore, need theology. In order to have possession of the truth of the various sciences, we must have the "whole truth." Theology is not just another subject, but it is the condition of general knowledge.[37] Such truth includes the "revealed truths" which enter into the provinces of science, philosophy, and literature. Every science is not

---

of questions about human nature and the ends of life philosophy and theology share. MacIntyre accordingly argues that theologians cannot do their work well in what they have to say about human affairs, divine providence, divine law, and redemption and grace without the work of philosophy. So theologians have to become philosophers if they are to speak intelligibly about human powers, reasoning, will and choice, and the relationship of human beings to their ultimate good (pp. 98–9). I have criticized MacIntyre for sometimes maintaining a far too rigid distinction between theology and philosophy, but I think he is exactly right about the theologians' need to do philosophy. In his paper on Newman's *Idea* at the University of Prince Edward Island conference, Ian Ker helpfully reminded us that by "philosophy" Newman meant that habit of mind characterized by equitableness, moderation, and wisdom rather than philosophy as a department in the university.

35 Newman, *The Idea of a University*, pp. 31–2.

36 Newman, *The Idea of a University*, p. 52. It may be objected that Newman's reference to "public schools" means what he says is not relevant to the university. Newman certainly argued that schools and colleges should rightly be concerned with "moral formation" in a manner that distinguished them from the university, but I do not think he is arguing that theology is only relevant to schools and colleges and not the universities. Newman also believes the "theology" he thinks necessary is natural theology, but he also says on the same page from which the quotation is taken that he has done so only to carry with him those who are not Catholic. He, moreover, suggests that much more must be about "revealed facts and principles" for theology to do its proper work.

37 Newman, *The Idea of a University*, p. 52. Newman claims that by "theology" he means "natural theology" because he wants to "carry along" those who are not Catholics. He

equally affected by the omission of theology. Pure mathematics will not suffer at all, chemistry will feel the difference less than politics, politics less than history, ethics, or metaphysics. But just to the extent the various subjects are connected with each other, the exclusion of theology will have a deleterious effect. Newman observes, for example, that "under the shadow of the church" philosophy does service to the cause of morality, but "when it is strong enough to have a will of its own" then it is tempted to form a system of ethics in a manner that serves the evils it should oppose.[38]

Moreover theology also needs the other sciences,[39] thus the title of Discourse IV of *The Idea of a University*, the "Bearing of Other Branches of Knowledge on Theology." For Newman the Catholic faith is true which means the church has no stake in trying to make every subject matter "Christian." For a university, even secular universities that may not have theology represented, cannot exist external to the Catholic pale as long as the quest to discover the truth in the connections is not lost.[40] Truth is truth. The Christian accepts truth where he or she finds it without feeling the need to claim possession of that truth.[41] After all the Christian believes that "all that is good, all that is true, all that is beautiful, all that is beneficent, be it great or small, be it perfect or

observes, however, "that no one can really set himself to master and to teach the doctrine of an intelligent Creator in its fullness, without going on a great deal farther than he at present dreams" (p. 52). Newman seems, therefore, to maintain that natural theology requires the truths of revelation which "furnishes facts to the other sciences, which those sciences, left to themselves, would never reach; and it invalidates apparent facts, which, left to themselves, they would imagine" (p. 54). Newman does not argue that theology can be part of the curriculum only as natural theology, but he rightly assumes "revealed theology" must be part of the curriculum (p. 54). By "fact" I do not think Newman meant that "facts" come uninterpreted, but rather are that which we only know by someone showing us the importance of this or that.

38 Newman, *The Idea of a University*, pp. 155–6.

39 Loughlin, I think, rightly characterizes Newman's views by noting that "the labour of knowledge is divided among the sciences, and when 'certain sciences are away' we have a 'defective apprehension' of the truth. All sciences are needed for the seeking of truth, in the university where it is sought. Thus Newman offers us a view of a unified existence, of creation in relation to creator, which must be studied by us – as particular, limited creatures – through a myriad of inter-related sciences: a truly interdisciplinary labor for the truth. And this common labour includes the co-dependence of theology on other disciplines, through which it learns of its own proper divine subject through their learning of the world which the creator has made and makes to be. On Newman's account, theology does not appear as the 'queen of the sciences,' but as the first amongst equals, for the truth which is to be known in theology is the fundamental condition of all knowledge" (pp. 18–19). Newman notes the church "fears no knowledge, but she purifies all; she represses no element of our nature, but cultivates the whole" (p. 178).

40 Newman, *The Idea of a University*, p. 163.

41 Newman observes "that the Church's true policy is not to aim at the exclusion of Literature from Secular Schools, but at her own admission into them. Let her do for Literature in one way what she does for Science in Another; each has its imperfection, and she has her remedy for each. She fears no knowledge, but she purifies all, she represses no element of our nature, but cultivates the whole" (*The Idea of a University*, p. 178).

fragmentary, natural as well as supernatural, moral as well as material, comes from Him."[42]

That the church feels no necessity to dominate the various sciences and literatures in the university does not mean that criticism cannot be made of science and literature. But such criticism is not about the work of science itself, but about theories and attitudes the scientist may have assumed that are not constitutive of the science. The problem is usually that a science tries to explain more than its method will allow. For example, if it is asserted that we are but products of an endless series of physical causes and effects, we have an indication something has seriously gone wrong with the science that makes such claims.[43]

The university, therefore, has a constitution and independence in relation to the church; but practically speaking the university cannot fulfill its task to teach "universal knowledge" without the church's assistance. The university cannot maintain its integrity without the church. For the university, like all creation, needs the gift that is superadded to its nature without which nature is incomplete.[44] Or as Newman puts it in *The Idea of a University*, the university has the office of intellectual education which is a good not requiring the church, but the church is necessary to steady the university in the performance of that office.[45]

I cannot pretend that I have done justice to Newman's subtle and complex account of the university and, in particular, the role of theology in the university; for I think Newman provides a quite helpful set of suggestions for how Christians can have a constructive role vis-à-vis the universities in which we find ourselves. I suspect that Newman, like John Milbank, would find the arrogance and insularity of many of the disciplines that comprise the university theologically problematic. But Newman, rightly I think, does not ask the various disciplines to submit to theology. Rather Newman helps us see that our theological task is to help the various disciplines of the university explore their limits, possibilities, and connections to other subjects. I do not think Newman thinks that such an enterprise will result in a unified account of all that is. The results will always be subject to further questions. The task of theology is quite rightly to force the questions to be asked.

Of course the last sentence Newman would not have written. He argues it is the philosopher's role to raise if not to force questions concerning limits, possibilities, and connections between disciplines. I have no reason to disagree with Newman about the role of philosophy. My hesitancy is that quite simply few philosophers now understand their task as Newman understood their task. The "professionalization" of philosophy is now a reality. Philosophers have become "experts." It, therefore, seems that the primary role of theologians vis-à-vis the universities is to ask that philosophers do the job they were set aside to do.

42 Newman, *The Idea of a University*, p. 50.
43 Newman, *The Idea of a University*, p. 44.
44 Newman, *Rise and Progress of Universities*, pp. 180–3.
45 Newman, *The Idea of a University*, p. XXXVII.

5. A CONCLUDING UNSATISFYING POSTSCRIPT

Is that all there is? Surely you must think that there has to be a bigger pay-off than the conclusion that theology needs philosophy if we are to find our way back into the university. I certainly think more can and needs to be said, but I do not think the significance of Newman's case for the importance of philosophy should be underestimated. Of course far more important than philosophy regaining its role in the university is the role itself, namely, that we must somehow recover in the university what Newman called the "teaching of universal knowledge." Yet in the university as we know it no persons, disciplines, or place exists charged with the responsibility to try to make what connections may and may not be able to be made. Connections are often made informally, but that is usually a happy accident that is not assumed to set a precedent.

In the light of the inability to make the kind of connections Newman thought the heart of the university, some think theology should assume that task. If theology would undertake the project of "pulling it all together," perhaps theology might be recognized as a legitimate knowledge of the university. I think, however, that would be a very unfortunate strategy. I do think theologians often exhibit a gregarious intellectual agenda that should commend their presence in the university. That theologians read more widely than many of our colleagues in other disciplines is because we are in the happy position, as the bottom feeders in the university, of having to know what others are thinking though they do not have to know what we are thinking. That theologians find themselves in the position of Hegel's slave I take to be a very good thing.

I think, however, there is another more important reason that theology is committed to "making the connections." The knowledge that theology names is knowledge of God. Of course theologians soon discover that such a knowledge is primarily negative, that is, theology is the ongoing discipline to teach us that most of what we have to say about God is that we do not know how to talk about God. But even to know what we cannot say means the theologian cannot divorce what is known and not known about God from all that we know. Indeed that is why I think Newman is right to suggest that theology not only potentially has something to say to other disciplines; but just as important, theology in order to be theology has to learn from other disciplines.[46]

To be sure, therefore, theology certainly is a "field" in which nothing that is known is irrelevant for the work theology must do. Yet, as I suggested above, I do not think that means theology should try to

[46] I am, therefore, sympathetic to Gustafson's argument in *An Examined Faith: The Grace of Self-Doubt* that theology cannot and should not avoid the challenge presented by the knowledges of the university. Gustafson, however, thinks such challenges are more easily located than I believe possible. Gustafson is surely right that any effort to integrate science and theology is futile, but Gustafson seems to think the results of science will always be a challenge to the theologian. I assume that some scientific results

establish its importance for the university by promising to be the subject that shows where everything "fits." Such an ambition would be foolhardy because we do not live in a time when it is obvious that all that we know in fact "fits." At best theologians, with the aid of the philosophers, need to help us understand why what we know is so often a jumble.

There is another reason, peculiar to my own theological convictions, that makes it unwise for theology to pretend to be the discipline that brings order to the disorder of the knowledges of the university. A project to try to pull it all together I fear could be a nostalgic attempt to reclaim the habits of Christendom. Christendom created the Christian university that made it seem natural that theology would be the supreme science just as the church was the supreme institution. I, of course, do think the church is that community that rightly commands our loyalty in a manner that relativizes all other loyalties. But the church does so because it can only rule as a servant. Accordingly theology is only a "queen" of the sciences if humility determines her work.

That is why I think the situation we confront concerning the role of theology in the curricula of universities is in many ways quite favorable to the task to which we are called as theologians. It is a good thing that theology bears the burden of proof before the epistemological conceits of the knowledges represented by the contemporary university. That challenge should not only make us more truthful and faithful theologians, but we might also discover different ways to think theologically because we cannot assume the way theology was once done is the way we must do theology. Of course theology should never be done to pass muster in the university. Theology must be done in a manner that glorifies God and serves God's people. It has always been my conviction that when theology is so done, those in the university will take notice because what we have to say is so interesting.

Moreover, as I suggested at the beginning of this chapter, I think we may well discover that theology cannot be relegated to the theology or religious studies department. I appreciate Newman's contention that the secular sciences should be allowed to be secular. But I think if Christians learn to take intellectually seriously the practices that should and do constitute the church, they may well find that how we think about economics, biology, or physics is different than how those subjects are now structured in the university. I think that is particularly true given the

may be a challenge, but it is the metaphysical presumptions that inform a science that are more likely to be the source of conflict. For example, if physics were thought to show that mechanistic causation "explains" all change, then I think there is a real conflict between theology and physics. Kenneth Miller, for example, quite rightly observes the "chance" that is assumed to be at the heart of a Darwinian account of the world is "not only consistent with the idea of God, it is the only way in which a truly independent physical reality can exist" (*Finding Darwin's God: A Scientist's Search for Common Ground Between God and Evolution* (New York: Harper, 1999), pp. 234–5). Miller has the good sense, as a scientist, not to make God part of the metaphysical furniture of the universe. He, therefore, quite rightly argues that "evolution is not rigged" and that his faith in God does not "require one to postulate a God who fixes the game" (p. 238).

intellectual paradigms that dominate fields like economics and political science.[47] The problem, of course, is not the university or the subjects that constitute the university. The problem is with those like myself who identify ourselves as Christians. Namely the challenge is whether any of us live lives as Christians that are sufficient to force us to think differently about what is and is not done in the university.

I am convinced, however, that theology becoming a subject in the modern university will not happen if Christians only take a negative view of the current university. I obviously think that the university as we know it is in deep trouble; but that does not mean we would be better off without the university. We need to remember that there is no *the* university, which means that every university will present a different challenge for the teaching of theology. In order that theology be recognized as a legitimate endeavor that every university should desire to have represented in the curriculum, theologians must do the work of theology without fear. For theology to be recognized as significant, theologians must have something of significance to say.

It is, moreover, hard to imagine that theologians do not have something interesting to say given the subject of our work. It is hard to make God boring or have little significance for the way we live and think. The challenge before us, therefore, is not really whether we can convince our colleagues in the rest of the university that theology matters. The challenge is whether we are capable of performing the work of theology with the joy and confidence the subject of theology requires.[48]

[47] I am, of course, thinking about the dominance of rational choice methods not only in economics but also in most of the social sciences. I am not suggesting that there is nothing to be learned from rational choice, but the "method" clearly seems to reproduce the liberal assumptions about human cooperation that should be challenged.

[48] Equally crucial is whether a people exist that demand the work of theology be done. I have focused this chapter on the university, but as important as the university is whether there is an educated public (or church) that not only wants the work of the university to be done, but needs such work. One of the deepest problems confronting the modern university is the loss of such a public. I think few have seen this more clearly than Alasdair MacIntyre who observes, "there is no type of institutional arena in our society in which plain persons – not academic philosophers or academic political theorists – are able to engage together in systematic reasoned debate designed to arrive at a rationally well-founded mind on these matters, a common mind which might then be given political expression. Indeed the dominant forms of organization of contemporary social life militate against the coming into existence of this type of institutional arena. And so do the dominant modes of what passes for political discourse. We do not have the kinds of reading public necessary to sustain practically effective social thought. What we have instead in contemporary society are a set of small-scale academic publics within each of which rational discourse is carried on, but whose discourse is of such a kind as to have no practical effect on the conduct of social life" ("Some Enlightenment Projects Reconsidered," in *Questioning Ethics: Contemporary Debates in Philosophy*, edited by Richard Kearney and Mark Dooley (London: Routledge, 1999), p. 257). MacIntyre has developed an exemplification of what a learned public might look like in his "The Idea of an Educated Public," in *Education and Values: The Richard Peters Lectures*, edited by Graham Hudson (London: University of London Institute of Education, 1987).

2

Leaving Ruins: The Gospel and Cultural Formations

1. IN IRELAND WITH BRUCE AND LOUISE

We were on the Dingle Peninsula, County Kerry, Ireland. This was our second vacation with Bruce and Louise Kaye. The first was a tour of the American West after they had come here for the wedding of their son Nigel to Cary. The American West has stunning scenery but the West is not noted for medieval cathedrals. In Arizona you can visit, as we did, the remarkable remains of the cliff dwellings made by the "ancient ones," but it is the Grand Canyon and Monument Valley that take your breath away. That is not the case in Ireland. The scenery in Ireland is beautiful, but that scenery is filled with remains of the past inhabitants.

Those inhabitants, moreover, often prove to be Christians. There is, of course, Neolithic Ireland with its circle forts and beehive huts, its dramatic dolmens, and mysterious stone circles, but it is the Christian remains that seem to call Paula and me back time and time again to Ireland. So it was a distinct pleasure that Bruce and Louise joined us for a holiday in Ireland in which we got to share with them our love of this remarkable country.

We had begun in Galway, driven through the Burren, and come to rest in Dingle. The Dingle Peninsula is not as well known as the Ring of Kerry, but though Dingle lacks the height of Kerry's mountains it has its own distinctive beauty. Moreover, Dingle is the home of the Gallarus Oratory, a remarkable church, built entirely of dry stone masonry with walls four feet thick. It seems to have been built sometime around the beginning of the seventh century. It testifies to the extraordinary development in Ireland of monks committed at once to prayer and learning. You cannot help but marvel, once you have seen St. Finnian's small rock hut on the Aran islands, how these monks managed to sustain their commitment to learning in such rough and isolated places. One suspects, however, that the monks that sought isolation so that they might continually pray would have thought these rocky places ideal for study.

We had not long left the Gallarus Oratory when we were in search of another monastic remains that was (as is often the case in Ireland) not well marked on the map, nor were the directions on the road well displayed. But with some diligence we found it. It was a modest ruin but had the classical early Irish monastic form of a circular enclosure containing a small rectangular church surrounded by circular stone huts. The form of these monasteries, perhaps most dramatically exemplified at Glendalough and Clonmacnoise, was the attempt of the Irish monks to sustain those committed to the vocation to prayer in community. To be in community, of course, was not only for theological reasons, but also out of the necessity to avoid being killed by the Norse and Viking marauders. Thus the need for the remarkable round stone towers in which the monks, and the villagers who so often lived around the monasteries, used to protect themselves from constant invasion.

The ruins of the small monastic community we found on Dingle had no grand round tower. All that was left was the foundations of the surrounding wall, the church, and the huts. We had walked through a farmer's field to the site of the monastery and we were, as is often the case in Ireland, surrounded by sheep. As we entered the enclosure, it was obvious that Bruce was visibly moved by this modest ruin left from the seventh century. He observed that because of these monks, because of their dedication to the life of prayer and scholarship, they had made it possible for us to be Christians. He suggested that we ought to sit down and thank God for these people and for the remains that we were privileged to see in this place. And that is what we did.

That Bruce would feel the necessity to thank God for these obscure Irish monks I think unsurprising. Bruce Kaye has been about trying to establish institutions for which Christians in the future might thank God.[1] That such a project is at the heart of all that Bruce does might lead some to think we are unlikely friends or worse that our friendship depends on not making certain differences explicit. Because of my anti-Constantinianism many think I am the last person to support the kind of project Bruce has been about. Is not Bruce about trying to establish Christian institutions and develop a Christian material culture that should make an anti-establishment Christian such as myself nervous? The answer is "No." What Bruce has been about not only does not make me nervous, but I hope that many years in the future some Christians

1 Bruce's reflections on the necessity as well as penultimate character of institutions can be found in his *Web of Meaning: The Role of Origins in Christian Faith* (Sydney: Aquila Press, 2000), pp. 115–57. Bruce's understanding of the significance of institutions is a correlate of his understanding of the centrality of the incarnation of God in the person of Jesus of Nazareth as the controlling theological conviction of Anglicanism. See, for example, his discussion of the incarnation in *Church Without Walls: Being Anglican in Australia* (North Blackburn, Victoria: Dove Publications, 1995), pp. 149–51. Bruce certainly emphasizes the significance of institutions, but he also never lets us forget that institutionality cannot "contain the power and the presence of the God who is Father, Son and Holy Spirit" (*Web of Meaning*, p. 131).

will – no doubt in a very different context than the ruins of a modest seventh-century monastery in Ireland – thank God for the good work Bruce has done to help Anglicans world wide, but particularly in Australia, to develop institutions in service to the Gospel.[2]

Yet one of the reasons I think the work Bruce has been about is so important is the similarity between early Ireland and Australia. Ireland may have become one great monastery, but that it did so took some doing. The Celts, diverse as they were, did not always naturally take to Christianity.[3] Of course Australia is on the other side of the triumph of Christianity, but that means it is all the more important to try to find ways, just as they had to find ways in ancient Ireland, for the habits of Christianity to be sustained across generations. Indeed it may be harder to establish such habits in Australia than it was in ancient Ireland exactly because Australia – a strikingly secular society whose secularity I find quite attractive – may have just enough Christianity left over to inoculate it from any attempt to establish a non-establishment practice of the faith.[4]

The assumed tension some may think exists between how Bruce and I understand the challenge before the church today is nicely embodied in our first "getting to know you." Out of the blue I received a letter from Bruce, as Master of New College at the University of New South Wales, to give the 1990 New College Lectures. I had no idea what it meant to be Master of New College, I had no idea what kind of university the University of New South Wales might be, I had almost no sense of

2 Perhaps none of these institutions is more important than Bruce's founding of the *Journal of Anglican Studies*. The purpose of the *Journal*, that is, "to foster a global scholarly conversation in the service of the renewal of this [Anglican] tradition of Christian faith," is constructive and helpful. (See "Editorial," *Journal of Anglican Studies* 1.1, August, 2003: p. 9.) Indeed, the very existence of the *Journal* is a sign of hope and catholicity. Just as the early church found itself dispersed throughout the world and struggling to find connections, so Anglicanism, a peculiar English church, now finds itself scattered throughout the world. This dispersion no doubt is the source of painful disunity and ambiguous forms of authority, but it is Bruce's great gift to help us all that our dispersion is also an opportunity for discerning the work of the Spirit.

3 Bruce, quite rightly I think, traces the beginnings of Anglicanism back to the Celtic church. See *A Church Without Walls* (pp. 14–15). Bruce's refusal to begin the story of Anglicanism with the Reformation is extremely important not only for helping us understand who we have been, who we may be, but also for what future we should want. Some may wonder at my use of "we" in the last sentence, given the assumption I am a Methodist. I am a Methodist, but I am a communicant of the Church of the Holy Family in Chapel Hill, North Carolina. Moreover Paula Gilbert, my spouse, is a Methodist minister who has been appointed by her bishop to Holy Family. Methodism is a reform movement in the Anglican communion and we like to think we are bringing that movement home.

4 I am aware, of course, that in *Web of Meaning*, Bruce suggests it is not helpful to describe Australia as secular because in Australia, in contrast to America, religious traditions were allowed to be involved in the affairs of government in a manner that defied the American "separation" of church and state. By calling Australia "secular," however, I am not thinking of legal arrangements, but rather the absence of any civil religion in Australia. So my use of the description "secular" is meant as a compliment.

what kind of country Australia is, but Paula and I shared in common the idea we would like to go to Australia. So I accepted the invitation with little idea of what I was getting myself into.

With Bruce's help, however, I did begin to read about Australia. Moreover once Paula and I arrived we began to understand what an extraordinary project Bruce was trying to pull off. In a society and university that is at best indifferent to Christianity, he was trying to institutionalize an unmistakable Christian voice that was not in perpetual and petulant mourning for a "lost Christendom." Of course I learned from Bruce that it would be odd for Australians to mourn a lost Christendom because there has never been an Australian Christendom except in the fervid imagination of a few Anglicans who were able to deny the obvious reality that Australia was a long way from England.

The title of the lectures I gave and subsequent book, *After Christendom?*, was probably a mistake given the character of Australian society.[5] If Locke was the semi-Christian public philosopher of America that allowed Americans to sustain the illusion that America had a Christian beginning, no such presumption was possible in Australia. Bentham, not Locke, is the public philosopher of Australia. In America I've thought my task to be helping Christians not confuse Christianity with America, which means I often have had to criticize those who confuse the effects of Christianity with the Gospel. Bruce, on the other hand, found himself in a society in which the church had not been all that successful in producing "effects."[6] Bruce seemed to be trying to build what I was trying to call into question.

However, I think there is a greater compatibility between our tasks than might seem apparent. I do not think the argument in *After Christendom?* is incompatible with the purpose Bruce was trying to accomplish by establishing the New College Lecture. I am convinced that he is right to think that the Gospel cannot help but be about the formation of a culture. Christians not only do, but also we must produce a material culture. The people of Israel, Jesus, and the church must take up space in the world. Accordingly, particularly in our time, we depend on ruins of the past that have survived the ravages of time and circumstance to help us, not only to survive, but also to live faithful to the Gospel. How I can think that to be the case and yet remain an anti-Constantinian I must now try to explain.

5 The book was originally published in 1991 by Abingdon Press. There is now a second edition of the book with a new "Preface" in which I try to explain why the book was misunderstood by those who persist in calling me a "sectarian."

6 I am not suggesting that the churches of Australia had no effect on Australian society or that the churches do not continue to make some difference. Yet the absence, for example, of any universities sponsored by the church is an indication that the challenge before Australian Christianity is quite different than that in America. Of course it is not at all clear that the universities established in America by Christians have been "a good thing."

2. THE GOSPEL AS CULTURAL FORMATION

"Modernity" is obviously a name for a complex reality. Charles Taylor rightly asks if we do not need to speak of "multiple modernities" in order to indicate that many non-western cultures have modernized in their own way making any general theory of modernity impossible.[7] Yet Taylor argues that "a certain kind of social imaginary" has shaped western societies. This imaginary, moreover, has become so self-evident we cannot conceive any alternatives to the world created by this imaginary. For example, the social forms correlative of this imaginary – that is, the market economy, the public sphere, and self-governing people – are simply assumed to be unquestionable "givens."

According to Taylor, the social imaginary that has shaped the world in which we now find ourselves "starts with individuals and conceives society as established for their sake. Political society is seen as an instrument for something pre-political."[8] Political society is understood to be the instrument to help individuals serve each other for mutual benefit by providing security and by fostering exchange and prosperity. Such societies emphasize the importance of rights which "reflects the holders' sense of their own agency and of the situation that agency normatively demands in the world, namely freedom."[9]

Taylor, however, suggests that the individual that enjoys such freedom is "disembodied." The individual that is "free" is no longer understood to live in an enchanted world in which they can only imagine who they are by locating their membership in a society that reflects an essential order.[10] The individual is now disembodied, requiring that they choose to be who they want to be. In my language, Taylor is suggesting that modernity names the time when a people are produced that believe they should have no story except the story they choose when they had no story. That is, modernity is the time when we assume our task is to defeat time. As a result modern humanism is, according to Taylor, unprecedented just to the extent that it is assumed that to flourish as an individual involves no relation to anything higher.[11]

One of the givens that sustains social orders determined by this imaginary is the distinction between the public and private. According to Taylor the public sphere (which is the attempt to sustain a context of

7 Charles Taylor, *Modern Social Imaginaries* (Durham: Duke University Press, 2004), p. 1.

8 Taylor, *Modern Social Imaginaries*, p. 19. In *Web of Meaning* Bruce rightly suggests "it is a silliness to imagine that a society is simply an agglomeration of individuals" (p. 148). I think he is right, but it is certainly the case that contemporary political theory in America seems committed to that "silliness." Bruce quite rightly I think argues that social pluralism is in reality the pluralism of groups and institutions.

9 Taylor, *Modern Social Imaginaries*, p. 21.

10 Taylor, *Modern Social Imaginaries*, pp. 49–67.

11 Taylor, *Modern Social Imaginaries*, p. 57.

debate free from social conflict to limit political power) must be radically secular. Such an understanding of the secular is radical because in contrast to assumptions that society must be founded on some divine foundation, this understanding of society assumes that the social order is constituted "in something that transcends contemporary common action."[12] In such societies time must be understood as "purely profane."[13]

In such a "modernity" Christians have found it next to impossible to avoid the presumption that Christianity is a set of beliefs necessary to make their lives "meaningful." Conservative and liberal Christians believe that they have a personal relation with God, a relation often associated with a decisive event or experience, which may or may not be enhanced by going to church. The crucial presumption is that "going to church" is clearly not at the heart of what it means to be a Christian. Therefore modernity names the time in which Christians have found it almost impossible to avoid the spiritualization of their faith. Ironically many Christians, who identify themselves as "conservative," that is, who assume it is very important that they have "been saved," fail to understand that their understanding of Christianity shares much with ancient gnosticism.[14]

This understanding of "where we are as Christians in modernity" I think can help us understand why the emphasis on the church, and in particular the visible church, in my and John Howard Yoder's work is so often misunderstood. Yoder argues that one of the results of the legalization of Christianity under Constantine was the invisibility of the church.[15] Yoder's work represents an attempt to reclaim the church's visibility as a necessary correlative of the eschatological character of the Gospel. The salvation wrought in Christ is not "spiritual," but rather the creation of a new community that constitutes an alternative to the world. According to Yoder:

> Jesus did not bring to faithful Israel any corrected ritual or any new theories about the being of God. He brought them a new peoplehood and a new way of living together. The very

[12] Taylor, *Modern Social Imaginaries*, p. 93.

[13] Taylor, *Modern Social Imaginaries*, p. 98.

[14] During our most recent visit with Bruce and Louise, a visit that allowed us to enjoy Tasmania together, and in particular the penguins at Bisheno, Bruce observed that his enemy has always been fundamentalism and my enemy has always been Protestant liberalism. I replied: "Same thing." Fundamentalism and Protestant liberalism are forms of Christianity, and note I assume fundamentalists and liberals are Christians, who reflect the formation of Christianity in modernity to be "beliefs" adhered to by an "individual." Both are the bastard stepchildren of pietism run amuck. See, for example, my argument that fundamentalism and historical-criticism are two sides of the same coin, in *Unleashing the Scripture: Freeing the Bible from Captivity to America* (Nashville: Abingdon Press, 1993).

[15] John Howard Yoder, "The Constantinian Sources of Western Social Ethics," in his *The Priestly Kingdom: Social Ethics as Gospel* (Notre Dame: University of Notre Dame Press, 2001), pp. 135–49.

> existence of such a group is itself a deep social change. Its very presence was such a threat that He had to be crucified. But such a group is not only by its existence a novelty on the social scene; if it lives faithfully, it is also the most powerful tool of social change.[16]

The challenge is how to enact this understanding of the necessary visibility of the church in a time when the politics that shapes Christians – the politics of Taylor's account of the modern imaginary – makes that effort appear unintelligible.[17] In such a time the ruins inherited from the past establishment of Christianity can provide imaginative ways to reclaim the visibility of the church.

For example, Yoder calls attention to "a form of Catholic discernment" in the early medieval period between the old Caesars and the new Carolingians, an age in which civilization had to survive without the support of righteous royalty that sustained Christian practices of holiness. Though Yoder does not mention the Irish, they certainly are among those engaged in the project to which he calls attention. He notes that during this time moral education consisted of telling the stories of holy people who lived lives of renunciation and withdrawal. But these same people were often called from their cave or from their role as abbot to be made a bishop. "It was an age when the bishop, through his control of the sacrament of absolution, was the community's main moral teacher and, through his administration of the right of sanctuary, was its most solid civil peacekeeper."[18]

16 John Howard Yoder, *The Original Revolution: Essays on Christian Pacifism* (Eugene, OR: Wipf and Stock, 1998), p. 31.

17 In *Performing the Faith: Bonhoeffer and the Practice of Nonviolence* (Grand Rapids: Brazos Press, 2004), I tried to show how at the heart of Bonhoeffer's work was an attempt to recover the visibility of the church. Yet Bonhoeffer's stress on the centrality of the church in no way entailed an abandonment of the world. Indeed the "worldliness" of *Letters and Papers from Prison* is but the outworking of his Christology. For example, in the *Ethics* he asks whether the world and human beings only exist for the sake of having faith in Jesus Christ. He says, "This question is to be answered affirmatively in the sense that Jesus Christ was there for the world and for human beings; this means that only where everything is directed toward Jesus Christ does the world become really the world and human beings become really human, according to Matt. 6:32(33). Only in recognizing that everything created is there for the sake of Christ and is sustained in Christ (Col. 1:16f.) are the world and human beings taken fully seriously. Given these presuppositions, the church indeed has a certain interest not only in the *puntum mathematicum* of faith, but also in empirical entities in the formation of a certain attitude concerning worldly questions, and in certain earthly conditions" (Dietrich Bonhoeffer, *Ethics*, translated by Ilse Todt, Heinz Ecuard Todt, Ernest Feil, and Clifford Green, edited by Clifford Green (Minneapolis: Fortress Press, 2005), p. 361). Bruce's insistence that the church must "take up space in the world" seems quite similar to Bonhoeffer's understanding of the necessary "worldliness" of the church.

18 John Howard Yoder, *For the Nations: Essays Public and Evangelical* (Grand Rapids: Eerdmans, 1997), pp. 212–13.

Yoder observes that our western moral universe has been impoverished by the Schoolmen, who looked for something more generalizable than the lives of the monks, and later by the Reformers, who denounced abuses associated with monasticism, and as a result we have been robbed of the place of hagiography in morality. Note: Yoder, the alleged "sectarian," here looks to the past to discover amid the ruins of the Christian past patterns of faithfulness, which includes the office of bishop, to shape our imagination for faithful living today. He does so because he rightly understands that the Christian faith requires the shaping of a visible community constituted by material practices that give us ways to go on when we are not sure where we are.[19]

Of course the forms of life that Christians produce necessary for faithful living are not created in order to leave ruins for the future. Indeed if Christians tried to insure that they would not be forgotten by Christians in the future they would betray a lack of trust in God. For we know that God is able to raise his people up from the "stones" (Matthew 3:9). Rather the ruins of the past are a resource exactly because they were not created to insure that future Christians would not have to be as creative as those that produced what we now cherish.[20] We now can assume the canon of the scripture is a great gift the church has been given; but that gift requires us to be as courageous and creative as those that gave us the canon.

It is instructive, in this respect, to contrast the ruins of the church with Hitler's architectural ambitions. Albert Speer, Hitler's architect who was to become the Minister of Armaments, tells of the attempt in the Third Reich to build buildings that would have a "ruin value." He notes that:

> the idea was that buildings of modern construction were poorly suited to form that "bridge of tradition" to future generations which Hitler was calling for. It was hard to imagine that rusting heaps of rubble could communicate these heroic inspirations which Hitler admired in the monuments of the past. By using special materials and by applying certain principles of statics, we should be able to build

[19] Oddly, I think, the often made charge that I am a "sectarian" takes no notice of the emphasis in my work on the materiality of the Christian faith. See, for example, my chapter "What Could it Mean for the Church to be Christ's Body?" in *In Good Company: The Church as Polis* (Notre Dame: University of Notre Dame Press, 1995), pp. 19–31.

[20] Goshen College, a Mennonite college in Goshen, Indiana, for many years did not have or attempt to raise an endowment on grounds that endowments work to relieve future generations of the moral commitments and sacrifices necessary to sustain the institution of the college. Such a commitment reflects the Mennonite conviction that to be a Christian one must make a voluntary decision. Though I am not convinced that what it means to be called to be a Christian is rightly understood to be "voluntary," the insight is one that is lost at our peril. Of course it is always a matter of judgment whether an "inheritance" may hinder or help sustain the commitments of future Christians.

> structures which even in a state of decay, after hundreds of (such were our reckonings) thousands of years would more or less resemble Roman models.[21]

Speer retrospectively acknowledges that the buildings so designed were monstrosities. They were so because they could not help but exhibit the prideful pretensions and ambitions of the Third Reich – prideful pretensions and ambitions too often shared by state regimes that are not as evil as the Third Reich. Christians have not been free of such pride and pretension, but the very character of our faith makes it difficult to avoid the exposure of our pride. The ruins the church produces cannot help but be the ruins of a ruined, that is, sinful people.[22] For Christians what lasts does so because it was not built or written or sung to last forever, but to glorify God. The fragile beauty of a Tintern Abbey, and the many abbeys like it, testifies to the willingness of monks to create a world shaped by humility.

Yoder's calling attention to the significance of the lives of the saints, and the office of the bishop necessary to sustain such lives, is but a reminder that a world was and can be sustained by the sacrament of reconciliation. The danger for Christians is to think that there is one form of architecture, one form of monasticism, one way to be holy, one way to think or write, one way to sing correlative to the Gospel. There came a time when the monastic form of Ireland needed reform. The round huts, not without a struggle, were replaced by the Cistercian church and cloisters.[23] For Christians change is not only inevitable and often painful but also necessary. It is so because the God we worship prohibits us from identifying the work of our own hands with the One that we seek to praise with the work of our hands. That conviction animates the work of Bruce Kaye as he has sought to produce work that testifies to the Christian joyful duty to be present in the world.

21 Albert Speer, *Inside the Third Reich*, translated by Richard and Clara Winston (New York: Avon Books, 1970), p. 93.

22 I am thinking, of course, of Rusty Reno's *In the Ruins of the Church: Sustaining Faith in an Age of Diminished Christianity* (Grand Rapids: Brazos Press, 2002). In response to the current controversies gripping the Anglican communion Reno suggests that "ruins are not unfit for Christian habitation," because in Christ Christians are not called to love strength, power, or beauty (p. 27). Reno makes an eloquent case for staying with the church in our current confusions, but there is a hint that there was a time in which the church was less in ruins or at least the church was otherwise ruined (p. 94). I have no difficulty with the latter, but I am not sure I think the church has ever been "less in ruins." No doubt Reno is right to call attention to our current lack of biblical literacy, the loss of the tradition and in particular the creed, as well as the failure of bishops to be signs of unity, but I remain unconvinced that there ever existed a church free of sin. Indeed it may be one of the gifts to the church in our time is to make unavoidable the acknowledgment of the pride that shaped the church's status in Christendom. If the church is currently being humiliated, that may well be a necessary condition if we are to lead lives of humility – and humor.

23 For an account of these reforms see James Lydon, *The Making of Ireland: From Ancient Times to the Present* (London: Routledge, 1998), pp. 37–61.

For Christians, particularly in the modernities of our time, must find the means to create space in the world if we are to serve the world in which we find ourselves. Such a space if produced with joy hopefully will become a resource for the imagination for Christians who face quite different challenges than those that produced the ruins we now inhabit. "Ruins" come in different forms and shapes requiring constant re-narration. Rock ruins seem particularly important in a time when Christians are tempted to spiritualize our faith. But any ruin, be it a building, book, or painting, requires memory. That memory, moreover, must be governed by the story that is the Christ. The peculiar challenge before us – that is, the Christians of modernity – is whether we have the resources to have our memories so determined. So I end with a memory.

3. IN LEADVILLE, COLORADO WITH BRUCE AND LOUISE

We were close to the end of our holiday in the American West. After the Grand Canyon and Monument Valley, we had turned north back into the Rockies. We had spent the night in the picturesque town of Silverton, Colorado. The beauty of the mountains surrounding Silverton made negotiating the hairpin curves necessary to get to Silverton worth it. We set out again planning to spend the night in Leadville, Colorado. Leadville turned out to be as unappealing as Silverton was appealing. Leadville was even higher than Silverton, but the scenery was not inspiring and the town was aptly named. It was an old mining town, but that lead was what they mined meant the town was, well, leaden.

What Leadville had instead of charm was a bicycle race with hundreds of contestants who had taken up most of the rooms. We were lucky to find a place to stay, but we had actually arrived earlier than we had anticipated and beat some of the crowd following the bicyclists. It was a Saturday, which meant that we would need to find a church for Sunday. Bruce and Louise have the principle that when on holiday you should go to the church that has historically been the church of the inhabitants of the country in which you are visiting. So they insisted, in spite of Paula's and my protestations, that on Sunday morning in Leadville we should go to the Methodist church.

So we began a search for the Methodist church having gotten the address from the phone directory. Leadville is a town of no more than two or three thousand, but finding the church was not easy. When we finally did find the small frame church it was boarded up, having some time before gone out of business. So Paula and I got what we wanted, namely, to find the Anglican church. Again the search proved complicated, but we did find the church. On the front door was the notice that the priest was coming from a town over a hundred miles away, which meant the service would begin around ten.

After breakfast we made our way to the church at the appointed time. There we discovered two other couples waiting for the service to begin. As we waited for the priest, we discovered that we were all from "out of town." We waited, assuming the priest would show up and he did, driving up in his four-wheel vehicle. He was quite apologetic about being late, but explained he had run into a violent thunderstorm as he had crossed the mountains to get to Leadville. He unlocked the church and invited us in. He then prepared the church for the liturgy.

He was dressed the way men dress in the American West. He had on jeans with a western shirt. I seem to remember, however, he put on a stole when he began the liturgy. Since the church did not have copies of the Book of Common Prayer, the liturgy consisted primarily of the reading of scripture, the sermon, and the Eucharist. The sermon was quite thoughtful and we were invited to respond. You could not help but be moved by the seriousness with which this priest took his duties for the six or seven of us who showed up to worship God in late summer in this little Anglican church in Leadville, Colorado.

Before we moved to the Eucharist we were invited to introduce ourselves with the usual indication of where we were from, what we were doing in Colorado, as well as what we did. We did so and in the process discovered that the only lay people in the congregation were Louise and myself. I have often observed that the Episcopal Church of America will be the first church in which every lay person has their own priest, because when an American Anglican gets serious about being a Christian they often assume they should be ordained. Here in Leadville, Colorado, that prediction seemed to be a reality – a reality, moreover, about which Bruce no doubt could not help but feel somewhat ambiguous, given his conviction that crucial to the church's witness is the role of the laity.

God knows what God is doing with the church in our time, but I believe that this Sunday liturgy in Leadville, Colorado, is not only a sign of hope, but also confirmation of the work Bruce has exemplified in his life. Leadville, Colorado, is not a natural home for Anglicans, but then neither is Australia. Indeed one of the reasons I like Australians is they are a lot like Texans, that is, they do not have anything to live up to. Those that inhabit the American West are a hard people made so by living in a hard land. Yet some people we do not know thought it important in Leadville, Colorado, to build and sustain, even to this day, a small frame building with an altar on which the Eucharist can be celebrated Sunday after Sunday. These unknown brothers and sisters made it possible for us to worship God in Leadville, Colorado. The confused and comprised Episcopal Church of America, moreover, produced a priest to celebrate the Eucharist on that memorable Sunday.

No doubt the building as well as the sustaining of the church in Leadville required great effort. But that is what Christians do. That is what Bruce has done not only in Australia, but also for Anglicanism around the world. For he has quite simply drawn on his experience in Australia, Germany, England, and America to help us discover the gifts from the past, gifts that often come as ruins, as resources for our life together. In the process he has helped us discover as a people marked by particular places and histories that we are friends just to the extent Sunday after Sunday we are drawn to Word and Table. By being an unapologetically Australian Christian, he has helped Christians around the world know better how to live so that hopefully in the future Christians will thank God we carried on even when we leave nothing more impressive than a small white frame church in Leadville, Colorado.

3

How Risky is *The Risk of Education*? Random Reflections from the American Context

1. WHAT TO DO WHEN YOU ARE NOT SURE YOU HAVE ANYTHING INTERESTING TO SAY

I find myself in an extremely embarrassing position. At least it is an extremely embarrassing position for me. I am one of those people who thinks it is better to have views than arguments. I suppose that a view is a kind of argument if you believe as I do that arguments depend on judgments that, if they are really judgments, are not arbitrary. So I seldom find myself without anything to say. Indeed most people think I have had far too much to say because I am far too willing to pronounce on almost anything. My weakness is that there is almost nothing in which I am not interested. My strength is that there is almost nothing in which I am not interested.

I am, moreover, not only interested in education but, in particular, the kind of innovative suggestions Reverend Luigi Giussani makes for reclaiming education as a Christian activity. I thought I would, therefore, have much to say about Giussani's book, *The Risk of Education.*[1] But alas, I find myself in such fundamental agreement with Giussani that it seems all I can do is say, "I wish I had said that." In truth, however, I have already said some of what Giussani has written in his book. What I have said has been primarily directed to the work of the university, but I think much of my criticism of contemporary universities is quite similar to Giussani's critique of secular educational practices in secondary schools.[2]

[1] Luigi Giussani, *The Risk Of Education: Discovering Our Ultimate Destiny*, translated by Rosanna Frongia (New York: Crossroad, 2001).

[2] Over the years I have written a series of essays about the church and the kind of education we find in modern universities. See, for example, my "How Christian Universities Contribute to the Corruption of the Youth," *Christian Existence Today: Essays on Church, World, and Living In Between* (Grand Rapids: Brazos Press, 2001), pp. 237–53; "The Politics of Witness: How We Educate Christians in Liberal Societies," in *After Christendom?* (Nashville: Abingdon, 1999), pp. 133–54; "Christians in

So I fear what follows is no more than my attempt to show how some of my concerns about the kind of education students receive in the colleges and universities of America confirm Giussani's critique of secular education. I am, of course, aware that the focus of Giussani's work is on the education of students at younger ages than college students. However, I think it is not unreasonable for me to focus on "higher education," not only because I know it best, but more importantly because what happens in universities usually has a direct effect on secondary education. Teachers in secondary education too often reproduce the mistakes they learned at the university. So the miseducation begun in college is passed on to students in lower grades, which means they will have no resources to challenge the education they later receive in college.

I think one of the reasons I find myself in sympathy with Giussani's work is that my reflections about education and, in particular, the education represented in the modern university has always been part of my project to reclaim the significance of the virtues for any account of the moral life. A focus on the virtues means you cannot easily separate what you come to know from how you come to know. Any knowledge worth having cannot help but shape who we are and accordingly our understanding of the world. Thus I use the description, "moral formation," rather than education, because I think all education, whether acknowledged or not, is moral formation. I think this is particularly true in courses that are *not* officially thought of as "ethics." For example, consider the moral seriousness of medical education in comparison to the training seminarians receive today. Students in seminaries too often think it more important for them to take courses in counseling (after all that is how you help people) rather than to take courses in Christology. In medical school, however, no student gets to decide whether she or he will or will not take anatomy. If you are going to be a doctor, you will take anatomy or give up your ambition to be a doctor. Anatomy may not sound like a course in ethics, but the kind of work young physicians are required to do if they are to study anatomy, I think, is rightly described as moral formation.

The intellectual and moral seriousness of medical education compared to seminary education, I think, can be attributed to a set of cultural presuppositions that are crucial for how we understand the training of students for medicine and for the ministry. Quite simply, no one believes in our day that an inadequately trained priest might damage their salvation; but people do believe an inadequately trained doctor can hurt them. Thus people are much more concerned about who their doctor may be than who is their priest. That such is the case, of course, indicates that no matter how seriously we may think of ourselves as

the Hands of Flaccid Secularists: Theology and 'Moral Inquiry' in the Modern University", "Christian Schooling, or Making Students Dysfunctional" in *Sanctify Them in the Truth: Holiness Exemplified* (Nashville: Abingdon, 1998), pp. 201–26.

Christians we may well be living lives that betray our conviction that God matters.

In his book, *The Restructuring of American Religion*, Robert Wuthnow observed that one of the trends in church life in America in the second half of the last century was the increasing growth of the laity who had college educations. He notes it was extremely rare in the 1950s for Baptist, Lutheran, or Catholic churches to have more than one in seven who had gone to college. Methodists and Presbyterians might have had a ratio of one to four. By the 1970s at least one person in four had been to college in most denominations, and in several the college educated were a clear majority. He suggests these "proportions would likely have been even larger had it not been for the fact that college educated people fled the churches in droves in the 1960s."[3] It seems, at least if Wuthnow's study is correct, that the single best indicator of whether as a person ages they will be identified with a church is determined by their having gone to a college or a university.[4]

There are many reasons that may account for this development. The social unrest of the 1960s associated with Vietnam or the change in sexual practices during the same period may have created the conditions that led many to think the church was irrelevant to their lives. No doubt the relation between college education and the increased earning power of those who have gone to college had and continues to have an effect if you believe – as I believe we are required to believe by the Gospel – that being wealthy is a disability for anyone who desires to be a Christian. I am sure no one factor is sufficient to account for the loss of membership in the mainline Protestant churches in America.

That said, however, I think it would be a mistake not to take seriously that what many learned, or thought they were learning, in colleges and universities led them to abandon Christianity. That students took course after course in which there was no discernible connection to Christian claims about the way things are surely created the conditions that made the conclusion that Christianity is at best irrelevant, and at worst false, hard to avoid. In other words I suspect that many people who leave their Christianity behind after they have gone to college do so because they have been created by God to desire the truth. Yet that desire has been formed by knowledges that seem to make it impossible for them to think that what Christians believe could be true. At best they assume the church may be important for spiritual or moral issues, but those spheres of life are not assumed to be about truth.

The strategy of many Christian colleges and universities, both Catholic and Protestant, unfortunately served to underwrite the presumption that the "Christian" part of education did not have to do with "truth."

3 Robert Wuthnow, *The Restructuring of American Religion* (Princeton: Princeton University Press, 1988), p. 160.

4 Even if the college educated continue to identify with a church, Wuthnow's study clearly indicates that they are less likely to identify with Christian orthodoxy.

What made a school "Christian" was not the content of the courses, but a concern for the "whole student." Student life, therefore, became the locus for any expression of Christianity. The relegation of strong religious beliefs to the "personal" side of life in modern universities reflected the distinction between the private and the public imposed on the church by liberal political regimes. Christian theologians aided this development by underwriting what Douglas Sloan identifies as a two-realm theory of truth.[5] Such a view distinguished the truths of science – which was thought to be objective and impersonal – from the truths of faith, which are then called subjective, grounded as they are in feelings, convention, or "common human experience."

These attempts to forge a "peace treaty" between the Christian faith and what were assumed to be more objective modes of knowledge that were the hallmark of the university are increasingly being called into question. Unfortunately, however, the critics that are challenging the forms of knowledge that so dominate the contemporary university are not drawing on the resources of Christian theology. Indeed the challenges too often seem to make problematic whether we can know anything at all. As a result, too often the critics of modernity only underwrite the fragmentation of the university curriculums. As a result, Alasdair MacIntyre observes:

> What the Catholic faith confronts today in American higher education and indeed in American education more generally is not primarily some range of alternative beliefs about the order of things, but rather a belief that there is no such thing as the order of things of which there could be a unified, if complex, understanding or even a movement toward such an understanding. There is on this contemporary view nothing to understanding except what is supplied by the specialized and professionalized disciplines and subdisciplines. Higher education has become a set of assorted and heterogeneous specialized enquiries into a set of assorted and heterogeneous subject-matters, and general education is a set of introductions to these enquiries together with a teaching of the basic skills necessary for initiation into them, something to be got through in order to advance beyond it into the specialized disciplines. The undergraduate major, when taught by those whose training has led them to presuppose this view – for it is often taken for granted, rather than explicitly stated – becomes increasingly no more than a prologue to graduate school, even for those who will never go to graduate school. And graduate school becomes a place where narrowness of mind is inculcated as a condition for success within each

5 Douglas Sloan, *Faith and Knowledge: Mainline Protestantism and Higher Education* (Louisville: Westminster/John Knox Press, 1994).

particular discipline in terms defined by its senior practitioners.[6]

MacIntyre makes clear he is not against specialization – because any discipline, even philosophy, cannot do its work well without detailed investigations. Yet in modern university curriculums, every course threatens to be an introductory course, because the faculties even in their individual disciplines cannot agree what needs to be learned first to make later learning possible. As a result every course a student takes has to begin with a beginning that from the student's perspective is constantly changing. This is particularly true in the humanities; but given the increasing specialized character of the individual sciences, they are beginning to suffer the same fate as the humanities.

From MacIntyre's perspective, the fragmentation of the curriculum makes it all the more important that Catholic universities recognize the significance of philosophy for any serious education that has any pretense to inculcate in students the skills necessary for those who would love the truth. According to MacIntyre, philosophy is the discipline committed to the inquiry necessary to understand how the disciplines that make up the university contribute to, but cannot themselves supply, an understanding of the order of things.[7] So a Catholic university cannot be such if it does not require students to study philosophy not only at the beginning of their study but also at the end.

Yet of equal importance, according to MacIntyre, is the study of theology. Catholic teaching rightly maintains that the natural order of things cannot be adequately understood by reason if reason is divorced from the recognition that all that is has been brought into being by God and is directed to the ends to which God orders creation. What is learned

6 Alasdair MacIntyre, "Catholic Universities: Dangers, Hopes, Choices," in *Higher Learning and Catholic Traditions*, edited by Robert E. Sullivan (Notre Dame: University of Notre Dame Press, 2001), pp. 5–8. MacIntyre provides a useful tool to test how far a university has moved to this fragmented condition. He asks whether a wonderful and effective undergraduate teacher who is able to communicate how his or her discipline contributes to an integrated account of things – but whose publishing consists of one original but brilliant article on how to teach – would receive tenure. Or would tenure be granted to a professor who is unable or unwilling to teach undergraduates, preferring to teach only advanced graduate students and engaged in "cutting-edge research." MacIntyre suggests if the answers to these two inquiries are "No" and "Yes," you can be sure you are at a university, at least if it is a Catholic university, in need of serious reform (p. 6). I feel quite confident that MacIntyre learned to put the matter this way by serving on the Appointment, Promotion, and Tenure Committee of Duke University. I am confident that this is the source of his understanding of the increasing subdisciplinary character of fields, because I also served on that committee for seven years. During that time I observed people becoming "leaders" in their fields by making their work so narrow that the "field" consisted of no more than five or six people. We would often hear from the chairs of the departments that they could not understand what the person was doing, but they were sure the person to be considered for tenure was the best "in his or her field."

7 MacIntyre, "Catholic Universities: Dangers, Hopes, Choices," p. 5.

from nature about God, MacIntyre notes, will always be meager as well as subject to the human limitations and distortions resulting from our sinfulness. Yet it remains the case that "universities always need both the enlargement of vision and the correction of error that can be provided only from a theological standpoint, one that brings truths of Christian revelation to bear on our studies."[8]

I am fundamentally in agreement with MacIntyre's account of the challenges facing us if we are to think seriously about what it means to reclaim education as a Christian enterprise. So I have nothing but sympathy for Giussani's attempt to help us see why and how Christians must reclaim education as a task of the church. The story he tells in "The Introduction to the 1995 Edition" about his first confrontation with students who did not believe matters of faith had anything to do with reason is a wonderful example of why education matters and why it matters for moral formation (p. 19).[9] I think Giussani, moreover, is right to insist that faith is "the highest form of rationality" (p. 19). But to so argue means you have to confront, as Giussani did, the deceits of modernity represented by the Professor Miccinesi's, that is, the teachers of the students who think faith has nothing to do with truth, of this world.[10] I fear Professor Miccinesi, moreover, is a nice exhibit of the challenge Christians face in education today. The problem quite simply is that the secular have become so stupid that they do not even recognize they do not and, indeed, cannot understand the commonplaces that make the Christian faith the Christian faith.

So I find myself in profound sympathy not only with the general argument about education Giussani makes, but also with the finer grained arguments he uses to sustain his overall perspective. That may seem strange because I am a Protestant, that is, a representative of that form of Christianity that according to Giussani separates "faith from following" (p. 116). Yet unfortunately I fear Giussani's characterization of Protestantism, at least the Protestantism that now exists, is correct. Put differently: Protestantism now names that form of Christianity that in the name of reform tried to separate the "essentials" of the Christian faith

8 MacIntyre, "Catholic Universities: Dangers, Hopes, Choices," p. 4.

9 I will make my references to Giussani in internal footnotes in the text.

10 Though I think MacIntyre would largely be in agreement with Giussani's position, I am not sure he would be willing to say as Giussani does that faith is the highest form of rationality. MacIntyre argues that philosophy is a strictly secular discipline, which means his arguments concerning how philosophy is properly understood do not draw on any theological presuppositions. According to MacIntyre "this is a universe that is at once Catholic and secular, in which purpose is at home, in which human and other goods are integral to the intelligible order of things, and in which the project of making that order of things intelligible to us through the activities of enquiry proper to universities is itself to be understood as a part of the order of things" (p. 4). I have no doubt that MacIntyre would not think this means that faith is irrational, but I am not sure if MacIntyre would think that faith is as rational as the "secular" discipline of philosophy. One catches a hint in MacIntyre from time to time that he may have a far too strict distinction between nature and grace.

from the contingent. The result was to turn Christianity into a belief system available to the individual without mediation by the church. Protestants, therefore, found themselves in modernity without resources to shape a way of life that can resist the forces that threaten to destroy any robust account of Christian "following" necessary for the education of young people as Christians. I fear this is particularly true of that most Protestant country yet founded, that is, the United States of America.

2. THE MATERIALITY OF THE CHRISTIAN FAITH AND THE DIFFERENCE IT MAKES IN EDUCATION

The comments made in this last paragraph, however, bring me to the most important challenge Giussani presents for those of us committed to education as moral formation in America. Giussani sees quite well that education is not possible if you restrict education to the classroom. This is particularly true if we are to sustain Christian education. Giussani puts it this way:

> The Christian fact is permanent throughout history. It has a structure that nothing can change because it is a definitive event. Nevertheless, the Christian who lives out this event, in dealing with the cultural, social, and political conditions of his times – unless he lacks intelligence or is totally slothful – cannot help but judge the prevailing ideas and structures from the point of view of his lived faith. As a result, the desire to create an alternative culture and alternative structures is unavoidable (p. 117).

Though I am often accused of being a "fideistic, sectarian, tribalist," I think Giussani is exactly right that the Christian faith requires expression in the everyday habits of life.[11] This, of course, is but the outworking of Giussani's claim above that faith requires a "following," that is, the "recognition of Christ, our love for him shaped by the parameters of time and space in which his event reaches us" (p. 116). I think, moreover, Giussani's insistence that faith is the highest form of rationality is a correlative of his claim that faith to be the Christian faith must be embodied in the practices of a community that will inexorably find itself in tension with the world.

I am aware that I may seem to be making Giussani sound very much like some of the arguments I have made about the necessity of the church to distance itself from the world in which we now find ourselves. But I trust those who know Giussani better than I do will correct me if they think I have misunderstood him. Yet I think my agreement with Giussani provides me with the means to say why I think some have so

11 See, for example, my *With the Grain of the Universe: The Church's Witness and Natural Theology* (Grand Rapids: Brazos Press, 2001).

misunderstood the kind of claims I have been making about why it is so important that the church not accept in liberal societies its relegation into the world of "spiritual." I fear my anti-Constantinianism has led some to think that I have tried to convince Christians to give up on the world by becoming "pure." Nothing could be further from the truth. The church that must exist, if the kinds of arguments I have tried to develop are to be intelligible, must be what Giussani says it must be, that is, a material reality shaping the equally material realities of politics, recreation, art, buying and selling, "personal" relations, in short, the whole of our lives.

I think this has particular importance for how we think about education. For if as Giussani maintains, "to educate means to help the human soul enter into the totality of the real" (p. 105), then the content of what is taught by Christians may appear quite different from secular subjects. MacIntyre rightly argues that what students have to learn from the standpoint of a Catholic university is that education in physics, history, or economics is incomplete "until it is to some degree illuminated by philosophical enquiry, and all education, including their philosophical education, is incomplete until it is illuminated by theologically grounded insight."[12] Yet I think Giussani is suggesting an even stronger case than that made by MacIntyre. For if Giussani is right about the fact of faith requiring an alternative culture, then it is at least possible that the very content of physics, history, or economics shaped by such a faith may be different.[13]

I need to be very clear about what I am saying about how the practices that comprise the Christian faith may shape the material conditions that make what Christians mean by physics quite different from what physics might mean if it is produced by those who do not share our faith. Am I really suggesting that there might be something like a "Christian physics" or a "Christian economics"? I can only say, "It depends on the character of what is meant by physics or economics in the societies in which the church finds herself." Christians can never fear what we have to learn from honest investigation of the world, even if such investigations are undertaken by those who have no identification as Christians.[14] Yet neither can Christians assume that knowledge of the world is a "given" to be uncritically accepted by Christians.

12 MacIntyre, "Catholic Universities: Dangers, Hopes, Choices," p. 8.

13 Guissani defines culture "as the critical, systematic development of an experience. An experience is an event that opens us up to the totality of reality: experience always implies a comparison between what one feels and what one believes to be the ultimate ideal or meaning. Culture works to unfold this implication for wholeness and totality which is part of every human experience" (p. 133). I am much more hesitant than Guissani to make culture depend on "experience" because, particularly in liberal Protestantism, "experience" replaces the church as the ultimate appeal.

14 The presence of Christians in an intellectual endeavor no more insures such work can be trusted to represent the "following" Giussani rightly thinks characteristic of Christian convictions. Moreover, work done by non-Christians may well reflect a more determined Christian perspective than that done by Christians. Which is a reminder that these are complex matters.

For example, if you believe as MacIntyre and I believe that usury is a practice that Christians must avoid, then how the knowledge called economics is understood may well be different from the understanding of those who do not share our views about usury. Or if you think that force can only be justified on just war grounds, then how you understand the relations between states may be very different from the assumptions of those that assume some form of a balance of power model is necessary for pursuing those research agendas called international relations. Or if you believe, as Christians do, that creation is a more fundamental notion than nature, that may well make a difference in the kind of distinction you think necessary between the study of botany and biology. Surely, for Christians who believe all that is created has purpose, the attempt to understand life mechanistically must be questioned.

MacIntyre is quite right to stress the significance of helping students acquire the intellectual skills necessary to see the interconnection between subjects; but I am suggesting that the very content of what is taught cannot be avoided if Christians are to take the "risk of education." The problem I think is that Christians in modernity have not been what Giussani says we must be, that is, people who create alternative cultures and structures. As a result, we have taught forms of knowledge in Christian schools that cannot help but undermine how Christians should understand the world in which we find ourselves. Giussani is surely right that "having children to educate is one of the greatest occasions God has given us for reawakening our faith" (p. 131). But I fear that we have failed as Christians, particularly in America, to show the difference the Christian willingness to have children should make for the wisdom that we are obligated to pass on to future generations.

For example, consider the implications of Giussani's almost throw-away observation – "Luckily, time makes us grow old" (p. 72) – for how medicine, and the sciences that serve medicine, should be understood. I think there is no denying that the current enthusiasm for "genomics" (that allegedly will make it possible to "treat" us before we become sick) draws on an extraordinary fear of suffering and death incompatible with Giussani's observation that *luckily* time makes us grow old. Our culture seems increasingly moving to the view that aging itself is an illness, and if it is possible, we ought to create and fund research that promises us that we may be able to get out of life alive. I find it hard to believe that such a science could be supported by a people who begin Lent by being told that we are dust and it is to dust we will return.

For Christians to create an alternative culture and alternative structures to the knowledges produced and taught in universities that are shaped by the fear of death, I think, is a challenge we cannot avoid. Moreover, to educate our children in such an alternative culture will mean that our children cannot presuppose that the education they receive will make it possible for them to be successful actors in a world shaped by a quite different culture. For Christians to educate our children for the world in which we now find ourselves means the education they receive will put them at risk. But at least they will have some chance to resist the lies that are assumed to be true because they are taught in university classrooms.

3. THE CULTURE OF DEMOCRACY AND THE CULTURE OF THE CHURCH

As I suggested above, some may think I am over-reading Giussani's suggestion that Christians should try to create an alternative culture and structure that shapes how we educate. Some may well think I have made Giussani sound as if he is advocating a more radical position than he in fact has. However, in my defense I want to end by calling attention to Giussani's remarks on democracy. His discussion of democracy is part of his argument that education is impossible without the recognition of the other. Such a recognition, he suggests, makes possible the dialogue necessary for me to come to a better understanding of who I am. But it is equally true that dialogue is impossible if we enter the dialogue without having some self-knowledge (pp. 93–4). We simply cannot begin any serious dialogue if we think we must begin by compromising our convictions in order to reach a common understanding.

Democracy is often defended as that form of social and political life that makes dialogue not only possible but also necessary. Yet Giussani argues that the relativism that the "prevailing mentality" so identifies with democracy makes dialogue impossible. He even reports that a "well-known university professor" dared to say to a select audience in Milan that "a Catholic, by the very fact that he is a Catholic, cannot be a citizen in a democratic state, for the Catholic claims to know the absolute truth. Therefore, it is not possible to have a dialogue or live with him in a democratic society" (p. 96). Giussani does not say if he agrees with this judgment, but he clearly thinks that the ideologies and practices often identified as democratic are in tension with the culture he thinks necessary to sustain Christian education.

Giussani has little use for the "values" taught in the name of sustaining a democratic ethos.[15] For example, he rightly calls into question any education that is based on the assumption that a person has "total autonomy." He clearly does not think that we ought to teach in a manner that allows students "to make up their own minds." To attempt such an education, as he puts it, only leaves "the teenager at the mercy of his likes and dislikes, his instincts, deprived of any standard of development" (p. 82). Giussani observes that an education that assumes the autonomy of the student cannot help but be one based on fear of confrontation with the world and as a result produces people incapable of dealing with a world gone mad.

[15] Indeed the very language of values – that is, the assumption that the moral life consists in subjective desires – is an indication that the language of economics has subverted serious moral judgments.

The rationalism that underwrites assumptions of autonomy "either forgets or denies that the self is fundamentally dependent; it either forgets or denies that evidence is a great, original surprise" (p. 69).[16] Ironically, the rationalism often defended as necessary for the sustaining of democratic societies can have the opposite effect. Rather than being educated with the openness required for ongoing inquiry, students feel unprepared to know how to go on because they can see no connection between their earlier education and more advanced subjects. Skepticism is the result, creating people who believe that the life choices they must make are arbitrary.

Ironically, such a people are incapable of sustaining democracy because as Giussani observes:

> the skepticism that shapes the soul is overcome in practice only by fanaticism – the intransigent assertion of a one-sided reality. This situation also applies to those students who come out of the fray still resolved to keep the religious and moral teachings they received. To save themselves they become defensive – as if retreating in a fortress, either out of caution or fear – and they shut out the environment that they feel is attacking them. Other similarly unprepared students will turn their backs on all received religious teaching without even examining it, determined to reject it (p. 61).

I think it is not hard to see how Giussani's characterization of the results of rationalistic education provides a quite accurate analysis of what has happened in America. The "religious right," for example, attempts to protect their religious convictions by supporting "democracy" but thereby fail to see that the form of life they are supporting often has the effect of undermining their faith. It does so because they are forced to compartmentalize their life, assuming that "faith" must be protected from the rationalism they rightly think is dominating the wider culture. Their very defense of Christianity too often makes the Christian faith appear to be a counter-rationalistic system. I often think the "religious right" are like canaries in coal mines. They rightly see something is wrong, but they fail to see that their own account of the Christian faith has been shaped by their enemies.

Alasdair MacIntyre's account of compartmentalization nicely complements Giussani's analysis of the results of how rationalism leads to skepticism. MacIntyre observes that

> the graduates of the best research universities tend to become narrowly focused professionals, immensely and even

[16] Alasdair MacIntyre wonderfully develops the interrelation of dependency and rationality in his *Dependent Rational Animals: Why Human Beings Need the Virtues* (Chicago: Open Court, 1999).

> obsessively hard working, disturbingly competitive and intent on success as it is measured within their own specialized professional sphere, often genuinely excellent at what they do; who read little worthwhile that is not relevant to their work; who, as the idiom insightfully puts it, "make time," sometimes with difficulty, for their family lives; and whose relaxation tends to consist of short strenuous bouts of competitive athletic activity and sometimes of therapeutic indulgence in the kind of religion that is well designed not to disrupt their working lives.[17]

Such lives are compartmentalized in at least two ways: (i) it is assumed that an individual passes through various spheres each with its own norms so the self is but a collection of different roles which (ii) makes it impossible for the individual to ever view her or his life as a whole.[18]

The fragmentation of the curriculum therefore becomes the institutional expression of the compartmentalized character of modern societies necessary to legitimate the form of life thought necessary to sustain democratic societies. For it is assumed that the kind of lives produced by modern university curriculums will be critical of everything, believing in nothing. Yet, if Guissani is right that skepticism is the breeding ground of fanaticism, then it is by no means clear that the rationalism that is the ideology of modern democratic regimes will be successful.

Modern democratic theory has been an attempt to give an account of democracies as just, without the people that constitute such a society having the virtue of justice. Of course, liberal democratic societies do form people in certain virtues, e.g. cynicism, but they seldom do so explicitly. The kind of training in virtue liberal educational practice involves cannot be acknowledged, because the neutrality that allegedly is required for education to be for anyone makes it impossible to make candid that any education is a moral education. It is unclear, however, if the kind of fragmented selves such an education produces are capable of being habituated in a manner necessary to sustain the virtues to form people of character.

These are obviously large issues, but they are at the heart of Guissani's account of the kind of education required by the Christian faith. I think, moreover, he is right to suggest that the education of Christians he is advocating can provide a more defensible account of democracy than that based on the rationalism of modernity. Indeed I find it quite interesting that Guissani, like John Paul II, is not afraid to say that what is required if we are to live in peace with one another is a "civilization of love" (*Centesimus Annus*, 10,2). To suggest that nothing less than love is at the heart of our contemporary challenges will no doubt be interpreted by many as an indication that Giussani has lost touch with

17 MacIntyre, *Dependent Rational Animals*, p. 15.
18 MacIntyre, *Dependent Rational Animals*, pp. 15–16.

reality. But that is the case only if you think the God Christians worship is not the God of Jesus Christ. Because Christians find our lives constituted by the confidence God gives us that the truth matters, we can continue – as Luigi Giussani argues we must – to take the "risk of education."

4

The End of "Religious Pluralism": A Tribute to David Burrell, C.S.C.

1. WHY "RELIGIOUS PLURALISM" DOES NOT EXIST[1]

Some years ago I was lecturing at Hendrix College in Conway, Arkansas. I no longer remember the lecture I gave, but I assume it was one of my attempts to suggest why Christians, if we are to be Christians, owe it to ourselves and our neighbors to quit fudging our belief that God matters. When I finished my lecture, one of the professors in the religion department at Hendrix had clearly had enough of me. He had been educated by John Cobb and, therefore, represented that peculiar mixture of Protestant liberalism and process theology. He reacted to my lecture by observing that my stress on the centrality of Christian convictions provided no theory that would enable Christians to talk with Buddhists. By "theory" people often mean the necessity of a third language to mediate between two traditions. Such a language is often said to be necessary in "pluralist" societies in order to mediate differences in the "public" square.[2]

I, however, apologized for being deficient of such theory, but asked, "How many Buddhists do you have here in Conway? Moreover if you

[1] This heading is meant to echo Stanley Fish's short but incisive essay, "Liberalism Doesn't Exist," that now appears in his book, *There's No Such Thing as Free Speech and It's a Good Thing Too* (New York: Oxford University Press, 1994), pp. 134–8. Fish argues that the liberal attempt to claim to represent a "rationality" free from beliefs about the world in order to secure a place free from "politics" is not a position anyone can inhabit. I will argue that in a similar fashion "no place" exists from which anyone might be able to describe "religious pluralism" in a non-persuasive manner.

[2] Calls for a third language fail to consider, however, that such languages are anything but neutral. Moreover, the assumption that traditions are airtight closed systems is a gross oversimplification. Significant traditions are amalgams of many influences that provide often surprising connection with other traditions. Before assuming the inability to communicate, you have to listen and look. Those concerned with "public theology" claim that a third language is necessary for the public business. Yet I suspect that calls for a third language, e.g., "rights," are attempting to underwrite the superiority of those who represent the third language in contrast to traditions that do not see the need for such translations. Those representatives of the "public" with "all humility" assume they are superior to other traditions because they can "appreciate" other traditions in a manner other traditions cannot appreciate themselves.

want to talk with them what good will a theory do you? I assume that if you want to talk with Buddhists, you would just go talk with them. You might begin by asking, for example, 'What in the world are you guys doing in Conway?' " I then suggested I suspected that the real challenge in Conway was not talking with Buddhists, but trying to talk with Christian fundamentalists. We should also ask whether we have anything interesting enough the Buddhist would even want to talk about with us.

I relate this story because the response I gave in Conway is more or less the same response I will give to the subject I address here, that is, "The New Religious Pluralism and Democracy." I am well aware that my response may be understood by many to be irresponsible, but then I am quite suspicious of attempts to have Christians take on "the burdens of running the world" in the name of "being responsible." I am, after all, a pacifist. I, of course, do not like the description "pacifism," not only because such a description suggests a far too "passive" response to violence, but more important, "pacifism" names for many a position regarding war and violence that can be abstracted from the Christological convictions I believe are necessary to make the stance of nonviolence intelligible.[3]

John Howard Yoder, the great representative of Christological pacifism, rightly challenged Reinhold Niebuhr's accusation that the pacifism of "the sects" was a coherent but irresponsible position.[4] Yoder pointed out that Niebuhr's appeal to responsibility was a disguised legitimating of "the necessity" to accept a Weberian understanding of politics. According to Yoder appeals to responsibility are used to imply that Christians have

> an inherent duty to take charge of the social order in the interest of its survival or its amelioration by the use of means dictated, not by love, but by the social order itself.

[3] I do not mean to denigrate forms of pacifism which are not Christologically determined. Rather I am simply indicating what I take to be the most defensible understanding of Christian nonviolence. For a wonderful account of the possibilities and limits of other forms of pacifism, see John Howard Yoder, *Nevertheless: The Varieties and Shortcomings of Religious Pacifism* (Revised and Expanded Edition; Scottdale, PA: Herald Press, 1992).

[4] Niebuhr's brilliant critique of pacifism was largely directed at liberal pacifism associated with mainstream Protestantism after World War I. He respected what he called "religious absolutism" in its apocalyptic or ascetic forms. The former he identified with the left wing of the reformation who, like Jesus, set "the absolute principles of the coming Kingdom of God, principles of uncompromising love and nonresistance, in sharp juxtaposition to the relativities of the economic and political order and assumes no responsibilities for the latter." Ascetics, such as Francis and Tolstoy, according to Niebuhr sharpen individual ideals of the spirit in contrast to a whole range of physical necessities. Niebuhr respected these alternatives as long as they acknowledged they must "withdraw from politics" (Reinhold Niebuhr, *Love and Justice*, edited by D. B. Robinson (New York: World Publishing Co., 1967), p. 261).

> This social order being sinful, the methods "necessary" to administer it will also be sinful. "Responsibility" thus becomes an autonomous moral absolute, sinful society is accepted as normative for ethics, and when society calls for violence the law of love is no longer decisive (except in the "discriminate" function of preferring the less nasty sorts of violence). Of course, according to pacifist belief, there exists a real responsibility for social order, but that responsibility is a derivative of Christian love, not a contradictory and self-defining ethical norm.[5]

At this point you may wonder if I have forgotten that the subject before us is not pacifism, but rather the "new religious pluralism and democracy." It will be, however, the burden of my remarks to show that the Christian response to the challenge of the "new religious pluralism" has everything to do with Christian nonviolence. Just as Yoder had to challenge the claim that Christian pacifists were "irresponsible" so I must challenge the very terms used to describe the challenge before us. From my perspective "pluralism" is the ideology used by Protestant liberals to give themselves the illusion they are still in control of, or at least have responsibility for, the future of America. "Religion" is the designation created to privatize strong convictions in order to render them harmless so that alleged democracies can continue to have the illusion they flourish on difference. Indeed, if there is anything "new" about the current situation it is that we are coming to the end of Protestant hegemony in America.

A strange claim to be sure, given the rise of the so-called "religious right" represented by the Bush Administration. Indeed I suspect some may associate my robust theological perspective with the aggressive Christianity associated with the religious right. As far as I know, however, no representative of the religious right has claimed me for an ally. That they have not so claimed me is certainly appropriate because I regard the religious right as representatives of a truncated, if not idolatrous form, of Christianity. Indeed I think the religious right is a desperate attempt of Protestantism to make sense of itself as a form of civil religion for America.[6] That is why the Christianity represented by the religious right is at once so strident and pathetic.

5 John Howard Yoder, *Reinhold Niebuhr and Christian Pacifism: A Church Peace Mission Pamphlet* (Scottdale, PA: Herald Press, 1968), p. 18.

6 In his *Democracy Matters: Winning the Fight Against Imperialism* (New York: Penguin Press, 2004) Cornel West rightly criticizes "conservative Christians" for their Constantinianism, but he praises Walter Rauschenbusch as a representative of prophetic Christianity (pp. 146–55). I also am a great admirer of Rauschenbusch but Rauschenbusch was in his day as implicated in the Constantinian project as the religious right is today. Christopher Evans suggests that toward the latter part of his life Rauschenbusch modified his call to "Christianizing the social order" but his project continued to assume the establishment of Protestant Christianity as necessary

In his book, *The First and the Last: The Claim of Jesus Christ and the Claims of Other Religious Traditions*, a book that very helpfully suggests how the Christian understanding of the final primacy of Christ does not close off an appreciative understanding of other traditions, George Sumner observes that the existence of other religious traditions became and has become "a problem for the Christian tradition at the very time that Christianity became a problem to itself."[7] Christians have always known that other religious traditions exist. Why has the knowledge that there are other religious traditions become such a problem?[8] Sumner suggests that the challenge of other religions is part of the more general Enlightenment challenge to religious particularism in the name of universal reason.[9] I have no doubt that Sumner is right that the very terms of how the challenge of other religions is now understood by

for the reform of America. See Christopher Evans, *The Kingdom is Always But Coming: A Life of Walter Rauschenbusch* (Grand Rapids: Eerdmans, 2004). What West fails to see is that the religious left are no less Constantinian than the right. For example in his recent book, *The World Calling: The Church's Witness in Politics and Society* (Louisville: Westminster John Knox, 2004), Tom Ogletree notes that the challenge before Christian social ethics is "to discover constructive ways of relating distinctively Christian social ideas to the civilizational ethic resident in a given social order. The underlying claim is that normative social teachings, Christian or otherwise, cannot become socially effective unless they can be rendered compatible with the organizational principles that structure particular societies. What is possible in one setting may be wholly unrealistic in another. The attainment of such compatibility requires a 'cultural synthesis,' that is, a creative combination of distinctively Christian values with core elements in a reigning 'civilizational ethic.' In the American context, for example, the question for a viable synthesis necessarily involves giving privileged standing to the 'blessing of liberty' celebrated in the Preamble to the U.S. Constitution" (p. 4). I cannot imagine a clearer account of cultural Christianity on behalf of the left. The Catholic right in an interesting way shares much with Ogletree's concerns. For example, in a recent article, "The Deist Minimum," in *First Things*, 149 (January, 2005), Avery Cardinal Dulles defends the minimal consensus deism represented because he doubts if pluralism goes unchecked, the nation will lack a corporate vision and collective purpose that have marked the American past (pp. 25–30).

7 George Sumner, *The First and the Last: The Claim of Jesus Christ and the Claims of Other Religious Traditions* (Grand Rapids: Eerdmans, 2004), p. 3.

8 For some reason Christians in our time seem to think that the existence of other traditions presents a decisive challenge to the truth and intelligibility of the Christian faith. I confess I simply do not understand why they seem to assume that what we believe is problematic unless everyone believes what we believe. As far as I can see there is no biblical reason for such a view. Indeed as I will suggest below, Christian scripture, and in particular the tower of Babel, implies that we should expect difference.

9 Sumner employs Alasdair MacIntyre's account of traditioned determined rationality and the possibility that traditions can create as well as recognize "epistemological crisis" as a way to display how religious traditions might be able to discover similarities as well as differences. Sumner, rightly, points to the logically odd and anomalous aspect of his use of MacIntyre, namely, he is "marshalling the philosophical proposal of MacIntyre in defense of understanding the thread of pluralism in a context-specific way, and, in what follows, in support of arguments located in a manner developed from the Christian theological tradition" (*The First and the Last*, p. 6). In other words "there is inherently an irony in defenses of the specificity and uniqueness of traditions

Christians is largely the result of the critiques of Christianity by Enlightenment thinkers. But it is very important to remember that what is now understood to be the Protestant right is as much the creature of Enlightenment developments as is Protestant liberalism.[10]

Sumner has rightly reminded us of the decisive importance to developments in Protestant theology for understanding the issue of "religious pluralism," but the "politics" of these developments cannot be overlooked if we are to understand the context in which these questions are raised. William Cavanaugh has provided an account of the fate of Christianity in modernity that is crucial if we are to understand why the very terms of analysis of the relation of Christianity to democratic societies betray how Christians should think about our faith. According to Cavanaugh the story of the modern state is a soteriological story in which the state is assumed necessary to save us from contentious religious factions spawned by the Reformation. The modern state is alleged to be necessary to stop Catholics and Protestants from killing one another in the name of doctrinal loyalties. The "privatization of religion," indeed the very creation of the notion of religion as more basic than any particularistic practice of a faith, was a necessary correlative of the development of the modern secular state whose task was to keep peace among warring religious factions.[11]

This story of the development of the modern state is a staple in modern political theory. Cavanaugh, for example, calls attention to Judith Shklar's account in her book *Ordinary Vices*:

> liberalism . . . was born out of the cruelties of the religious wars, which forever rendered the claims of Christian charity a rebuke to all religious institutions and parties. If the faith was to survive at all, it would do so privately. The alternative then set, and still before us, is not one between classical virtue and liberal self-indulgence, but between cruel military and moral repression and violence, and self-restraining tolerance that fences in the powerful to protect the freedom and safety of every Christian.[12]

---

that appeal to general observation about the nature of human knowing (e.g., that it is tradition-specific) or human community (e.g., about practices embedded in a unique form of life" pp. 10–11). Sumner sees quite clearly that the only thing a Christian theologian in response to this tension can do is display how particular Christian convictions do or do not relate to different communities. The tension Sumner identifies as inherent in his project I have long thought to be a tension in MacIntyre's attempt to maintain a too strict distinction between philosophy and theology.

10 For my account of the common roots of Protestant liberalism and fundamentalism see *Unleashing the Scripture: Freeing the Bible From Captivity to America* (Nashville: Abingdon Press, 1993).

11 William Cavanaugh, *Theopolitical Imagination: Discovering the Liturgy as a Political Act in an Age of Global Consumerism* (New York: T&T Clark, 2002), pp. 20–1.

12 Cavanaugh, *Theopolitical Imagination*, p. 21.

This story of how the modern state saved us from religious anarchy and violence has been repeated so often it is assumed to have canonical status. There is only one problem with the story. It is not true. Drawing on the work of Quentin Skinner, Charles Tilly, and Richard Dunn, Cavanaugh argues that the so-called "wars of religion" were not the events that gave birth to the modern state, but rather were the birth pangs of the creation of such states.[13] Protestants killed Protestants and Catholics killed Catholics in the interest of the new power configurations developing after the demise of the medieval order. What was crucial for the development of state power was the redescription of Protestantism and Catholicism as religion. Religion, moreover, is now understood as "beliefs," personal convictions, which can exist separately from one's public loyalty to the state. "The creation of religion, and thus the privatization of the Church, is correlative to the rise of the state."[14]

It may be objected that Cavanaugh is making far too much of the description "religion." After all, that description is but an attempt to make sense of the diversity of human behavior that seems to deal with, in Christian Smith's words, "superempirical orders."[15] However, such definitions of religion cannot help but die the death of infinite qualifications. For example, it is very hard to make sense of Christianity as a "superempirical order" given the Christian belief in the Incarnation. Moreover, anyone familiar with attempts to make sense of religion by religious studies departments in the contemporary university cannot help but be aware that at best religion is understood as an inexact term to describe diverse subject matters that have very little in common.[16] Put more polemically, the creation of religious studies departments can be

13 Cavanaugh, *Theopolitical Imagination*, p. 22.

14 Cavanaugh, *Theopolitical Imagination*, p. 31. In their extraordinary book, *Blood Sacrifice and the Nation* (Cambridge: Cambridge University Press, 1999), Carolyn Marvin and David Ingle observe "in the religiously plural society of the United States, sectarian faith is optional for citizens, as everyone knows. Americans have rarely bled, sacrificed or died for Christianity or any other sectarian faith. Americans have often bled, sacrificed and died for their country. This fact is an important clue to its (the country's) religious power. Though denominations are permitted to exist in the United States, they are not permitted to kill, for their beliefs are not officially true. What is really true in any society is what is worth killing for, and what citizens may be compelled to sacrifice their lives for" (p. 9). I take this to be the outworking of the process of state formation Cavanaugh describes. The result is perhaps most apparent in expressions often heard such as, "I believe that Jesus Christ redeemed the world, but that is just my personal opinion." You can be sure that people formed to express such drivel lack the capacity to resist state power.

15 Christian Smith, *Moral, Believing Animals: Human Personhood and Culture* (New York: Oxford University Press, 2003), p. 98.

16 For an excellent discussion of the difficulty of coming to any agreement for how "religion" can be understood, see Paul Griffiths, *Problems of Religious Diversity* (Oxford: Blackwell, 2001), pp. 12–16. Griffiths argues that even if there are natural kinds in religions, we are not in a position to know what they are or where their boundaries lie, which means that if we persist in sorting religions into kinds, such sorting ought to be viewed as useful fictions. For the most adequate attempt to

understood as the ongoing development of universities to provide legitimating knowledges for state power.[17]

The problematic character of the concept of religion, however, is a reflection of any attempt to make sense of pluralism. I suggested above that pluralism is the ideology of people in power to comfort themselves with the presumption that they are in control of the world in which they find themselves. For example, John Milbank argues that the very terms of discourse which provide the privileged categories for encounters between significant traditions as well as the criteria for the acceptable limits of the pluralist embrace, that is, terms such as dialogue and pluralism, are themselves embedded in a wider western discourse that presumes global dominance. As a result the celebration of other cultures and traditions is at the same time the "obliteration of other cultures by western norms and categories, with their freight of Christian influence."[18]

Some may find Milbank's argument exaggerated, but Milbank's argument that pluralism is a rhetoric to avoid difference is not peculiar to him or his work. For example Ken Surin, drawing on the work of the anthropologist Bernard McGrane, argues that the transition from the Christian attempt to understand the non-European "other," through the Enlightenment understanding of the other as "unenlightened," to our current attempt to see the other as culturally different has been an ongoing project of cultural imperialism. What Surin calls the "democratization" of "difference" is the exemplification of that imperialism. Such democratization seems like an advance because the non-European other is no longer understood to be in the depths of some petrified past, but "with this radical democratization of difference he or she is thus now our contemporary. ... Non-European others are still different of course, but now they are *merely* different."[19]

According to Surin this celebration of difference in the name of pluralism underwrites the universalistic ideology of the "American way of life" in a manner that mimics how the McDonald's hamburger has become the first universal food. As a result, Surin argues, the dominant ideology of the new world order declares nations, cultures, religions obsolete if they maintain their old forms as fixed in intractable

provide a "delineation" of religion in response to Asad's critique see Bruce Lincoln's *Holy Terrors: Thinking About Religion After September 11* (Chicago: University of Chicago Press, 2003), pp. 5–8.

17 For the development of this claim, see Timothy Fitzgerald, *The Ideology of Religious Studies* (New York: Oxford University Press, 2000). It would, of course, be a mistake to single out religious studies as the discipline in the modern university peculiarly in service to state interest. It is hard to find any discipline in the university not so determined.

18 John Milbank, "The End of Dialogue," in *Christian Uniqueness Reconsidered: The Myth of a Pluralistic Theology of Religions*, edited by Gavin D'Costa (Maryknoll, NY: Orbis, 1990), p. 175.

19 Kenneth Surin, "A 'Politics of Speech': Religious Pluralism in the Age of the McDonald Hamburger," in *Christian Uniqueness Reconsidered*, p. 198.

particularities.[20] This new-world reality and ideological concomitants, that is, that which makes McDonald's into a universal food and sustains the world ecumenism advocated by exponents of religious pluralism,

> creates the *episteme* or paradigm which renders both sets of phenomena intelligible. To resist the cultural encroachment represented by the McDonald's hamburger, therefore is of a piece with resisting the similar depredation constituted by this world ecumenism. It is to seek to resist the world view which makes both possible. The question is: How do we theorize relationships between Hindus, Buddhists, Sikhs, Jews, Christians, and Muslims without underwriting this *episteme*? How can such people talk to each other without endorsing, even if only tacitly, the presumptions embodied in the formulations of the Kraemers, Rahners, Cantwell Smiths and Hicks of this world? What is needed here, I am trying to suggest, can ultimately be nothing less than the displacement of a whole mode of discourse.[21]

The Kraemers, the Rahners, the Cantwell Smiths, and John Hicks are those Christians identified by Joseph Dinoia, O.P. as inclusivist, that is, they are Christians who "espouse some version of the view that all religious communities implicitly aim at salvation that the Christian community most adequately commends, or at least that salvation is a present possibility for the members of non-Christian communities."[22] According to Dinoia pluralists are but a variation of the inclusivist type who believe that all religious communities aim at salvation but do so under a variety of scheme-specific descriptions. Yet Surin, rightly I think, has no use for either of these types, believing that even the attempt to develop such typologies betrays ideological presumptions.

Yet if I agree with Cavanaugh, Milbank, and Surin that religion and pluralism are mystifications that hide from us their ideological functions, where does that leave me? Should I try to supply a "whole mode of discourse" Surin suggests we need? It would seem that is exactly what we need if we are democratically to find a way to negotiate our religious differences. If I fail to provide such an account it would seem only to confirm Jeff Stout's assessment of my work as

20 Cavanaugh makes a similar point about the power of the universal in service to the state. He notes that "globalization does not signal the demise of the nation-state but is in fact a hyperextension of the nation-state's project of subsuming the local under the universal. The rise of the modern state is marked by the triumph of the universal over the local in the sovereign state's usurpation of power from the Church, the nobility, guilds, clans, and towns" (*Theopolitical Imagination*, p. 99).

21 Surin, "A 'Politics of Speech,' " p. 201.

22 Joseph Dinoia, O.P., *The Diversity of Religions* (Washington, DC: Catholic University Press of America, 1992), p. 37.

decidedly anti-democratic.[23] I cannot, however, supply the discourse Surin thinks we need to engage other traditions. I certainly do not have the intellectual power for that task, but even more I cannot be a representative of the "we" that thinks such a task necessary. Nor do I have any moral or policy recommendations to make to suggest how religious differences might be negotiated in this allegedly democratic society. However, by drawing on the work of John Howard Yoder I will at least try to suggest how Yoder's understanding of a non-Constantinian Christianity provides an alternative, at least for Christians, when confronted by the religious "other."

2. THE DISAVOWAL OF CONSTANTINE: JOHN HOWARD YODER'S UNDERSTANDING OF INTERFAITH DIALOGUE[24]

In 1976 John Howard Yoder was on sabbatical at the Ecumenical Institute for Advanced Theological Studies at Tantur/Jerusalem where he delivered a lecture entitled "The Disavowal of Constantine: An Alternative Perspective on Interfaith Dialogue."[25] That Yoder was in Jerusalem – the site of conflict between Judaism, Christianity, and Islam – influenced how Yoder approached his task. But it is also the case that Yoder used this occasion to explore the difference his understanding of a non-Constantinian form of Christianity might make for interfaith relations. Yoder took as his task to "ask what difference it makes or would make for interfaith dialogue, if instead of every 'religion' as represented by its most powerful 'establishment,' the disavowal of the establishment of religion were restored as part of a specifically Christian witness."[26]

According to Yoder Christianity had been transformed by what he called "the Constantinian shift." Yoder's understanding of the significance of that shift did not entail speculation concerning Constantine's sincerity, but rather Yoder was much more interested in the Christological and ecclesiological implications of the church becoming the legitimating institution for empire. For example, prior to establishment Yoder observed Christians were confident that God was present in the

23 Jeff Stout, *Democracy and Tradition* (Princeton: Princeton University Press, 2004), pp. 140–61. For my initial response to Stout, see *Performing the Faith: Bonhoeffer and the Practice of Nonviolence* (Grand Rapids: Brazos Press, 2004), pp. 215–41.

24 I am aware that Yoder's use of "dialogue" is open to Milbank's critique. I can only ask the reader to be patient before making that association, for I hope to show that given Yoder's understanding of the conditions necessary for dialogue, the hegemonic implications Milbank associate with the word "dialogue" do not apply.

25 John Howard Yoder, "The Disavowal of Constantine: An Alternative Perspective on Interfaith Dialogue," in *The Royal Priesthood: Essays Ecclesiological and Ecumenical*, edited by Michael Cartwright (Grand Rapids: Eerdmans, 1994), pp. 242–61. The above information is provided by Michael Cartwright's introduction to this essay. We are indebted to Cartwright for putting these essays of Yoder's between two covers as well as for writing one of the best introductory essays we have on Yoder.

26 Yoder, "The Disavowal of Constantine," p. 247.

church, but they had to believe that God was also active in the world. After establishment, given the mixed character of the church, Christians were confident that God was active in the world, but they had to believe that God was present in the church. In particular when Theodosius made it a civil offense not to be a Christian, Christianity was fundamentally transformed from a nonviolent faith, that is, prior to Theodosius you could only become a Christian through conversion. After Theodosius to become a Christian could not help but be coercive.

The nonviolent character of Christian conversion for Yoder is a correlate of his Christology. For at the heart of Yoder's understanding of Christianity is a "concern for the particular, historical, and therefore Jewish quality and substance of New Testament faith in Jesus."[27] Yoder is, therefore, an uncompromising "particularist" which means, in George Lindbeck's terms, Yoder is a "Christological maximalist," that is, he assumes that every possible importance should be ascribed to Jesus that is not inconsistent with the rule that there is only one God, the God of Abraham, Isaac, Jacob, and Jesus.[28] Yoder, I think, would also be in agreement with George Sumner who, as I suggested above, argues that Christian approaches to interfaith dialogue must be governed by a pattern he describes as the "final primacy" of Jesus Christ. That is as Christians confront "alien claims" and communities they must do so in confidence that "Christ is the One toward whom the narratives run and from whom their truth (to the extent that they are true) derives. He is at once the *final legis* (the end of the law) and the *prima veritas* (the first truth)."[29]

Accordingly Christians cannot avoid being in mission to witness what they believe God has done in Christ. Yoder notes that the word "mission" has become a negative word for many because of its colonial history, but the very grammar of the Christian faith requires that Christians be heralds. Christians must be heralds because they announce an event that can only be known through its announcement. Moreover they believe what they announce is true. Yoder observes:

27 Yoder, "The Disavowal of Constantine," p. 247.

28 George Lindbeck, *The Nature of Doctrine: Religion and Theology in a Postliberal Age* (Philadelphia: The Westminster Press, 1984), p. 94.

29 George Sumner, *The First and the Last: The Claim of Jesus Christ and the Claims of Other Religious Traditions*, pp. 6–17. Yoder observes that Christians are often tempted to jettison the particular, the local, the specific biblical content in an attempt to correct the Christian imperialism associated with Christian Europe. Universality and commonality with other traditions is sought at the price of specificity. But he notes there is another way. "It would be possible to say that the error in the age of triumphalism was not that it was tied to Jesus but that it denied him, precisely in its power and disrespect for the neighbor. Then the corrective would be not to search for a new consensus but to critique the old one. Its error was not that it propagated Christianity around the world but that what it propagated was not Christian enough. Then the adjustment to Christendom's loss of elan and credibility is not to talk less about Jesus and more about religion but the contrary" ("The Disavowal of Constantine," p. 257).

> If it were not true the herald would not be raising his or her voice. Yet, no one is forced to believe. What the herald reports is not permanent, timeless logical insights but contingent, particular events. If those events are true, and if others join the herald to carry the word along, they will with time develop a doctrinal system, to help distinguish between more or less adequate ways of proclaiming; but that system, those formulae, will not become what they proclaim.[30]

Yoder's Christological maximalism requires, therefore, that the herald, the witness, must remain non-coercive if it is to be true to that which it is a witness. You never have to believe it because (i) the message concerns a contingent event with the challengeable relativity of historical reporting and (ii) you do not have to believe it because the herald cannot have the power to force you to believe it. The herald cannot be in a position to make anyone who refuses to believe be destroyed or persecuted. It is the herald who must be vulnerable. "What makes the herald renounce coercion is not doubt or being unsettled by the tug of older views. The herald believes in accepting weakness, because the message is about a Suffering Servant whose meekness it is that brings justice to the nations."[31]

30 Yoder, "The Disavowal of Constantine," p. 256. For Yoder's understanding of "doctrine" see his *Preface to Theology* (Grand Rapids: Brazos Press, 2002). Yoder's Christological center does not entail a strong distinction between reason and revelation. Indeed I suspect that Yoder would have no reason to deny Denys Turner's recent attempt to defend the possibility of a "natural theology." In defense of Aquinas, Turner observes "that to prove the existence of God is to prove the existence of a mystery, that to show God to exist is to show how, in the end, the human mind loses its grip on the meaning of 'exists'; such a demonstration is therefore designed to show that within creation itself, with our deepest human experience of the world, the mystery of unknowable existence is somehow always present with the world simply in its character of being created" (*Faith, Reason, and the Existence of God* (Cambridge: Cambridge University Press, 2004), p. xiv). What is remarkable about Turner's defense of "natural theology" is how he understands such a defense of reason is made imperative by Christological commitments. If I had had Turner's book when I wrote *With the Grain of the Universe: The Church's Witness and Natural Theology* (Grand Rapids: Brazos Press, 2001), I would have been better able to show how John Paul II's reclaiming of the Christological center for Catholic theology is not irrelevant to the argument of *Fides et Ratio*.

31 Yoder, "The Disavowal of Constantine," p. 256. Rom Coles has called my attention to the radical implications of this perspective made clear by Yoder in the page prior to this quote when he says, "We are all 'nominal adherents.' No one's faith is final in this life. It may be the Islamist Kenneth Craig who for some time has made most poignant the insight that I have only really understood another's faith if I begin to feel I could be at home in it, if its tug at me questions my prior (Christian) allegiance anew. Likewise, I am only validly exposing my own faith if I can imagine my interlocutors coming to share it. Perhaps the word mission has been rendered unusable in some contexts by abuse, but respect for the genuineness of dialogue demands in both directions that there be no disavowal in principle of my witness becoming an open option for the other. Mission and dialogue are not alternatives; each is valid only within the other, properly understood" (p. 255).

For Yoder, therefore, for Christians to disavow Constantine requires communal repentance. The Constantinian assumption of the indefectibility of the church must be challenged. But that challenge cannot take the form of saying, "We still think we are right, but you may be right, too" or "Yes, that is a wrong idea, but this is what we really meant." Such responses generate notions (like Rahner's account of other people as "anonymous Christians") which for their good will, are attempts to maintain Constantinian power in a tolerant mode.[32] Rather, Christians must say, "We were wrong. The picture you have been given of Jesus by the Empire, by the Crusades, by struggles over the holy sites, and by wars in the name of the 'Christian West' is not only something to forget but something to forgive."[33]

Such forgiveness cannot simply be remorse for the wrongs of the past, but requires *mentanoia*. The discovery of a new way to be for Christians may well come through being reminded by "outsiders" of our past failures, but "at least for Christians, the continuing pertinence of the historical memory of Jesus, via the New Testament, as a lever for continuing critique, is part of the message itself. The capacity for, or in fact the demand for, self-critique is part of what must be shared with people of other faiths and ideologies."[34]

Yoder, therefore, does not try to develop or recommend a general theory or strategy for Christian conversations with other faiths or traditions. He cannot because such theories or strategies would only reproduce Constantinian habits. "By the nature of the case," he observes, "it is not possible to establish, either speculatively or from historical samples, a consistent anti-Constantinian model. The prophetic denunciation of paganization must always be missionary and ad hoc; it will be in language as local and as timely as the abuses it critiques."[35] The way forward must be fragmentary and occasional. For the "affirmative alternative underlying the critique of paganization is the concreteness of the visible community created by the renewed message. The alternative to hierarchical definition is local definition."[36]

32 Paul Knitter certainly represents the best attempt from a Rahnerian point of view to do justice to religious difference. See his *No Other Name: A Critical Survey of Christian Attitudes Toward the World Religions* (Maryknoll, NY: Orbis, 2003).

33 Yoder, "The Disavowal of Constantine," p. 250.

34 Yoder, "The Disavowal of Constantine," p. 251.

35 Yoder, "The Disavowal of Constantine," p. 250.

36 Yoder, "The Disavowal of Constantine," p. 253. Sheldon Wolin ends the second edition of *Politics and Vision* by suggesting that democratic politics will depend on the recovery of localism. For Wolin, only by attending to the concrete can we recover political experience necessary to challenge the superpower character of America. The convergence of Wolin's and Yoder's understanding of politics is quite remarkable. See Sheldon Wolin, *Politics and Vision* (Expanded Edition; Princeton: Princeton University Press, 2004), pp. 601–6.

Yoder's "localism" is not some strategy to avoid conversation with other traditions.[37] Rather it is an attempt to shift the focus from questions about the truth content or validity of the ideas or experiences of other religions as systems or performances in order to attend to "the uncoercible dignity of the interlocutor as person and one's solidarity (civil, social, economic) with him or her as neighbor is what must (and can) be defined first."[38] For Yoder to ask in the abstract the status of, for example, Buddhism vis-à-vis the Christian faith is a Constantinian question. I certainly do not think he would object to the kind of close study of other traditions represented by Paul Griffiths, Joseph Dinoia, and George Sumner.[39] Indeed Yoder would have every reason to encourage the close reading of the texts of other traditions. Yet that kind of scholarship can never replace the concrete encounter with the neighbor who is different from me.

At the heart of Yoder's account is his understanding of the story of the tower of Babel in Genesis 11. From Yoder's perspective too often God's destruction of the tower of Babel is interpreted as punishment. But such a reading, according to Yoder, fails to appreciate that the first meaning of Babel was the effort of a human community to absolutize itself. Those who built the tower were attempting to resist God's will that there be a diversity of cultures. Rebellious humanity sought to replace their dependence on God by creating their own heaven. "They were the first foundationalists, seeking by purposeful focusing of their own cultural power to overcome historically developing diversity."[40]

God's scattering of the people from Babel was therefore a benevolent act. At least that is the way Paul saw what happened at Babel as reported by Luke in the Book of Acts (14; 16ff; 17:26f). The "confusion" of Babel is such only when measured against the simplicity of an imperially enforced uniformity. Babel is, therefore, a gracious intervention by God to continue the process of dispersion and diversification through

37 Yoder was particularly concerned to renew the conversation between Christianity and Judaism. See his *The Jewish–Christian Schism Revisited*, edited by Michael Cartwright and Peter Ochs (Grand Rapids: Eerdmans, 2003).

38 Yoder, "The Disavowal of Constantine," p. 256.

39 I suspect, however, that Yoder might well prefer Griffiths' *Religious Reading: The Place of Reading in the Practice of Religion* (New York: Oxford, 1999) to Griffiths' *Problems of Religious Diversity* (Oxford: Blackwell, 2001). Yoder would, I think, be attracted to Griffiths' attention to the actual practice of reading in the former book. Yoder would also be quite sympathetic with the attempt to discover how religious claims might come into conflict. I suspect, however, he would have found that William Christian's *Oppositions of Religious Doctrines: A Study in the Logic of Dialogue Among Religions* (New York: Herder and Herder, 1972) isolated "beliefs" from practices in a way that failed to do justice to the complexity of a tradition. In a letter responding to this essay, Paul Griffiths reminds me that this criticism of isolating beliefs from practices does not mean that what people believe can be, as near as possible, stated with precision and critically engaged.

40 John Howard Yoder, *For the Nations: Essays Public and Evangelical* (Grand Rapids: Eerdmans, 1997), p. 63.

which we are forced to learn to respect the other and learn humility. "Thus the 'confusion of tongues' is not a punishment or a tragedy but the gift of new beginnings, liberation from a blind alley."[41]

For Yoder, therefore, the existence of other significant traditions is not a "problem" for Christians, but rather a gift. That is why Christian missionaries who went and continue to go to make Christ present to those they assumed did not know Christ so often return confessing they discovered Christ in those they went to serve. The great missionary effort of the nineteenth century was no doubt sometimes sponsored by a western arrogance, but it may well turn out to be one of the ways God used to humble that same arrogance.[42] At the very least the missions served to remind Christians we rightly are a minority religion. The result Yoder would think providential.

In summary Yoder does not recommend that Christians disavow Constantine

> Because we enjoy concern with either our guilt or our innocence, and still less out of denominational self-righteousness, but because all that we ultimately have to contribute to interfaith dialogue is our capacity to get out of the way so that instead of, or beyond, us or our ancestors, us or our language systems, us or our strengths or weaknesses, the people we converse with might see Jesus. It is that simple: but that is not simple. It will not happen without repentance. If we mean that Jesus of history, the Jewish Jesus of the New Testament, then even here in the land of his birth – to say nothing of Benares or Peking or Timbuktu – there is no

41 Yoder, *For the Nations*, p. 63. Lamin Sanneh has argued quite persuasively that the missionary enterprise, without necessarily intended to do so, had the effect often of strengthening indigenous cultures through a revitalization of the mother tongue made necessary for the translation of the Bible. See his *Whose Religion is Christianity? The Gospel Beyond the West* (Grand Rapids: Eerdmans, 2003), pp. 24–5. On Yoder's grounds Christians must always desire conversation with those that are not Christian, but we cannot assume that those to whom we wish to talk will want to talk with us. Our first task as Christians is to live faithfully to what makes us Christians in the hope that others will want to know more about what makes us tick.

42 Lamin Sanneh provides an interesting account of the new reality of world Christianity in his *Whose Religion is Christianity?* It would be extremely interesting to know what Yoder would make of his suggestion that the world church is subject to persecution, but that the response should not take the form of state protection. But churches should, when confronted as they often are with low public confidence in state institutions, break with the tradition of religious privatization in order to have an impact in "public ethics" (p. 29). I suspect Yoder might find Sanneh's understanding of "public ethics" problematic, but that does not mean he would reject Sanneh's suggestion about the church's public role in the world. Yoder would simply want to know more. For a fascinating study of how Catholicism provided some resistance to colonialism see Damian Costello, *Black Elk: Colonialism and Lakota Catholicism* (Maryknoll, NY: Orbis, 2005). Costello convincingly argues that Neihardt's famous account of Black Elk excluded Black Elk's Catholicism.

> alternative but painstakingly, feebly, repentantly, patiently, locally, to disentangle that Jesus from the Christ of Byzantium and of Torquemada. The disavowal of Constantine is then not a distraction but the condition of the historical seriousness of the confession that Jesus Christ who is Lord.[43]

3. A TRIBUTE TO DAVID BURRELL, C.S.C.

My account of Yoder's understanding of what implications might follow from the Christian disavowal of Constantine for interfaith dialogue I am sure will seem to some an attempt to avoid the subject before us. Yoder's criticism of Constantinianism may seem interesting, but not relevant to the challenge the "new religious pluralism" presents to the American society. At best Yoder represents an inner-Christian debate, but that debate does not translate into implications for broader public policy. Of course I never promised you a rose garden. More important, however, is to understand why, if Yoder is right about what it means to disavow Constantine, I cannot meet the expectations to articulate a public policy in response to the increasing religious diversity of America.

I suppose one of the ways to try to make the analysis I have provided "relevant" would be to work all the harder for the disestablishment of Christianity politically and socially in America. The First Amendment gives American Christians the presumption that Christianity is not established in law, but in fact Christianity still enjoys a cultural establishment that makes legal establishment unnecessary. If, as some have maintained, American is becoming culturally a more secular society that (at least if Yoder is right) is not necessarily bad news for a Christian recovery of what contribution we might have for interfaith interactions.[44]

I do believe that Christians even in America can make a contribution for better interfaith understanding once we are free from the presumption that we have a peculiar role or special position in America. That contribution is quite simply people who are committed to having their lives exposed to other faiths. In particular I have in mind my friend and former colleague David Burrell, C.S.C. David Burrell was chair of the department of theology when I taught at Notre Dame from 1970 to 1984. He is a distinguished philosophical theologian who has written ground-breaking books on Aquinas. In particular he is often credited as being among the first to offer fresh readings of Aquinas, and in particular how Aquinas' understanding of analogy made possible Wittgenstein.[45]

43 Yoder, "The Disavowal of Constantine," p. 261.

44 I have no intention to enter the debates about "secularization." Stout, I think, does a good job of clarifying the different accounts of the secularization thesis in *Democracy and Tradition*, pp. 92–117.

45 Burrell's first book on Aquinas was *Analogy and Philosophical Language* (New Haven: Yale University Press, 1973), but his *Aquinas: God and Action* (London: Routledge and Kegan Paul, 1979) is regarded as his most important book on

During Burrell's tenure, money was given to establish a chair in Judaica. The temptation presented by such a chair was to make Judaism an exotic other. However, Burrell was determined to avoid such a development because he had come to understand, an understanding schooled by colleagues such as Joe Blenkinsopp and Robert Wilken, that for reasons internal to Christian theology Judaism could not be relegated to the role of being an antecedent to Christianity.[46] Accordingly the position in Judaica was structured into the curriculum in a manner that made clear the work done by our colleague in Judaica was crucial for Christian theology.

During this time Burrell was also involved with helping Father Hesburgh, C.S.C., the president of Notre Dame, set up the Ecumenical Center in Jerusalem. Father Hesburgh had been asked by Paul VI to establish an ecumenical center in the hope that Catholic, Protestant, and Orthodox scholars would be able to study and interact in Israel, where (as Paul VI put it) "We were all once one." As a result Burrell was a frequent visitor to Jerusalem and even served, after finishing his term as chair of theology at Notre Dame, as the director of the Center. Once there, he found himself increasingly immersed in the lives of Jews, but also sympathetic with the plight of the Palestinians.[47]

Given Burrell's scholarly excellence you can almost forget that he is first and foremost a priest. The university, while important to him, was not always the most conducive context for the expression of his priesthood. As a result in 1975 he responded eagerly to his Provincial Superior's request to teach in the seminary in Bangladesh where his congregation had been present for more than a century. There he encountered Muslims whose way of life he could not help but be impressed. As a result he wanted to read the Koran. But he realized he could not read the Koran without learning Arabic. Accordingly once he had taken up residence in Israel, his practice of saying Mass in Hebrew gave him the opportunity to study Arabic.

Burrell, of course, could not forget he was an Aquinas scholar. Aquinas, moreover, was a student of Ibn-Sina and Maimonides. It is not surprising, therefore, that Burrell drew on his increasing knowledge of Judaism and Islam to write *Knowing the Unknowable God: Ibn-Sina,*

Aquinas. For the best book on the relationship between Wittgenstein and Aquinas see *Grammar and Grace: Reformulations of Aquinas and Wittgenstein*, edited by Jeffrey Stout and Robert MacSwain (London: SCM Press, 2004).

46 The Catholic character of Notre Dame had everything to do with Burrell's way of understanding Judaism. Catholics understood they often became for Protestants the Jews, that is, Catholics had been surpassed. Nowhere was this more apparent than in the scholarly guilds surrounding the study of scripture in which Second Temple Judaism became the dead priest-ridden religion that the charismatic Christianity of the New Testament replaced. Protestant biblical scholarship simply reproduced that story with their triumph in the Reformation.

47 Burrell is very sympathetic with the position developed by Jonathan Sacks in his book, *The Dignity of Difference: How to Avoid the Clash of Civilizations* (London: Continuum, 2002).

Maimonides, Aquinas.[48] In this book Burrell explored how these thinkers, each in their distinctive way, maintained the crucial distinction between essence and existence in the order of finite beings as crucial for maintaining the difference that creation makes. Without trying to force these traditions "to learn from one another," Burrell was able to show in fact some of Aquinas' most fundamental moves came from Jewish and Islamic scholars.

However, as a student of Aristotle and Aquinas, Burrell never forgets that metaphysical questions are in service to friendship, and in particular, friendship with God. Thus his wonderful chapter in *Friendship and Ways to Truth* entitled, "Friendship with God in al-Ghazali and Aquinas."[49] In this chapter Burrell shows how both theologians draw on their respective scriptures to display that as creatures we are necessarily related to our creator in a manner that makes possible the living of our lives as the gift life is. In this essay we begin to see Burrell becoming so internal to Islamic theology he is able to suggest that al-Ghazali's proposal of a mutual love between Muslims and the one God challenges those stereotypes of Islam overdetermined by the translation of Islam as "submission." Burrell's investment in Islam now even extends to translating Al-Ghazali's *Ninety-nine Beautiful Names of God*.

Burrell is obviously a remarkable mind and spirit, but I do not think he is exceptional. Rather I think his life has been made possible because he exemplifies the opportunity opened by the disavowal of Constantine. A strange claim, perhaps, given that Burrell is a Roman Catholic priest. What could be more Constantinian than being a Roman Catholic priest, particularly one that has spent a lifetime teaching at the University of Notre Dame? Yet as Burrell reminds us in *Friendship and Ways to Truth*, it was Karl Rahner (the same Rahner of "anonymous Christianity") who argued that the real point of Vatican II was to sound the end of 19 centuries of "western European Christianity" in order to present Christianity vis-à-vis other faiths in a fashion quite different from anything in history since Christianity had parted ways with Judaism.[50]

That David Burrell has been drawn into the lives of Jews and Muslims is not because he is a cosmopolitan. Rather he has been drawn into the lives of Jews and Muslims because he is a Catholic. He exemplifies Yoder's contention that the closer we are drawn to Jesus the closer we must be drawn to those who do not pray as Christians do to the Father, Son, and Holy Spirit. Yet Burrell has learned that Jews and Muslims recognize in Christians who pray something of their own lives. In that recognition, moreover, is the hope that we are not doomed to reject one another out of fear.

48 David Burrell, C.S.C., *Knowing the Unknowable God: Ibn-Sina, Maimonides, Aquinas* (Notre Dame: University of Notre Dame Press, 1986).

49 David Burrell, C.S.C., *Friendship and Ways to Truth* (Notre Dame: University of Notre Dame Press, 2000), pp. 67–86.

50 Burrell, *Friendship and Ways to Truth*, p. 38.

As a Christian I have no theory or policy to solve the problem of "the new religious pluralism." But I do have something to give. I give you the example of David Burrell. Some may not think that sufficient to resolve the challenge before democracies. I am confident, however, that if people like David Burrell do not exist, appeals to democracy will be of no help.

5

The Pathos of the University: The Case of Stanley Fish

1. SETTING THE STAGE

There are two questions seldom asked by the faculty and administrators of universities: "What are universities for?" and "Who do they serve?" There are, no doubt, many reasons why these questions are not asked. Some may not ask these questions because they assume the answer or answers to the questions are so obvious they do not need to be raised. Moreover universities are doing so well, everyone thinks it a good thing to be educated, these questions do not need to be explored. It may also be the case that many assume that answers to these questions are so various, particularly given the multi-university, any answer is too complex to be of much use.

Yet I think a more straightforward reason is behind the unwillingness to ask these questions, that is, we do not ask them because we sense we, that is, those of us who administer and teach at universities, have no ready answers to give. The university may pride itself as being the place that embodies the proposition that the unexamined life is not worth living, but like most people and institutions we know that to be false. As the novelist Peter DeVries observed the unexamined life may not be worth living but the examined life is no bowl of cherries either.[1]

Those that run and those that teach in the modern university simply have no idea what or how they might provide an answer to the question of what the university is for or who it is to serve. As a result we are content to comfort ourselves by repeating familiar slogans about the importance of being an educated person who can think critically. Which, as I will suggest below, means that those who have gone to university, particularly top-tier universities, will have greater earning power.

[1] Peter Euben pointed out to me that these questions may not be asked because those who administer and teach at universities have a profound stake in being ignorant of any answers we might find. He observes that universities tend to absent themselves from the questions they insist other institutions ask and answer.

I need to be clear I am not blaming anyone for this state of affairs. It is just the way the world, and in particular, the world of the university, has gone. But neither do I think the inability of those at universities to raise or explore the answers to these questions is good for the health or survival of the university. When we do not know how to approach these questions – and explore the ways in which they are related – too often answers are given that tend to make universities something they should not be.

In order to show why this is the case I will explore the case made by Stanley Fish in a series of editorials in the *Chronicle of Higher Education* that suggest the university does not need to answer questions of purpose or service. I do so because no one makes the case more clearly than Fish that the purpose and justification of the university is quite simply to support Stanley Fish's work as a literary critic. I focus on the case Stanley Fish makes for the university because what he has to say is so marvelously candid. Fish simply says what I think anyone should say that accepts the world in which we find it, that is a world in which there no longer exists any common judgments about the true, the good, and the beautiful. In such a world the university at best is conceived as a lovely poem that creates its own meaning. You do not need to ask what it is for or who it serves because such questions threaten its very character.

I will argue, however, that the university so understood cannot be sustained or justified. Fish's understanding of the university is betrayed by the subservience of the university to money. But money is merely the medium to name the necessary service the university should perform for those who care about what universities can and should be. Which is but another way to say that universities cannot avoid questions concerning what they are and who they serve.[2]

I need to be candid about my own agenda in trying to force question of use and service. I am trying to think through what difference it might make that a university should be in service to an institution called the church. I want to explore the difference it might make for a university that gains its purpose from a people who worship God for how knowledges are conceived and related. I hope to show Stanley Fish that given what he loves he would be better off teaching at a university that wants him to study Milton because Milton thought God matters.

Though I will be critical of the case Stanley Fish makes for the university, I hope my criticisms will reflect my profound admiration for him and his work. Indeed I am not only an admirer, I am honored

[2] That I shifted the grammar in this sentence to the plural is significant. To focus on *the* university can imply that the university has an "essence" that all universities and colleges share. I simply do not believe such an essence exists. There are no doubt family resemblances between universities that may be useful to name, but to talk about "the university" *too often* is an attempt to avoid questions of purpose and consistency.

that Stanley counts me as a friend. We were not only neighbors for many years, but also colleagues at Duke University. During Stanley's tenure as the director of the Duke University Press I was chair of the Duke University Press Board. So I hope those reading this will understand my criticism of Stanley's position to be a conversation between friends.

2. FISH'S DEFENSE OF THE UNIVERSITY

In the editorials Stanley wrote in the *Chronicle of Higher Education* he argues that neither professors nor administrators in the modern university should take a stand on any social, political, or moral issue.[3] In the first editorial entitled, "Save the World in Your Own Time," Fish criticizes Bob Kerrey, president of New School University, for calling for a regime change in Iraq. Fish has no objection to Kerrey taking such a position as a citizen, but according to Fish if Kerrey was speaking as a university president he betrayed his role as a representative of the university.[4] He did so because according to Fish "it is immoral for academics or for academic institutions to proclaim moral views."

It is important to note that Fish is not suggesting that the university has no moral purpose. He quite clearly says that "it is immoral" for academics to proclaim moral views. So he is making a moral argument against those who want to use the university to support moral causes that are not intrinsic to the purpose of the university. Such purpose Fish identifies as that made in a 1967 faculty report to the president of the University of Chicago, that is, that the "university exists only for the limited purposes of teaching and research." The report, therefore, concluded that, "since the university is a community only for those limited and distinctive purposes, it is a community which cannot take collective action on the issues of the day without endangering the conditions for its existence and effectiveness."

Fish argues that the university can and should take action on issues relevant to its educational mission, that is, the integrity of scholarship, the evil of plagiarism, and the value of a liberal education. But he argues against those that suggest the university must be a "free speech zone" in the interest of sustaining liberal democracies. Nor should universities use

3 Fish's editorials appeared in the *Chronical Careers* on January 23, 2003, May 16, 2003, and July 11, 2003. There was also an editorial in the *New York Times* entitled, "Why We Build the Ivory Tower," on June 1, 2004. I will not give page references to these editorials because I am using online texts.

4 Fish seems to assume that the category of "citizen" is intelligible – an assumption that certainly requires defense. Colleges and universities often claim they are educating the young to be "global citizens" but such a claim is unintelligible. Citizenship only makes sense in terms of role responsibilities correlative of a particular history and place. "Global" denotes universal pretensions that should challenge the assumptions necessary to sustain an intelligible account of citizenship. That universities use the language of "global" and "citizenship" to define their purpose is but an indication of the false consciousness that dominates university life.

their wealth to put pressure on South Africa or Israel to be more just. The crucial question to determine any action contemplated by the university, actions such as providing places and times for controversial speakers or causes, is whether the decision to do so is justified on educational grounds.

This applies also to the classroom. The moral responsibility of professors is to teach their subjects. Their task is not to teach peace or war, to advocate nationalism or antinationalism, or to try to enlist students in their favorite causes. Such matters may be part of their teaching only if they are intrinsic to their field of study. The only advocacy appropriate to the classroom is that identified with the intellectual virtues of "thoroughness, perseverance, intellectual honesty," which are necessary for the pursuit of the truth. That is what the American public expects of teachers; that is, to pursue truth, and if you are not in the pursuit of truth you should not be in the university.[5]

In a subsequent editorial entitled "Aim Low," Fish develops his position by warning against confusing democratic values with academic one. The task of an academic should not be trying to produce students who have a commitment to moral and civic responsibility. It may be a good thing for students to have respect for others, but the development of such respect is not and should not be the goal of academic training. Indeed if such a goal is made central for the work of the university Fish contends that what the university should fundamentally be about will likely be slighted. Even more important, however, Fish argues that the university should only try to aim for that which it *can* do. It is simply beyond the power of those who make up the university to promise to provide moral and civic education. What has to be recognized is that democratic and educational values are not the same and to confuse them can corrupt the educational mission.

Finally Fish argues in an editorial entitled "The Same Old Song" that the argument he has been making concerning the university is but a version of the case he has made for some time in defense of the hermetic narrowness of disciplines. A discipline becomes a discipline, at least a discipline that deserves recognition in the university, by having distinct focus that allows its practitioners to prove the utility of their subject to other academics. In short a discipline becomes important just to the extent those in the discipline represent knowledge unavailable without the narrow focus they represent.

Moreover what is true of disciplines should be true of the university as a whole. Of course the university is under pressure from parents and politicians to achieve goals they desire, e.g. a higher paying job or conservative political positions. But the university should resist those who would demand that the university be what it cannot be. Rather the university's purpose is "quite simply to produce and disseminate

[5] Fish seems to think this "as such" is not "political." A very odd position for someone as politically astute as Fish.

(through teaching and publication) academic knowledge and to train those who will take up that task in the future." The university is in the business of the search for truth as an end in itself and fidelity to that task means the university cannot be in the business of forming character or fashioning citizens. In short the university is a "self-consuming" artifact.

3. THE BACKGROUND OF FISH'S ARGUMENT CONCERNING THE UNIVERSITY

Fish's argument in defense of the apolitical character of the university is but a footnote to the case he makes in his book, *Professional Correctness: Literary Studies and Political Change*.[6] In his book Fish takes aim at the new historicist and those in cultural studies who think their task to be the study of literature in the interest of political change. In contrast Fish argues that the literary critic is not nor should be an organic intellectual (Gramsci), but rather should aspire to be "a specialist, defined and limited by the traditions of his craft, and it is a condition of his labors, at least as they are exerted in the United States, that he remain distanced from any effort to work changes in the structure of society" (p. 1).

Literary criticism must, therefore, be a distinctive enterprise. By distinctive Fish means simply that it must be what it is in itself and not something else. To be so distinctive secures autonomy for the discipline, but autonomy means simply that those engaging in literary criticism have responsibility "for doing a job the society wants done" (p. 20).[7] Fish observes at one time some pursued a literary life to secure a position at court, but that day is long past. Now

> literary activity is increasingly pursued in the academy where proficiency is measured by academic standards and rewarded by the gatekeepers of an academic guild. The name for this is professionalism, a form of organization in which membership is acquired by a course of special training whose end is the production of persons who recognize one another not because they regularly meet at the same ceremonial occasions (unless one equates an MLA meeting with the Elizabethan court), but because they perform the same "moves" in the same "game." That is, they participate in the same "immanent intelligibility" whose content is the same set of "internal" – not foreign – purposes (p. 32).

6 Stanley Fish, *Professional Correctness: Literary Studies and Political Change* (Oxford: Clarendon Press, 1995). (Page references to this book will appear in the text.)

7 One might wish Fish would have a more extensive account of how disciplines are autonomous yet do a job society wants done. At the very least Fish owes us an account of the history of the development of "disciplines" just to the extent such a history reveals the quite contingent contexts that make and unmake the disciplines and the knowledges they represent.

Fish acknowledges that the emergence of the profession of literary studies has been a recent development of the last hundred years. Moreover there have been costs for this development not the least being the "difficulty of connecting up specifically literary work with the larger arenas in which it was once able to intervene" (p. 43). Some may lament this development, but Fish argues that you cannot reverse what has happened. Those in cultural studies who think they can change society by focusing their attention on television rather than poetry will only be frustrated. The new historicist's desire to substitute political agendas for the standards appropriate to the academy are simply unrealizable.

Fish does not deny that if enough literary scholars work with an eye for immediate political effect and call what they do literary criticism then literary criticism will be what they do. But Fish argues such a development would come at a great loss, that is, the skills of close reading that now give a distinctive identity to the profession of literary studies will suffer. Fish does not claim that the close reading learned from new criticism cannot be replaced by the new historicist, but such a replacement means that literary critics will no longer be doing what he does (p. 69).

With his usual candor Fish tells us that the reason he does his work in the manner he does it is because "I like the way I feel when I am doing it" (p. 110). He claims this is quite similar to virtue being its own reward. Because, like virtue, literary criticism can be difficult, but it is the very difficulty that draws Fish to engage in it. He says,

> I like being brought up short by an effect I have experienced but do not yet understand analytically. I like trying to describe in flatly prosaic words the achievement of words that are anything but flat and prosaic. I like savoring the physical "taste" of language at the same time that I work to lay bare its physics. And when those pleasures have been (temporarily) exhausted, I like linking one moment in a poem to others and then to moments in other works, works by the same author or by his predecessors or contemporaries or successors. It doesn't finally matter which, so long as I can *keep going*, reaping the cognitive and tactile harvest of an activity as self-reflexive as I become when I engage in it (p. 110).

Fish does not try, just as he argues that universities should not try, to provide an external justification for his work as a literary critic. The only justification is the practice of literary criticism itself. Those that might object that there must be a normative structure to which any such practice can be assessed simply fail to see that no such structure exists. Rather justification can only be provided within the history of the discipline. "Justification never starts from scratch, and can only begin if everything it seeks to demonstrate is already taken for granted" (p. 113).

Accordingly no one, Fish argues, ever chooses a profession or a discipline because of moral and philosophical considerations. You discover your life's work after many false starts by one day finding "yourself in the middle of doing something, enmeshed in its routines, extending in every action its assumptions. And when the request for justification comes, your respond *from the middle*, respond with the phrases and platitudes of disciplinary self-congratulation . . . Justification is not a chain of inferences, but a circle, and it proceeds, if that is the word, by telling a story in which every detail is an instantiation of an informing spirit that is known only in the details but always exceeds them" (p. 113).

Fish's arguments against attempts to justify the work of the university on grounds other than what the university can and should do is obviously but an extension of his understanding of his discipline of literary criticism. He does not deny that the relationship between academic practices and social and political change is a matter of degree. For example the introduction of noncanonical texts into the curriculum may have had an effect on students in their roles as citizens, churchgoers, parents, and so on. But the problem with such "success" is they cannot be counted on, particularly in the United States.

Some may say so much the worse for the United States, but Fish observes that being "sequestered" in the university has advantages. Thus many academics, who have recently sought increased attention by the wider society in the name of progressive causes, have instead had to endure a right-wing backlash. Fish observes, therefore, that it may not be a "bad thing after all that in the United States those who operate the levers of commerce and government do not give much heed to what goes on in our classrooms or in our learned journals" (p. 96). This, I take, is the reason Fish argues in his editorials in the *Chronicle of Higher Education* that administrators and professors should not use their positions to argue for social and political causes. He desires the university to be politically irrelevant in order to save the university from politics. That is, from having to say who the university serves and what it is for.

4. MONEY

Yet something seems missing from this picture. What I think is missing is money. A strange absence given Fish's avowal that he is a dedicated consumer. You need money to be a consumer and Stanley Fish has never apologized for being well paid. He also wants his fellow academics to be well paid. So he is acutely aware that the university runs on money, but the need for money does not seem to enter into his account of the nature of the university.

He does acknowledge that many parents send their children to the university in the hope that the education they receive will increase their ability to make money. Fish has no reason to deny that such a result may be a byproduct of a university education, but he seems to object to making the earning of money the purpose of the university. But it is not clear why those that think that university should be about helping their children make more money should be persuaded by Fish's justification of the university. Why, for example, should anyone pay Stanley Fish to gain such pleasure from his reading of Milton?[8]

Fish may object that his account of the university is meant to defeat such questions, but I do not think even on his own grounds he is able to do so. In his justification for the university he appeals to "the value of a liberal education" as well as the academic virtue of the conscientious "pursuit of truth." But for whom is liberal education a "value" and why is the pleasure Fish gets from his study of Milton to be identified with the "pursuit of truth?" If liberal education is a value then surely some account is needed to explain for whom it is a value. Moreover whoever it is that values liberal education needs to sustain that education with the only measure we have of value, that is, money.

In a review of *Professional Correctness* Terry Eagleton observes that Fish's argument is "a plea for old-style New Critical textual autonomy, but one couched in the terms of the very theory such 'close readers' find most unpalatable. As such *Professional Correctness* repeats its author's customary maneuver of deploying sophisticated theory for anti-theoretical ends, wheeling up avant-garde notions to defend the status quo."[9] Eagleton argues this leaves Fish without any justification for his work as a literary critic. Fish has rejected the humanist case for studying literature (it makes you a better person) as well as the radical case (it aids political liberation) leaving him with what is essentially a hedonist avowal of how he feels when he does literary criticism.

In this respect Fish's adherence to close reading may be open to Frank Lentricchia's criticism of modernist poets. Lentricchia argues that

8 Fish loves to challenge students who express admiration for Milton's poetry by pointing out that Milton did not want their admiration. He wanted their souls. Fish, therefore, insists for anyone that would understand Milton's poetry must remember that his poetry is only conflicted, tragic, paradoxical, or inconclusive if you forget that for Milton "God is God and not one of a number of contending forces" (*How Milton Works* (Cambridge: Belknap Press, 2001), p. 14). I think Fish is right about this, but it does raise a question about his justification for his understanding of literary criticism. Why should Milton be read as a "literary" text? Milton, as Fish often does so well, should be read in the context of Christian theology. That Milton is often not read by Christian theologians is one of the reasons that Milton has become the property of English departments, but this is a reminder of the failure of theology.

9 Terry Eagleton, "The Death of Self-Criticism," *Times Literary Supplement* (November 25, 1995), p. 6. Eagleton's critique is a challenge to Fish's contention that theory has no consequences. See, for example, Fish's important essay, "Consequences" in his book, *Doing What Comes Naturally: Change, Rhetoric, and the Practice of Theory in Literary and Legal Studies* (Durham: Duke University Press, 1989), pp. 315–41. I am quite sympathetic with Fish's argument against theory on grounds that the general can never be substituted for the local. Indeed my criticism of his defense of the university is that he fails to adequately locate the "local" that makes the university intelligible to itself.

modernist writers like Frost and Eliot defined themselves against the standards of the mass market by becoming champions of radical originality and the maker of "a one in a kind text." But their very attempt to preserve an independent selfhood against the market, against money, was subverted by the market, not because they wrote according to popular formulas, but because they gave us "their poems as delicious experiences of voyeurism, illusions of direct access to the life and thought of the famous writer, with the poet inside the poem like a rare animal in a zoo. This was the only commodity Frost and Eliot were capable of producing: the modernist phenomenon as product, mass-culture's ultimate revenge on those who would scorn it."[10]

In like manner Fish's attempt to preserve the autonomy of the university can result in the self-deceptive strategy of hiding from those that administer and teach in the university whose interests they are serving even though they claiming to serve none, if they are as honest as Fish, but themselves. Fish's account of the university simply avoids the reality, the reality money names, of the universities in which Fish taught and administered. James Engell and Anthony Dangerfield have, I think, named that reality in an admirably straightforward manner when they observe:

> The fastest-expanding and often strongest motivation in American higher education is now money. While other aims and functions certainly persist, they are increasingly eclipsed by this ultimate goal of wealth accumulation. Money, rather than a means, is becoming the chief end of higher education. With growing frequency, the ends are not cultural values or critical thinking, ethical convictions or intellectual skills. When these goals are pursued, it is often not because they offer multiple uses and relevance but because they might be converted into cash.[11]

Engell and Dangerfield provide evidence for this development by calling attention to the implication money has had on the preferred fields of study in the contemporary university. Fish's account of the professional development of disciplines simply betrays the fact that the disciplines that flourish in the contemporary university are those that study money (economics), are the source of money (sciences), or are linked, often it seems mistakenly, to future chances of being in an occupation or profession that promises a high earning standard (p. 89). As a result Engell and Dangerfield argue the humanities' "vital signs are poor…Since the late 1960s the humanities have been neglected,

[10] Frank Lentricchia, *Modernist Quartet* (Cambridge: Cambridge University Press, 1994), pp. 112–13.

[11] James Engell and Anthony Dangerfield, *Saving Higher Education in the Age of Money* (Charlottesville: University of Virginia Press, 2005), p. 2. Page references will appear in the text.

downgraded, and forced to retrench, all at a time when other areas of higher education have grown in numbers, wealth, and influence" (p. 88).

Engell and Dangerfield observe humanists have often been complicit in the loss of the central role of the humanities in the university. "Just as the cult of money was laying siege to the culture of learning, many beleaguered exponents of humanistic study divided into parties and embarked on a series of unedifying public disputes, including ones that degraded the name, 'humanist' " (p. 98). At the same time many in the humanities discovered they were "interdisciplinary," they often tried to be so in a manner that resulted in studies that were so specialized they became unintelligible to anyone "outside" their discipline. What was lost was any attempt to show how the humanities have as one of their essential tasks to incorporate results from other areas of endeavor, not the least being science, through judgments of human value, relevance, and significance (p. 99).[12]

Unlike Fish, however, Engell and Dangerfield argue that the university cannot survive if the purpose for its existence is disavowed. First of all the university cannot exist as a loose aggregate of its separate parts quite simply because the university is not a capital market. The university serves other purposes, which may not be inimical to the market, indeed they may even be beneficial to the market, but the university is constitutive of goods too complex to be subjected to questions of employment. Universities simply cannot avoid decisions about what forms of knowledge are most worth having.[13] Therefore it may be that the university must insist certain disciplines be developed and taught because they are necessary for making us a better people.

Engell and Dangerfield argue that the most determinative corruption of the university money creates is that the moral purpose of the

12 Engell and Dangerfield do not believe, as Fish does not believe, that the humanities can guarantee a moral outcome. They observe "like the uses of all knowledge, the uses of literature *guarantee* nothing. Its knowledge acts as an instrumentality. Like a scalpel or laser, it can heal or lance a cavity swollen with prejudice. It can also destroy, kill or justify killing. Many SS officers were well educated" (p. 166).

13 Engell and Dangerfield quote Mark Yudof, who is the former president of the University of Michigan, that "The unvarnished truth is that the extraordinary compact between state governments and their flagship universities appears to be dead – or at least on life support. For more than a century, these two parties had a deal: In return for financial support from taxpayers, these universities would keep tuition low and provide broad access for undergraduates from all economic strata, train graduate and professional students, promote arts and culture, help solve local problems, and perform groundbreaking research. Unfortunately, the agreement between the states and their flagship universities has deteriorated for 25 years, leaving public research universities in a purgatory of insufficient resources – low tuition and flat appropriations" (p. 186). I think at least one of the reasons for this development is the inability of the university to articulate for itself and for those it served the moral purpose of the university. Instead the sciences were held up to promise that the university would cure this or that disease or to give us power over "nature." But how do you provide an account of the moral purposes of the university in a social order no longer sure what its moral character is or should be.

university is lost. The power of money works, to be sure in a manner often difficult to discern, to undermine by degrees the essential goals and independent functions of the university. These are goals and functions, moreover, that other institutions either do not pursue or do not pursue nearly so well (p. 20). Those goals and functions Engell and Dangerfield suggest are captured by Edward Shils' claim that "the discovery and transmission of truth is the distinctive task of the academic profession" (p. 102).

But is that not what Fish also says? Engell and Dangerfield at least seem to differ from Fish because they think the future of democracies depends on universities producing people who can steer us, as they put it, "through these complex and perilous times." Such people must be those who have mastered language, who can put together sound arguments, who have learned from the past,

> and who have witnessed the treacheries and glories of human experience profoundly revealed by writers and artists. The humanities can and should be broadly instrumental, as well as existing for pleasure and aesthetic pursuits. Their functions are multiple. Especially with regard to the uses of language, history, and ethical reflection – as well as alerting everyone to their abuses – the humanities can keep our collective capacities for thinking flexible, adaptable, inquisitive, tolerant, and open, and not only open to reasoned discourse but actively involved in shaping the best expression of that discourse (p. 103).

This may well be, however, what Fish means when he appeals to the value of a liberal education. Yet Engell and Dangerfield in a manner unlike Fish argue that it is not enough for the university to be about the pursuit and preservation of knowledge, but it must also consider that knowledge in the light of its potential for the human good. They quite rightly have a chapter critical of ethics becoming another specialized discipline of the university. Instead they argue that "ethics" is inseparable from every subject and activity of the university.[14] Appealing to Cardinal Newman they remind us that though Newman is often used to justify the pursuit of knowledge for its own sake, he actually sets a higher and final goal, that is, that "all knowledge, whether applied or

[14] In particular they argue that history is particularly important. "Commercial leadership without historical imagination produces inefficiency, repetition of failed strategies, lack of situational awareness, and strategic miscalculation of long-term behaviors. When people successful in business have amassed fortunes and are prepared to aid society through philanthropy, a historical perspective helps ensure effective, meaningful gifts of lasting impact. Scientific leadership without knowledge of history of science risks unethical applications. Political leadership without historical consciousness results, at best, in blunders and ineffectiveness, at worst in fiasco and tragedy" (p. 121).

relished alone, is to be considered in light of ethical conduct and human good" (p. 131).

I suspect that Fish will not find the case Engell and Dangerfield make to try to save the university from the subversion of money to be an interesting alternative to the position he developed in his editorials in the *Chronicle*. Engell and Dangerfield may have called attention to a subversion of the university which belies Fish's account, but Fish without contradiction can acknowledge that the university may well not conform to his "ideal." Fish can even acknowledge that Engell and Dangerfield's suggestion that all knowledge is to be considered in the light of the human good is not foreign to his understanding of the university. He did say that it was "immoral" for academics to proclaim moral views.

Moreover Engell and Dangerfield do not, just as Fish does not, suggest who is going to pay for the university they think is in danger of being lost. They begin their book noting that they are not advocating "a return to some era when money exerted little or no force in higher education" (p. 1). Indeed one wonders if such a time ever existed, but they do not tell us who will pay for the university they think should exist. Money is but a name for people the university is meant to serve. "What is the university for?" and "Who does the university serve?" are questions the fundraisers for universities cannot avoid.[15] Yet it is not clear if Engell and Dangerfield have provided, in the world as we know it, any better answers to those questions than Fish has done. For in effect Fish has said in a world in which such questions cannot be answered it is best not to ask them in the hope that those that support and those that come to universities will let us do what we like to do. Engell and Dangerfield, however, can argue that Fish's refusal to justify the university as a moral enterprise for the societal good means Fish can have no objection to the transformation of university curriculums by money. Engell and Dangerfield believe that if the university is to be the place of truthful speech it is important that the university be, for example, committed to teaching students Milton. Yet that is the kind of justification that Fish seems to want to avoid.

In contrast to Fish, Engell and Dangerfield are right to insist that the university must have a moral purpose, but it is not clear that their understanding of that purpose is an advance beyond Fish. At the very least they owe us an account of whose moral purpose the university represents. Vague appeals to the importance of the university for democracy are not sufficient. Even more important Engell and Dangerfield need to tell us if those who represent the moral purpose they identify as

15 Academics generally disdain the fundraising side of the university, but I have long thought that "development" is the most determinative form of the university's educational task. Teaching people why they should want to give money to the university is an ongoing test of the education the university provided to its alumnae. Those raising money must hope that those from whom they must ask to give money were well enough educated to understand why they should want to fund an institution that teaches that making money cannot be what constitutes a good life.

the heart of the university i.e., the formation of people of truth, are willing to support that purpose with money.

5. WHY VIRTUE IS NOT ITS OWN REWARD

I noted above that Stanley Fish defends his understanding of what he does as a literary critic on grounds that virtue is its own reward. But Aristotle did not think that virtue was its own reward. Aristotle's account of the virtues requires that one be well brought up in a manner that in becoming virtuous you reflect back to the community that which was assumed to be a good life. In contrast the Stoics thought that virtue was its own reward because the polis that at least imaginatively informed Aristotle's account of virtue no longer existed. Empire not polis shaped the world in which the Stoics had to think through what a worthy life might entail. Virtue had to become its own reward because there no longer existed any politics necessary to name as well as make intelligible a virtuous life. The Stoics provided the best account available for the moral formation of bureaucrats destined to serve an empire.

I am aware that the suggestion that Fish's advocacy of virtue as its own reward reflects a Stoic-like account of morality may seem far-fetched, but I am much less interested in what Fish may have meant by his appeal to virtue than the context his remarks reflect. That context I take to be the social order called America that is determinatively shaped by liberal political practice. "Liberal" names the assumption that a social order should be constituted by procedural arrangements that require no account of goods held in common. Those procedural arrangements are often articulated by "values" such as freedom and equality that are assumed to be universals that all people share. That is why America can be an imperial power without recognizing it is so because Americans believe that all people if they had our money and education would want to be just like us.

Fish, of course, has been an unrelenting critic of the epistemological conceits that have been used to justify liberal political arrangements.[16] Yet, as Eagleton suggests in his review of *Professional Correctness*, the relativist Fish occasionally remembers that his position is provincially American. Eagleton, noting that Fish would not put it this way, "represents the perilous situation of American intellectuals bleakly marooned in an extravagantly philistine, money-obsessed society."[17] Eagleton's comment, which is overly harsh, nonetheless suggests that the justification that Fish has given for the university, as well as his kind of literary

[16] See, for example, his wonderful response to Stephen Carter entitled "Liberalism Doesn't Exist," in *There's No Such Thing As Free Speech . . . And It's a Good Thing Too* (New York: Oxford University Press, 1994), pp. 134–8. Fish's critique of liberalism is a correlative of his attack on all forms of formalism.

[17] Eagleton, p. 6.

criticism, in spite of his criticism of liberalism, is a reflection as well as a reproduction of liberal theory and practice. The only way to justify reading Milton, or the other texts in the humanities, in a world that no longer believes in the God Milton believed in, is to make the text a self-consuming artifact. I need to be clear that I am not criticizing Fish for this result. What else can he do given the fact there is no alternative?

The alternative that is missing, the alternative I suspect Fish might desire, is what Alasdair MacIntyre has called "the idea of an educated public."[18] MacIntyre notes that the purpose of the modern university, by which he means the university since the eighteenth century, has been to form young people to assume some social role and function that will require ongoing recruits. The second purpose is to teach the young how to think for themselves. These aims depend on the purposes of the university finding articulation in the platitudes of the age as well as providing the final answer to a chain of questions of the form, "For the sake of what is that being done?" (p. 17).

MacIntyre argues, however, that these two aims, which are not necessarily incompatible, are incompatible in modernity. They are so because what modernity excludes is the existence of an educated public that represents judgments in answer to the question of "for the sake of what is being done?". According to MacIntyre the existence of such a public depends on three conditions being met: (i) that a large number of individuals, educated into the habit and opportunity of active debate, exist to discern how the debate has implications for their shared social existence; (ii) that there is a shared assent to standards to which the success or failure of any argument is to be judged; (iii) and that an educated community exists in which there is a shared background of beliefs informed by the widespread reading of a common body of texts which have canonical status within that particular community. The last condition requires that there is also a tradition of interpreted understanding of how the texts are to be read (p. 19).

MacIntyre thinks eighteenth-century Scotland exemplified the kind of educated public that made intelligible the great university reforms of Scotland. However, he argues that the Scottish achievement was subverted in a manner that illumines our current situation. According to MacIntyre, the developments in philosophy of common sense resulted in a professionalization of philosophy in which the work of philosophy ceased to be intelligible to the common educated mind. Societal developments also played a role as the size of the population made it increasingly difficult for the virtues to flourish. Economic developments, in particular the specialization into different trades and professions, eroded

18 Alasdair MacIntyre, "The Idea of an Educated Public," in *Education and Values: The Richard Peters Lectures*, edited by Graham Haydon (London: University of London Press, 1987), pp. 15–36. Page references will appear in the text.

civic virtues as well as how individuals might understand their primary loyalties to society as a whole.

The results of these developments were magnified by the effect of economic growth on the class structure of the society in which the educated class was impotent and functionless in the face of the class conflicts between laboring and manufacturing classes. At the same time the growth of specialization and the division of labor not only had an effect in industry but also was reflected in the realm of knowledge and the curriculum of the university. The increasing professionalization make the specialized content of each discipline a subject matter that did not require knowledge of other disciplines. As a result the university could not help but become the exemplification of so many different and incompatible modes of justification that made and makes it impossible for us to arrive at a common mind even about what we should be quarreling about (pp. 26–8). In short, we got the university Stanley Fish celebrates.

MacIntyre notes that someone might object that even if he has shown what brought an end to an educated public in Scotland, he has not shown that the making and remaking of an educated public is in fact presupposed by the modern educational system. He responds, however, noting that if you take away the presumption of such a public with shared standards of justification, with a shared view of the past of the society, with a shared ability to participate in a public debate, the result will be that knowledges represented by the liberal arts and sciences, so far as those who are not specialist, cannot help but be transformed into passively received consumer products (p. 29).

One may well think MacIntyre's account of the educated Scottish public to be an exercise in romantic nostalgia, but I think it provides a useful contrast to help us understand why Stanley Fish does not try to justify the university as an institution in the business of the moral formation of students. I think MacIntyre's analysis also helps us understand why Engell and Dangerfield, who think the knowledges of the university should be in service to ethical conduct, must leave what they mean by "ethical conduct" vague. Fish, Engell, and Dangerfield simply lack the authority made possible by an educated public to make the arguments necessary for the university to serve moral ends.

Which finally brings me to the difference it might make if a university had or may even have some relation to the church. For at the very least Christianity names an ongoing argument across centuries of a tradition which has established why some texts must be read and read in relation to other texts. Christians for all their shortcomings still represent an ongoing educated public that means they must, as MacIntyre suggests any educated public must, have agreements that make their disagreements intelligible. As a result Christians should, if they are not intimidated by the secular academy, produce knowledges and the interconnection of those knowledges that can appropriately form students.[19]

Christians should know what their universities are for. They are to shape people in the love of God. Christians should know who their universities serve. They serve a people who must recognize that the university, at its best the kind of university Stanley Fish is willing to defend, is not the kind of university we should want. If Christians are a people with an alternative history of judgments about what is true and good they cannot help but produce an alternative university. Which means Christians must be those who are ready to match their convictions with their money. If one of the most important questions you can ask is who a university serves then it becomes all the more important that those who are served are also those who support the university with money.

It is not at all clear what a university supported by Christians might look like in our day. But I am convinced if Christians had the will and imagination to try to create such a university, a creation that no doubt would use the resources of universities that now claim to be Christian, we would not only surprise ourselves at how interesting such a university would be but we might also discover that Stanley Fish might want to teach at such an institution. For a university so constituted would be able to provide reasons to justify why no one graduating from the university should be ignorant of how Stanley Fish teaches us to read Milton.

19 What this means for Christians, like me, who teach at secular universities is an ongoing challenge. Such a challenge can be avoided by taking refuge in institutional arrangements i.e., I teach in a seminary not a university. But that is a far too easy escape. That my university has a seminary is a testimony to the historical background of the university as a Methodist institution. And this history should matter. But more important is the argument that Duke is a better university because the seminary is one of its educational units. That is an argument for another time. I would, however, argue that Christians in the undergraduate college should not avoid exploring what difference their convictions might make for why they do what they do. That difference will, of course, vary from subject to subject but surely such an investigation is the kind of work a university should sponsor. I obviously think that would be true of those working in other religious and nonreligious traditions. Of course, such work would make the university more conflictual but I see no reason why that is a disadvantage.

6

What Would a Christian University Look Like? Some Tentative Answers Inspired by Wendell Berry

The most fundamental kind of thinking is invariably provincial, in one form or another.

Robert Pogue Harrison[1]

1. THE CHALLENGE BEFORE US

"There are also violent and nonviolent ways to milk cows," I observed in a sermon on the occasion of the Installation of Dr. Gerald Gerbrandt as President of the Canadian Mennonite University on September 28, 2003.[2] I made the comment to commend the parochial character of the Canadian Mennonite University. The Canadian Mennonite University, as its name suggests, is Mennonite and Canadian and you cannot get more parochial than that. My comment about milk, therefore, was meant to praise why such a university would have no reason to distinguish between theoretical and practical forms of knowledge.

My sermon, and I think it important to observe that this is a university that assumes it is appropriate to have a sermon as part of its inaugural event for the first president of this institution, expressed my hope that the Canadian Mennonite University would not be just another "Christian liberal arts college." I think it is now clear that Christian liberal arts colleges have turned out to be more liberal than Christian. It is not my particular interest in this chapter to try to understand why the Christian liberal arts college has failed to sustain itself as Christian, but rather to begin to explore what a university responsive to the church might look like.[3]

[1] Robert Pogue Harrison, *Forests: The Shadow of Civilization* (Chicago: University of Chicago Press, 1992), p. 246.

[2] The sermon entitled "On Milk and Jesus" can be found in my book, *Disrupting Time: Sermons, Prayers, and Sundries* (Eugene, OR: Cascade Books, 2004), pp. 142–8.

[3] This way of putting the matter often raises the questions, "Which church?" and "Does such a church exist?" The answer is, "The Church of the Holy Family (Chapel Hill, North Carolina) is a church and it exists."

"To begin to explore what a Christian university might look like" is, of course, a far too grand project. What I am really interested in is to try to spell out what difference there may be between violent and nonviolent ways to milk cows. The focus on milking cows might suggest I assume that university curriculums should not be determined by presumptions about the necessity to sustain "high culture." I think it important, however, that universities teach Plato, Aquinas, Dante, and Darwin because I think one of the tasks of the university is to be a memory of a people. But too often Christian justifications of the university focused on the need to preserve the "classics" of western civilization have created universities that serve class interests more than Christian purpose. Why and how Plato is read at the Canadian Mennonite University may be quite different from why and how Plato is read at Duke University.

I think, moreover, Wendell Berry's criticism of the university is very important to help us understand the difference between violent and nonviolent ways to milk cows. Berry is an unrelenting critic of the contemporary university. I am deeply sympathetic with his criticisms of the university as we know it, but his criticisms are so radical it is not unreasonable to conclude that Berry has no hope that the university can be reclaimed for humane – much less Christian – purposes. I hope to show that Berry's work also suggests how we need to begin to live and, thus, think if we are to begin to imagine what a university shaped by Christian practices might look like.

I have, like Berry, often been a critic of the contemporary university. Of course to be a critic of the university is to mark oneself as a university person. After all, universities are often associated with people who think thinking – if it is to be thinking – must be "critical." So critics of the university often discover that their criticisms of the university are criticisms that only people trained at universities could produce. Therefore our very critiques reproduce the practices that we critique. The truth of the matter is that in America it is very hard to sustain a life of study without being parasitic on the university. I am more than willing, therefore, to acknowledge that my criticisms of the university, I hope, reveal my profound love of the university.

I hope I am a Christian, but the university has been more my home than the church. I went to Southwestern University in Georgetown, Texas in September, 1962. As they say, "the rest is history," because from that time to the present I have always lived in a university. The only way I know to make a living is to be at a university. I did not necessarily set out to be a university person. My life just worked out that way. I was brought up to be a bricklayer – honest work. I have tried not to forget what it means to be "in the trades," but for better or worse I am an academic.

After Southwestern I spent six years at Yale Divinity School and Yale Graduate School where I received the Bachelor of Divinity degree and my Ph.D. I taught two years at Augustana College in Rock Island, Illinois, fourteen years at the University of Notre Dame, and I am now in my twenty-third year of teaching in the Divinity School at Duke. My life has been made possible by people who care about sustaining the university. I no doubt owe the university more than I know.

Yet the history recounted in the last paragraphs is not one characteristic of those who have sought to have an academic career. I have always served the university, I have always used as well as been used by the university, because I am a Christian. I am a theologian. Theology is not generally considered a legitimate field in the university. Of course that was not the official position at Augustana or Notre Dame. Lutherans and Catholics still thought and think that theology should matter though how it matters is in dispute. Theology is tolerated at Duke because we are a Divinity School, but the Divinity School is regarded by many at Duke as a "cultural lag." Theologians in the modern university bear the burden of proof, which turns out to be very good for theology, because if you are a theologian you need to know what your colleagues in other disciplines know but they do not have to know what you know.

Yet my identity as a theologian means I have always been in the university but not of it. Berry has been more "out" of the university than "in" the university. Berry, of course, would not be Berry without the university. He is a graduate of a university. He has a graduate degree. He has taught at the University of Kentucky and other universities from time to time. But Berry has clearly chosen to "think" and write outside the university. I may, therefore, have more of a stake in making the university "work" than Berry may have. Nonetheless I hope to show how Berry can help us begin to rethink what a university might look like in order to be of service to the church. Having said this, I should warn the reader that I may also be using Berry's work to sustain a project that Berry thinks hopeless.

2. BERRY ON THE UNIVERSITY

"Abstraction is the enemy *wherever* it is found."[4] If any sentence could sum up Berry's work and, in particular, his criticism of the modern university it is this one. In order to appropriately appreciate Berry's criticism of abstraction, however, I think it wise to attend to his early,

[4] Wendell Berry, *Sex, Economy, Freedom, and Community* (New York: Pantheon Books, 1992), p. 23. Not to be missed are the implications about power involved by presumptions concerning the necessity of abstractions. No one has seen this more clearly than Sheldon Wolin who observes that modern power is reflected materially in the structure and attributes of theoretical knowledge as understood by the knowledges represented by the development of the mathematical sciences. Wolin notes this conception of power was unlimited because "the knowledge that made power reproducible had selected nature as its object and conceived it to be a field of inexhaustible forces...abstraction and dehistorization conjoined to clear the way for a form of knowledge that could freely construct its objects and their relationships" (*Tocqueville between Two Worlds: The Making of a Political and Theoretical Life* (Princeton: Princeton University Press, 2001), pp. 20–1).

but very important essay, "Standing by Words."[5] Berry is very careful not to reproduce dualisms that only create the problem he is trying to help us avoid. He is not, for example, advocating subjectivity as an alternative to objectivity nor is he recommending the particular over the universal. Rather he is trying to help us resist our tendency to speak nonsense.

Berry seldom betrays any knowledge of philosophy or philosophers. I suspect, like many poets, he is suspicious of philosophers. But his understanding of language, the criticism of the abstractions that we are taught to speak at universities, cannot help but remind some of us of lessons we have learned from Wittgenstein. In "Standing by Words" Berry argues that the disintegration of communities and persons in our time is a correlative of our loss of accountability in our use of language.

According to Berry, for any statement to be complete or comprehensible three conditions are required:

1. It must designate its object precisely.
2. Its speaker must stand by it: must believe it, be accountable for it, be willing to act on it.
3. This relation of speaker, word, and object must be conventional; the community must know what it is.[6]

Berry suggests that these common assumptions are becoming uncommon through the development of specialization. As a result language is increasingly seen as a weapon to gain power over others or as a medium of play. Or some, even poets such as Shelley, think the subjectivity of language must be emphasized in order to resist objectification. Yet, according to Berry, when that unhappy choice is accepted only pathos can result making language nothing more than a medium of self-pity.

It is extremely important to note that Berry is not denying the need for generalization. There is truth in the claim that "the particular has no language" – but there are nonetheless two forms of precision that allow the particular to be communicated. The first form of precision is the speech of people who share the same knowledge of place and history. "The old hollow beech blew down last night." Berry calls this community speech which he praises because it is precise and open to ongoing testing against its objects. Such speech is the "very root and foundation of language."[7]

The second form of precision is that which "comes of tension either between a statement and a prepared context or, within a single statement, between more or less conflicting feelings, or ideas."[8] To illustrate

5 Wendell Berry, *Standing by Words* (Washington, DC: Shoemaker and Hoard, 1983), pp. 24–63.
6 Berry, *Standing by Words*, p. 25.
7 Berry, *Standing by Words*, p. 33. Note Berry does not say the "particular" defies all language.
8 Berry, *Standing by Words*, p. 34.

this form of precision Berry contrasts Shelley's complaint against our mortality, "I could lie down like a tired child," with Robert Herrick's "Out of the world he must, who once comes in . . . ," observing the latter satisfies our need for complexity and thus does justice to our actual experience.[9] Such precision is hard won requiring us to battle against our proclivities to engage in fantasies.

One form such fantasies take is to produce sentences that try to be "objective" by avoiding all personal biases and considerations. Berry thinks such language is often used by scientists. He gives the example of transcribed conversations of members of the Nuclear Regulatory Commission during the crisis of Three Mile Island, who worked to "engineer a press release" to avoid frightening the public that a meltdown might happen. Thus one commissioner suggested they say, "in the unlikely event that this occurred (i.e., the meltdown) temperatures would result and possible further fuel damage." Berry observes what is remarkable and frightening about such language is the inability of those who speak in such a way to acknowledge what it is they are talking about.[10]

The perversion of speech illustrated by attempts to be "objective" serves the political purpose of securing the power of those who use it without their being held accountable. They say such speech aims to bring people together for some common project. Accordingly they try to create the illusion we all speak the same language – meaning either that they will agree with the government or be quiet, as in communist and fascist states, or that they will politely ignore their disagreements or disagree "provisionally," as in American universities. But the result – though power may survive for a while in spite of it – is confusion and dispersal. Real language, real discourse are destroyed. People lose understanding of each other, are divided and scattered. Speech of whatever kind begins to resemble the speech of drunkenness or madness.[11]

Berry offers another example of this passion for objectivity that interestingly enough has to do with cows. In an article entitled, "The Evolution and Future of American Animal Agriculture," G.W. Salisbury and R.G. Hart argue for the importance of the transformation of American agriculture from an art to a science. Art, they suggest, is only concerned with the "hows," but science with the "whys." Accordingly they recommend that a cow be described as "an appropriate manufacturing unit of the twentieth century." Berry notes that such language relieves those

9 Berry, *Standing by Words*, p. 35.

10 Berry, *Standing by Words*, p. 38. James Scott provides ample documentation to show how this kind of language is a correlative of state power designed to destroy the concrete. Scott identifies "the old hollow beech blew down last night" with *methis*, that is, speech that requires exemplification in concrete situations. *Methis*, in other words, is close to what Aristotle meant by practical reason. See Scott, *Seeing Like a State: How Certain Schemes to Improve the Human Condition Fail* (New Haven: Yale University Press, 1998), pp. 319, 335.

11 Berry, *Standing by Words*, p. 40.

who use it of any accountability indicated by a farmer's statement, "Be good to the cow, for she is our companion."[12]

The latter sentence, Berry observes, requires a world that is organized in a hierarchical sequence of nature, agriculture, community, family, person. Such a hierarchy is based on the assumption that these systems are interrelated and whatever affects one will affect the other. The former sentence, that is, the cow as "an appropriate manufacturing unit," reverses this hierarchy with one that runs from industrial economy, agriculture, dairy, dairyman. This latter hierarchy is meant to disintegrate the connecting disciplines by turning farming into a profession and a profession into a career.

Berry's subsequent criticism of the university can now be seen as the development of his concern that in the university we are taught to speak in a manner in which we are unable to "stand by our words." Thus my claim that the two questions you cannot ask in the modern university are: "What is the university for?" and "Who does it serve?" That the university has no "learned public" to serve – and a learned public might be one that knows how to milk cows – is at the heart of our problem.

Berry thinks the modern university is at least one of the institutions that should be held responsible for the corruption of our language. The university at once legitimates as well as reproduces the disintegration of the life of the mind and of communities through increasing specialization. According to Berry,

> The various specialties are moving ever outward from any center of interest or common ground, becoming ever farther apart, and ever more unintelligible to one another. Among the causes, I think, none is more prominent than the by now ubiquitous and nearly exclusive emphasis upon originality and innovation. The emphasis, operating within the "channels" of administration, affects in the most direct and practical ways all the lives within the university. It imposes the choice of work over life, exacting not only the personal costs spoken of in Yeats' poem ("The Choice"), but very substantial costs to the community as well.[13]

12 Berry, *Standing by Words*, pp. 43–4.

13 Wendell Berry, *Life is a Miracle: An Essay Against Modern Superstition* (Washington, DC: Counterpoint, 2000), p. 61. Yeats' poem reads:

> The intellect of man is forced to choose
> Perfection of the life, or of the work,
> And if it take the second must refuse
> A heavenly mansion, raging in the dark.
>
> When all that story's finished, what's the news?
> In luck or out the toil has left its mark:
> That old perplexity an empty purse,
> Or the day's vanity, the night's remorse.

Specialization of the disciplines, however, Berry argues is thought to be crucial if the university is to receive the support it needs from a capitalist society. If universities are to grow, and the assumption is that they must always grow, they will need money. But equally important, universities must accept the fundamental economic principle of the opposition of money to goods. Berry, who otherwise betrays no Marxist sympathies, seems to know in his bones that there is no "abstraction" more abstract than money. Labor is not only appropriated from the worker in the name of money, but the worker is expected to use that money to buy goods that cannot be represented by money.

The incoherence of university curriculums reflects the university's commitment to legitimate the abstraction effected by money. For example, it is crucial that the university insure that learning be organized not to be a conversation between disciplines, but rather that disciplines be representatives of competing opposites. As a result accountability is lost. The sciences are sectioned off from one another so they might serve their respective corporations. "The so-called humanities, which might have supplied at least a corrective or chastening remembrance of the good that humans have sometimes accomplished, have been dismembered into utter fecklessness, turning out 'communicators' who have nothing to say and 'educators' who have nothing to teach."[14] Indeed universities no longer are sources of literacy. Accordingly the English department itself has become a "specialty" and even in those departments writing has become a subspecialty of the freshman writing program. The result is the clear message that to write well is not necessary.[15]

Berry confesses he has no idea how the disciplines might be reorganized, but he is doubtful that anyone knows how to do that. However, he is convinced that the standards and goals of the disciplines need to be changed. He observes

> It used to be that we thought of the disciplines as ways of being useful to ourselves, for we needed to earn a living, but also and more importantly we thought of them as ways of being useful to one another. As long as the idea of vocation was still viable among us, I don't believe it was ever understood that a person was "called" to be rich or powerful or even successful. People were taught the disciplines at home or in school for two reasons: to enable them to live and work both as self-sustaining individuals and as useful members of their communities, and to see that the disciplines themselves survived the passing of the generations.[16]

14 Berry, *Life is a Miracle*, p. 123.
15 Berry, *Life is a Miracle*, p. 68.
16 Berry, *Life is a Miracle*, p. 130.

The incoherence of university curriculums reflects the acceptance of the assumption that there is nothing odd about unlimited economic growth or consumption in a limited world. Education is now job preparation for a career in a profession.[17] But work, whether it is done in the academy, a profession, or industry, is now designed so that the workers are separated from the effects of their work. The workers are permitted "to think that they are working nowhere or anywhere – in their careers or specialties, perhaps, or in 'cyberspace.' "[18] The university, therefore, becomes the home for the homeless, or in Wallace Stegner's wonderful description, the "boomers."[19]

The dominance of science in the modern university reflects the captivity of universities to industrial societies. For the abstractions of science are readily assimilated to the abstractions of industry in which

> everything is interchangeable with or replaceable by something else.... One place is as good as another, one use is as good as another, one life is as good as another – if the price is right. This is the industrial doctrine of the interchangeability of parts, and we apply it to places, to creatures, and to our fellow humans as if it were the law of the world, using all the while a sort of middling language, imitated from the sciences, that cannot speak of heaven or earth, but only of concepts. This is the rhetoric of nowhere, which forbids a passionate interest in, let alone a love of, anything in particular.[20]

For Berry the assumption that education is the solution to all our problems is a correlate to the increasing violence of what is taught. Berry thinks the violence of education is, as we should suspect from his analysis in *Standing by Words*, to be found in the destruction of language and community. Berry observes that "education has become increasingly useless as it has become increasingly public. Real education is determined by community needs, not by public tests."[21]

Berry's distinction between community and public may seem odd given the assumption that the public names the goods of the community, but Berry understands the term "public" to mean simply people abstracted from any personal responsibility or belonging. Thus a public

[17] Wendell Berry, *Another Turn of the Crank* (Washington, DC: Counterpoint, 1995), pp. 13–14.

[18] Wendell Berry, *Citizenship Papers* (Washington, DC: Shoemaker and Hoard, 2003), p. 33.

[19] Berry, *Another Turn of the Crank*, p. 82. Berry reports that boomers are people "who expect or demand that the world conform to their desires. They either succeed and thus damage the world, or they fail and thus damage their family and themselves."

[20] Berry, *Life is a Miracle*, pp. 41–2. Berry's characterization of science unfortunately too often is accurate, but science can be one of the most exciting disciplines through which to see the beauty of the particulars.

[21] Berry, *Sex, Economy, Freedom, and Community*, p. 123.

building is one that belongs to everyone, but no one in particular. A community, in contrast, "has to do first of all with belonging; it is a group of people who belong to one another and to their place. We would say, 'We belong to our community,' but never 'We belong to our public.' "[22]

Berry does not deny that under certain circumstances the public and the community might be compatible, but under the economic and technological monoculture in which we live they cannot help but be at odds. A community is centered on the household, which means it is always concerned with a place and time. The public, when it is rightly formed, is concerned about justice and is centered on the individual. The problem we confront is that the emphasis on individual liberty has made the freedom of the community impossible. Paradoxically, as a result the more the emphasis has been on individual freedom the less liberty and power has been available to most individuals.[23]

In his novel *Hannah Coulter* Berry describes the effects of the university on Caleb Coulter, the son of Hannah and Nathan. Hannah and Nathan are hard-working farmers who have managed to create a life from an unforgiving ground. Caleb was the last born of their three children all of whom went to college. Hannah observes that you send your children to college in order to do the best for them, but neither do you want to burden them with your expectations. Hannah confesses that you hope they will go away and study and learn and then come back and you will have them for a neighbor. However, Hannah observes, while their children were at the university there always "came a time when we would feel the distance opening to them, pulling them away. It was like sitting snug in the house, and a door is opened somewhere, and suddenly you feel a draft."[24]

Caleb even became Dr. Coulter, a professor, who taught agriculture to fewer students who were actually going to farm. Hannah describes him this way,

> He became an expert with a laboratory and experimental plots, a man of reputation. But as I know, and as he knows in his own heart and thoughts, Caleb is incomplete. He didn't love farming enough to be a farmer, much as he loved it, but he loved it too much to be entirely happy doing anything else. He is disappointed in himself... Caleb is well respected, and I am glad of that. He brings me what he calls his "publications," written in the Unknown Tongue. He wants me to be proud of them. And I am, but with the sadness of wishing I could be prouder. I read all of his publications that he brings

22 Berry, *Sex, Economy, Freedom, and Community*, pp. 147–8.
23 Berry, *Sex, Economy, Freedom, and Community*, pp. 147–55.
24 Wendell Berry, *Hannah Coulter* (Washington, DC: Shoemaker and Hoard, 2004), p. 120.

> me, and I have to say that they don't make me happy. I can't hear Caleb talking in them. And they speak of everything according to its general classification. Reading them always makes me think of this farm and how it emerged, out of "agriculture" and its "soil types" and its collection of "species," as itself, our place, a place like no other, yielding to Nathan and me a life like no other.[25]

The novel *Hannah Coulter* expresses Berry's deepest worry about the contemporary university, which is what an "education" does to people. It is a mistake to accuse him of being anti-technological or against all forms of specialization. His problem with technology and specialization is when they become ends in themselves producing people with no ends. As he puts it in *Another Turn of the Crank*, he is not " 'against technology' so much as I am for community. When the choice is between the health of a community and technological innovation, I choose the health of the community."[26] Technology, particularly in industrial economies, too easily becomes abstracted from the purposes that it was to serve.

Nor is Berry against science. Science has a proper place in relation to the other disciplines, particularly when all the disciplines are equally regarded and given equal time to talk no matter what the market may be in "jobs" or "intellectual property." Indeed it is one of the tasks of the university to foster such a conversation between disciplines so that our whole humanity may be embodied in and by the university. So Berry thinks the university has an appropriate task, he is simply doubtful that any university exists committed to accomplishing that task.[27]

That task, moreover, requires that "a system" exist that secures the conviction that the truth can be known, but never all truth. Such a conviction Berry calls "religious" to indicate that the world in which we find ourselves is a mystery making possible accountable speech and behavior. For I hope it is now clear that Berry's criticisms of the university are but further implications of his concern that we hold one another accountable for what we say. From his perspective the university has become the source of speech determined by abstractions which are no longer accountable to any community of purpose. Berry does not claim that the fate of the modern university is the result of the loss of mystery, but he is sure that all "answers" put forward in the university

> must be worked out within a limit of humility and restraint, so that the initiative to act would always imply a knowing acceptance of accountability for the results. The establishment and maintenance of this limit seems to me the ultimate empirical problem – the real "frontier" of science, or at least

25 Berry, *Hannah Coulter*, pp. 131–2.
26 Berry, *Another Turn of the Crank*, p. 90.
27 Berry, *Citizenship Papers*, p. 189.

> of the definition of the possibility of a *moral* science. It would place science under the rule of the old concern for propriety, correct proportion, proper scale – from which, in modern times, even the arts have been "liberated." That is, it would return to all work, artistic or scientific, the possibility of an external standard or quality.[28]

Berry's criticisms of the university are clearer than the alternative he offers. That is probably the way it should be. Who knows what a Berry-inspired university might look like? It may well sound too "artsy," but Berry, I think, would want the center of a university to be the practice of poetry. For only through poetry, speech tied closely to community, place, and time can we avoid the abstractions that have become our way of life.

Berry reports he was raised by agrarians, but he did not know he was an agrarian until he was a sophomore in college. He seems to think it a good thing he was taught he was an agrarian. Indeed to learn he was an agrarian could be considered a poetic development. Learning he was an agrarian meant he was able to distinguish between industrialism which is based on monetary capital from agrarianism which is based on land. Moreover it was partly Berry's education that made it possible for him to trace the lineage of agrarian thought through Virgil, Spenser, Shakespeare, and Pope. According to Berry it is from poets like these you learn you should not work until you have looked and seen where you are in a manner that honors Nature not only as your grandmother, but as teacher and judge.[29]

As critical as Berry is of the university as we know it, and certainly any of us who live in the university recognize the university exists that he criticizes, he still remains a lover of the university. After all it was in a university he learned to read Virgil, Spenser, Shakespeare, Pope, and Jefferson. Yet he seems to hold out little hope that the kind of university he would like to exist could be a reality. No doubt he assumes that his university might exist in pockets of any university, but that

28 Berry, *Standing by Words*, pp. 49–50.

29 Berry, *Citizenship Papers*, pp. 118–19. To cultivate and nurture beauty I believe is one of the central tasks of the university. The sheer ugliness as well as the dominance of kitsch in contemporary life is surely an indication that those of us in the university are not doing our job. Andrius Bielskis has argued the culture of kitsch is a correlative of the dominance of liberal democratic societies. Bielskis observes, "if the role of strong moral judgments and rational deliberation about what it is to live the good life decreases within the public sphere (and the psychological marketing techniques used by politicians illustrate this), then the sphere of democratic politics become dangerously irrational which means we lack the means to resist the sentimentality kitsch represents" (Andrius Bielskis, *Towards a Post-Modern Understanding of the Political: From Genealogy to Hermeneutics* (New York: Palgrave, 2005), pp. 92–3). Bielskis' argument is shaped by quite interesting readings of Nietzsche, Foucault, and especially MacIntyre.

such an existence depends on people existing that defy the abstractions that are so tempting. It would be silly to suggest that the church might offer the possibility of making a Berry-like university a reality, but I at least want to explore how we might imagine that possibility.

3. WHY BERRY NEEDS A CHURCH

Christians are a people who worship the God of the Jews. We are a people who worship Jesus, the messiah, the Incarnation of the Word of God. The God we worship is flesh so our cardinal action is to eat and drink the body and blood of Christ. The God we worship is, therefore, only known through a story as concrete as "the old hollow beech blew down last night." We learn about the old hollow beech by being told by another it was blown down. In similar fashion we know about Jesus by being told by another. Witness is constitutive of the character of what Christians believe. For the Christian witness to be truthful requires that Christians distrust all abstractions not disciplined by the Word that is Christ.

However, well before the development of the kind of abstraction Berry finds so destructive, Christians developed their own form of abstraction. Jesus commanded his disciples to "Go therefore and make disciples of all nations, baptizing them in the name of the Father and of the Son and of the Holy Spirit, and teaching them to obey everything that I have commanded you" (Matthew 28:19–20). Jesus' command to be a witness to the nations, a task that should force Christians to recognize as well as criticize the infinite and unending forms of abstraction, has also tempted Christians to confuse the pretentious universalism of "the nation" with the Gospel.

The politics of Christian abstraction has taken many different forms. But at least one name for such a politics is called "Constantinianism." Constantinianism is the attempt by the church to use the power of the "state," and the "state" is an abstraction, to impose the Gospel on others without the vulnerability of witness. Because the church is obligated to be a witness to all nations she has sometimes confused the universalism of the speech of empire, speech that by necessity is shaped by abstraction, with the concreteness of the Gospel.

Christians, particularly in modernity, have forgotten that our name for universal is "catholic." The office that enacts the catholic character of the church is called "bishop." The task of the bishop is to insure that the stories that make a church the church are shared by other churches across time and space so that our speech is tested by how other Christians have learned they must speak to one another as well as those who do not speak as we speak. Theologians are servants to the Bishop charged with the task of maintaining the memory of the church so that the church may be one. Theologians are, therefore, "answerable to a specific locality or very often multiple specific localities, such that [their] sense of perpetuating a history must be combined with [their] sense of carrying out an archaeology and mapping a geography."[30]

If Christians are to support the development of a Berry-like university we will need to be freed of our Constantinian pretensions. That freedom, moreover, will come only by the intensification of the catholic character of the church. For the abstractions that bewitch our speech as Christians can only be located and resisted by word care made possible by being challenged by our brothers and sisters across time and place. As John Howard Yoder has observed the alternative to the confusion of paganism and Christianity so often the result of Constantinianism is "the concreteness of the visible community created by the renewed message. The alternative to hierarchical definition is local definition."[31]

Modern universities, whether Christian or secular, have been servants of the emerging nation-state system. That nation-state system, moreover, has been the enemy of locality. Local communities are not and cannot be efficient given the need to organize "populations."[32] The abstractions Berry identifies as the enemy are those necessary to legitimate the public organizations that claim to serve our interests. The very language of "interest," of course, is but an exemplification of the kind of abstraction Berry deplores.

Berry's appeal to a religious sense of mystery for maintaining some sense of the "whole" is important, but a sense of mystery cannot be sustained absent a community in which the mystery is materially enacted. A university able to resist the mystifications legitimated by the abstractions of our social order will depend on a people shaped by fundamental practices necessary for truthful speech. In short, without the church, a church capable of demythologizing the false idealism that possess our imaginations, there is no possibility that a university can exist capable of educating a Caleb Coulter who might return home.

30 John Milbank, "The Last of the Last: Theology in the Church," in *Conflicting Allegiances: The Church-Based University in a Liberal Democratic Society*, edited by Michael Budde and John Wright (Grand Rapids: Brazos Press, 2004), p. 250.

31 John Howard Yoder, "The Disavowal of Constantine: An Alternative Perspective on Interfaith Dialogue," in *The Royal Priesthood: Essays Ecclesiological and Ecumenical*, edited by Michael Cartwright (Grand Rapids: Eerdmans, 1994), p. 253. Yoder's alternative of localism finds support in the late work of Sheldon Wolin who argues that "small scale is the only scale commensurate with the kind and amount of power that democracy is capable of mobilizing, given the political limitations imposed by the prevailing modes of economic organization. The power of democratic politics lies in the multiplicity of modest sites dispersed among local governments and institutions under local control and in the ingenuity of ordinary people in inventing temporary forms to meet their needs. Multiplicity is anti totality politics: small politics, small projects, small business, much improvisation, and fierce anathema to centralization whether of centralized state or of the huge corporations" (*Politics and Vision* (Expanded Edition), (Princeton: Princeton University Press, 2004), p. 603).

32 For an analysis of the significance of the creation of the nation of "populations" see my chapter "The Christian Difference: Or Surviving Postmodernism" in *A Better Hope: Resources for a Church Confronting Capitalism, Democracy, and Postmodernity* (Grand Rapids: Brazos Press, 2000), pp. 35–46.

These are, of course, highly theoretical remarks. Do they have any implications for what a church-based university might look like? Some are beginning to try to imagine what such a university might entail. For example many of the essays in *Conflicting Allegiances: The Church-Based University in a Liberal Democratic Society* are not content to explore how the contemporary university might be reformed to be more responsive to Christian practice. As Michael Budde puts it: "The purpose of ecclesially based higher education is to make participants more fully into disciples shaped by the priorities and practices of Jesus Christ; to help them discern their vocation as members of the transnational body of Christ; and to contribute to the mission of the church – to help the church serve more fully and faithfully as a foretaste of the promised kingdom of God, on earth as in heaven."[33]

Budde observes this is a difficult task because our imaginations are possessed by what is assumed to be normative assumptions about higher education. Indeed the very language of "higher" may be misleading just to the extent it presumes that knowing how to milk is not a "higher knowledge." Budde, however, would readily agree that the use of "higher" to distinguish university subjects from the knowledge represented by "milking" is part of the problem. Accordingly, many of the essays in *Conflicting Allegiances* challenge the (dis-)organization of knowledges characteristic of the contemporary university. For example Therese Lysaught asks what form the life sciences might take if they were organized on the principle that Christians are obligated to love our enemy even the enemy of death.[34]

The problem is not whether we lack the imagination to begin to think what a university shaped by Christian practice might look like, but rather whether the church exists that can provide the material conditions that can make such an alternative university possible. By material conditions I do not mean only money, but rather whether churches are constituted by the practices, and no practice is more important than the habits of our speech, habits nurtured by worship, that require the development of knowledges that can challenge the abstractions that are legitimated in and by the current university. Have Christians learned to milk nonviolently? So oddly enough we will not know how to think about the character of the university without thinking about the character of the church.

But we cannot wait. Many of us, as I suggested above concerning my own life, continue to teach in universities that exemplify the pathologies Berry describes. Should Christians continue to teach in universities,

33 Michael Budde, "Assessing What Doesn't Exist: Reflections on the Impact of an Ecclesially Based University," in *Conflicting Allegiances: The Church-Based University in a Liberal Democratic Society*, p. 256.

34 Therese Lysaught, "Love Your Enemies: The Life Sciences in the Ecclesially Based University," in *Conflicting Allegiances: The Church-Based University in a Liberal Democratic Society*, pp. 109–27.

universities that are often identified as "church-related," in which students are shaped by abstractions that serve quite a different reality than that of the church? Do Christian academics, in spite of their criticisms of the university, legitimate those universities by our very presence?

Any attempt to justify Christian participation in the university as we know it is an invitation to self-deception. Yet in his 2004 Oxford University Commemoration Day Sermon, Rowan Williams provides some helpful reminders that can point us in a constructive direction.[35] Williams observes that Oxford began as a cell of the Catholic church for the study of canon law, but by the fourteenth and fifteenth centuries Oxford's survival depended on forming people who would govern the kingdom. He notes this will confirm the worst fears of some that assume Oxford is primarily an institution committed to serving the elite. Yet Williams points out that it was assumed "that to govern a kingdom you needed to know how language worked, what difference was between good and bad arguments, and how you might persuade people to morally defensible action." Accordingly you needed tools of thought that were organized in a hierarchy of learning.

Williams acknowledges that much has changed at Oxford. An abstract understanding of rationality has displaced what many now consider the "authoritarian" character of the medieval university. Yet Williams argues to the extent the university maintains a commitment to disciplined argument there remains a sense of the capacity to respond with justice and accuracy to the inner structure of creation thus testifying to the divine image constitutive of each of us. Williams, therefore, thinks he is justified to "insist upon the university's role in nourishing honest and hopeful speech, for the sake of a properly reasonable culture and politics." He, therefore, concludes that what the church has to say to the university is:

> Don't be afraid of assuming that your task is to equip people to take authority. In a democratic age, this is not the authority of a royal counsellor or imperial proconsul; it is the authority of the literate and educated person to contribute to the public reason. And don't be afraid in encouraging in whatever way is available the calling both to scientific research and to public service, administration and politics and social care; law and medicine, those ancient and persistent elements in the pattern of public life; the service, in one calling or another of the Body of Christ. Avoid the false polarisation between disinterested research and the world of target setting and assessment; remember that all properly intellectual work can be a form of witness to public values.

35 Williams's sermon can be found on the Archbishop of Canterbury website (www.archbishopofcanterbury.org).

I have no idea if Berry would find Williams's understanding of the task of the university compatible with his understanding of what universities ought to be about. However, I suspect Berry might find congenial Williams's suggestion that the university's task is to train literate people capable of recognizing a good from a bad argument. No doubt the study of poetry helps the development of such a skill, but so can the study of a science. I am sure, moreover, that poets and scientists exist at every university committed to such a task. What remains unclear is whether a people exist that care whether such poets or scientists exist. At the very least Christians are obligated to care because we believe we have been given the great privilege to stand by the Word.

"To stand by the Word," moreover, might help us maintain the connection between the labor of the university with those that labor outside the university. Fritz Oehlschlaeger, in a letter responding to my essay, "Theological Knowledge and the Knowledges of the University," observes that intellectual work, even at its most strenuous, is not as difficult as physical labor. How then, he asks, can we ever justify those like ourselves who think the work we do in the university is important. Oehlschlaeger, who teaches in the English Department at Virginia Tech,[36] responds to his question observing:

> It seems to me this requires active memory and recognition by the intellectual of the labor that sustains his/her ability to pursue knowledge. The best way to ensure this is for the intellectual to come into the presence of others, to make offering with them of their labor, and to receive the truly priceless food provided by the One whose love can only be understood as pure gift. Thus we learn that utility in meeting needs can never be a sufficient standard, as we cannot produce the very thing we need most. And the Eucharist perhaps also disciplines the intellectual to recognize his bonds to those whose labors make his work possible – so that any pursuit of knowledge for its own sake carries also the memory of the labor that sustains it. Intellectuals formed within a community nourished by the milk of Jesus seem much more likely to think what they do as requiring a community to receive it... Maybe there's a role, then, for Christian intellectuals who might mediate among the disciplines and between disciplines and public in ways that would not occur to the market-driven knowledge-producers on today's faculties.

Hopefully, "maybe there's a role," is hopeful speech.

36 Oehlschlaeger has begun the difficult task to think what a Christian reading of literature might mean in his *Love and Good Reasons: Postliberal Approaches to Christian Ethics and Literature* (Durham, NC: Duke University Press, 2003).

7

Carving Stone or Learning to Speak Christian

1. LEARNING TO BE A STONE CARVER

I was raised a bricklayer. Actually, that is not quite true. I was raised to labor for bricklayers. I eventually learned to lay brick, but not with the skill of my father who was a master craftsman. In truth I was a better laborer than I was a bricklayer because to be a master craftsman requires years in the trade. It is important to remember, however, that while the laborer may not have the skill of the bricklayer no one can become a bricklayer, at least a bricklayer who is a craftsman, who has not learned to labor. For to lay brick well requires that you have learned subsidiary skills such as how to chop (mix) mortar. Bricklaying, like all significant tasks, involves a hierarchy of tasks requiring that those who would practice the craft learn those skills in an appropriate order.[1]

Attention to the training necessary for crafts such as laying brick I believe is crucial if we are to understand the role theology might have in education, or, as I would prefer, moral formation. Too often I fear we associate education with teaching students how to think. We think, moreover, that thinking is a linguistic activity. Education certainly involves learning how to think and we do think linguistically, but it is important that we not think of thinking as something that goes on in our "minds." By observing the language two stone carvers use to reflect on their craft I hope to display why learning to think, as well as learning a language constitutive of thinking, is rightly understood as work done with our hands.

[1] I have a more extensive account of laying brick as a model for learning to be a disciple in *After Christendom?* (Nashville: Abingdon Press, 1999), pp. 101–11. My account of how learning to lay bricks might illumine moral formation drew on Alasdair MacIntyre's account of what it means to be trained in a craft to display the character of moral rationality in his *Three Rival Versions of Moral Enquiry: Encyclopedia, Genealogy, and Tradition* (Notre Dame: University of Notre Dame Press, 1990), pp. 63–8. My account of the stone carvers in this chapter continues to be informed by MacIntyre's account of the necessity of a master for an account of moral education as well as the innovative character of a tradition.

Such a view may seem quite odd in a conference designed to investigate what role theology, and in particular moral theology, may have in educating and forming lives.[2] Theologians are not usually associated with hard work or physical labor. I suspect theologians are more like laborers than bricklayers; that is, the theologian's task is to serve those who are masters of the craft of being Christian. Yet if that craft is constituted, as I think it is, by language, then it becomes all the more important that some are trained in the hard work of teaching the language of the craft. In particular it is crucial that those charged with the task of teaching not forget that teaching and learning a language, particularly the language of prayer, is as physical as learning to carve stone. A remark, however, I can only develop by saying more about learning a craft and, in particular, the craft of stone carving.

In *The Stone Carvers: Master Craftsmen of Washington National Cathedral*, Marjorie Hunt tells the story of two Italian American master stone carvers – Roger Morigi and Vincent Palumbo.[3] These men were born and trained in Italy, but like other Italian carvers they came to America because they had skills necessary for the completion of buildings like the Cathedral Church of Saint Peter and Saint Paul in Washington, DC, which is more generally known as the National Cathedral of the American Episcopal Church.[4] Roger began work at the Cathedral in 1956 and was joined by Vincent in 1978.

Both Roger and Vincent were born into families of stone carvers. For them to be a stone carver was to be made part of a tradition whose habits of memory, the stories of carving stone, were inseparable from the stories of the family.[5] For example, as Vincent Palumbo carves he reports the memories of the years he spent being guided by his father noting:

2 This chapter was written for a colloquium on the topic, "The Way of Life: Education, a Challenge for Morality," sponsored by the Pontifical John Paul II Institute in Rome, 2006.

3 Marjorie Hunt, *The Stone Carvers: Master Craftsmen of Washington National Cathedral* (Washington: Smithsonian Institution Press, 1999). All references to *The Stone Carvers* will appear in the text.

4 That the Cathedral is qualified by "National" should be an embarrassment for any Anglican. Unfortunately that does not seem to be the case.

5 These are the kind of memories that W. James Booth calls "thick memories," that is, they are habits that are often non-explicit behaviors that constitute "the geological deposit of enduring relationships. This habit-memory is itself a form of persistence of the past" (*Communities of Memory: On Witness, Identity, and Justice* (Ithaca: Cornell University Press, 2006), pp. xi–xii). Booth argues that "there is an intuition which belongs to the keeping of such forms of memory that they should be preserved and transmitted as a kind of bearing witness, as a debt owed to the community. This obligation in certain respects is closely kindred to justice and might be described as a kind of indebtedness: what is owed within the context of an enduring community, an obligation incumbent on us as persons sharing a life in common" (p. xii). Witness is the word Booth uses to name this aspect of memory, that is, because we are members of persisting communities of accountability we must bear witness to both good and bad memories.

> When I was working with my father on a job we don't feel we were father and son, but just partners. We talk a variation of things – how to do the best. He always teach me the secrets how to give the master touch, how always he wants me – even if stone is dead material – still he was telling me how to make the stone look like life, almost talk, look realistic. Especially to give that small detail, so when we were carving flowers, the petals of the flowers look like moving. That was the *best* part. And I'm trying to do the best I can in his memory (p. 5).

Vincent and Roger take pride in their family tradition because they understand their families to represent the longer tradition of stone carving. To carve stone is to contribute to an ongoing tradition nestled within larger narratives that give purpose to the craft. That they are carving stone for a Cathedral means that they do not understand what they do to be just another job, but rather they participate in the story that constitutes their and our existence. Thus Vincent's claim that "Even God gave Moses the ten laws on stone. He carved the Ten Commandments on stone. So this is the oldest trade in the world" (p. 3).

Roger was the master carver at the National Cathedral for 23 years. He reports it was a task he cherished above all others. "To me," he says, "the Cathedral is like my home. Next to my home, it is home. When you say that, you say everything. You get attached to a place. This may be just stone to most people, but to me it's alive" (p. 37). Hunt reports that Roger's last carving for the Cathedral was a life-size statue of Adam. Roger's comment on his life work was, "I finished where God began" (p. 37). That he would describe his work so wonderfully witnesses to his understanding of how his craft fits within a larger purpose.

Roger and Vincent were brought up in families of stone carvers, but they still had to be apprenticed to a master stone carver if they were to become masters of the craft. To be sure carving involves some formal instruction, but according to Roger you cannot teach anybody to carve. Rather

> You give them the fundamentals of carving, like you take a hammer and a point and you hit, you take a chisel and cut. But the main thing in carving, you steal carving. When I say steal, you see, like you're in the shop and there are seven or eight apprentice boys. One would be a little better than the other, and you have two or three carvers working in the same place, so you watch one, you watch the other; you steal a little bit from one, you steal a little bit from the other. Then you put it all together yourself. You develop your own technique (p. 41).

Roger and Vincent make clear, however, that within the community of stone carvers there is a clear and essential hierarchy determined on the basis of skill and seniority. They therefore describe their learning to be stone carvers as "coming up" in the trade to indicate the long process required to work through the levels from apprentice and journeyman in order to finally become a master of the craft. Such a process is necessary because to be a good carver you need to be able to do everything associated with obtaining the stone from the quarry to putting the carved stone in place on the building. Thus a carver must be "almost perfect as a stonecutter, which means you've got to be able to put a straight face on a slab of stone maybe two and a half meters long by a meter, meter and a half wide, with different kinds of tools – we call a six-teeth or an eight-teeth point" (p. 68).

For stone carvers apprenticeship is imperative, but the master, at least at the beginning, is not expected to pay his apprentice. As the apprentice improves the master may start to pay the apprentice, but again that is at the master's discretion. According to Roger and Vincent such an arrangement is more than fair: "You have to consider this," Roger says, "the guy who taught you, what he gives you, he gives you a gift. And if you dedicate yourself enough to learn, to make something of it, he gives you a gift that nobody can steal from you. What he give you money can't buy" (p. 51).

Though the apprentice learns by imitating the master, this imitation does not mean one slavishly copies the master's way of working. Rather one must develop, in Roger's words, "something of your own." Therefore the master "should correct you if you make mistakes, but they should allow you to use your own techniques, what you think, what you feel about it" (p. 72). Those just beginning to learn, therefore, must travel to other shops of stone cutters in order to learn how to work with different materials and tools.

A good stone carver is, in a manner, forced to be innovative because they soon learn that every stone is different, requiring different tools.[6] So there is no one right way to carving in general, but rather the stone carver must be ready to do what works best for each particular stone. Roger reports his father used to tell him, "If it works to wipe it with your ass, do that!" (p. 71). Stone carvers must be ready to work with a wide

6 MacIntyre puts it this way: "The authority of a master within a craft is both more and other than a matter of exemplifying the best standards so far. It is also and most importantly a matter of knowing how to go further and especially how to direct others toward going further, using what can be learned from the tradition afforded by the past to move toward the *telos* of fully perfected work. It is in thus knowing how to link past and future that those with authority are able to draw upon tradition, to interpret and reinterpret it, so that its directedness towards the *telos* of the particular craft becomes apparent in new and characteristically unexpected ways. And it is by the ability to teach others how to learn this type of knowing how that the power of the master within the community of a craft is legitimated as a rational activity" (*Three Rival Versions of Moral Enquiry*, pp. 65–6). Masters are often not the most talented in a craft. I suspect the reason many mediocre baseball players become managers is because they have had to study the game as well as learn the skills of the game more thoroughly than those who are naturally gifted.

range of material, but because it is their task to transform raw material into art, they hate nothing more than having to work on a poor grade of stone. If the stone is "crumbly" in Vincent's words, "it ruins your ambition because you work and work, and it don't come up too good" (p. 104).

The stone carver, therefore, must constantly adjust his tools to the stone. For example Roger observes that pink Tennessee marble is "sensitive" because "it resents the tools" whereas Botticino stone is like "working glass, it's sharp, it snaps like anything." In contrast Carrara marble is the kind of material that every little hit with a chisel brings life (p. 105).[7] This means that not only must the carver adjust to the stone, but he must know his tools well because if a tool is tempered too hard it will cut the stone, particularly limestone, too roughly.

And so the precarious nature of the craft, the constant need to rethink one's approach, means also that one learns to be a stone carver through talk. Vincent says he was nourished in the craft in his home and in the discourse of daily life. He describes it this way:

> When you come from a traditional family you learn from talking. What happened to me, we was in that trade. We was talking about work anytime; at breakfast, dinner, supper, most of the subject was work. Think about this stone, how we gonna do this, who was gonna do that, we gotta use this trick. So you're growing, and you listen, and your mind, it gets drunk with all those things, and then, when it comes time, you remember (pp. 20–1).

Stories are, therefore, crucial for learning to carve stone. Through tales of personal experience and stories passed from one generation to another, stone carvers learn habits, attitudes, and standards "that lie at the heart of who they are and what they do" (p. 56). The stories, moreover, name as well as constitute the virtues required to be a carver

[7] Questions of "idealism" and "realism" would appear quite differently I believe if those concerned with such issues would attend to learning a craft. MacIntyre argues, for example, that "it is from *within* the practice of painting in each case that shared standards are discovered, standards which enable transcultural judgments of sameness and difference to be made, both about works of art and about the standards governing artistic practice and aesthetic evaluation" ("Colors, Cultures, and Practices," in *The Tasks of Philosophy: Selected Essays*, Volume 1 (Cambridge: Cambridge University Press, 2006), pp. 47–8). MacIntyre argues, therefore, that color names are not arbitrary, at least, they are not arbitrary if we are to account for a painter like Turner.

Andrew Moore puts it this way: "Christians only ever have reality under a description. We know God as he gives himself to us in Jesus Christ and by his Holy Spirit grants us faith. So to say we have his reality under a description is emphatically not to imply that the description constructs a reality that would not be in existence without it. However it is to say that it is not possible for us to adopt a stance external to this (or any other) perspective so as to give a complete metaphysical description of the universe and its creator" (*Realism and the Christian Faith* (Cambridge: Cambridge University Press, 2003), p. 214).

of stone. Vincent observes, to carve stone "it requires 100 percent concentration" because, according to Roger, "You've got to be patient and not overestimate the stone, because when you overestimate the stone, it comes back and bites you" (p. 100).

To learn to carve stone, therefore, is not like learning a language – to learn to carve stone is a language that is inseparable from the work itself. Hunt describes Vincent's formation as a child this way: "like a child learning a language, Vincent began to acquire a grammar of stone carving; he began to piece together knowledge of the various elements of the craft and the underlying principles that governed them" (p. 21). In Vincent's words he learned the music of stone carving:

> I remember this clear, especially when I was young and I was there (in his grandfather's shop) trying to learn stonecutting. I remember we was about eight or nine stonecutters. We was three or four kids like me and then the old masters. As we say, all the work was done by hand. We gotta put a face on this big slab of stone with a brush hammer and things like that. And what happened while we were working one of the guys start to sing. While he's singing, all the rest they start singing, too. And so what happened, we work by the tune of the music, of the singing. So we beat the bush hammer on the stone to make some kind of music; it was according to the singing. And we make more production because you can't stop, you can't split the singing. And it's many times like that (p. 62).

Vincent draws on the analogy of music to describe what he understands a stone carver to be, that is, a performer. Just as a composer can write a beautiful symphony it remains the case that the beauty of the symphony depends on it being played well by the musicians. So it is with carving. "The sculptor makes a beautiful piece, but it's up to the carver to make the work on stone look really good or to ruin the thing because he does not know how to carve" (p. 97). According to Vincent stone carving is the art of reduction in which the carver brings into view what was hidden in the block of stone. But to reveal what was hidden, Vincent suggests, is miraculous. He puts it this way: "The sculptor is the creator. He creates on clay. And then when they cast on plaster is the death. And the carving is the resurrection. That is the motto of our branch of the stone business" (p. 98).

2. WHAT VINCENT, ROGER, AND ALASDAIR MACINTYRE HAVE TO TEACH US

If we are to recover a determinative understanding of the contribution theology might make for the formation of Christians I think we best think of education more like teaching people how to carve stone rather than what we usually associate with the education provided by academic institutions.[8] This is particularly the case if education is about forming people in the habits of speech that make possible the virtues constitutive of the Christian tradition. The problem with the knowledge so often taught in our schools is that in such a setting Christian convictions cannot help but be presented as information. But information, by its very nature, is not meant to do any work and is thereby open to ideological distortions.[9]

That is why I think it important to make explicit what Vincent and Roger have to teach us – not only about how to carve stone but what is entailed in learning any significant way of life. They were fortunate, of course, to be born into families in which the tradition of stone cutting was, so to speak, in the air they breathed and in the food they ate. The habits of hard work were not foreign to them. Yet it was not sufficient for them to be born into families of stone carvers. In order to become master stone carvers it was necessary for them to become apprenticed to masters of the craft. Through their apprenticeships they acquired the more basic skills necessary to perform at the highest level of stone carving. In the process they learned to be patient because without patience they could not have learned how to carve the stone.

That apprentices acquire the virtues in the process of learning the basic skills of stone carving has important implications for how education should be understood. Not only should there be a clear hierarchy of

8 Of course it will be objected that universities are not in the business of teaching crafts. I am suggesting, however, that stone carving provides a fruitful analogy for helping us think through the pursuit of intellectual disciplines in the university. And yet by invoking analogy I by no means want to undermine the rigorous discipline and intellectual merit of learning a craft such as stone carving. Indeed I would argue that stone carving should be taught in universities where such a discipline would serve to teach and preserve a particular tradition.

9 By drawing our attention to stone carving, therefore, I am challenging the assumption that education is merely the transference of information from an "expert" to a "non-expert." I am, thereby, calling into question the model of the university or school where the goods of "knowledge" are obtained through students' acquisition of intellectual disciplines as though the mastering of a "discipline" could be acquired through the pursuit of the isolated individual. This is not only a point about pedagogy, but rather speaks to the very character of knowledge that should be at the heart of any institution that claims to be Christian. No one has made this case more forcefully than Peter Candler in his *Theology, Rhetoric, Manuduction, or Reading Scripture Together on the Path to God* (Grand Rapids: Eerdmans, 2006). By contrasting Aquinas's understanding of reading as participation in the life of God to modern modes of reading that isolate texts qua texts, Candler helps us see how current practices of reading distort the character of what is read. Candler argues, therefore, that the very form of the *Summa* makes clear that Aquinas understood theology not only as a craft but as a trade in which the student received from the hand of the master the bodily habits – none more important than speech – that would lead the student to God. Candler shows how crucial to Aquinas's understanding of the "art of memory" was the role of memory shaped by the Eucharist in which time is quite literally a reenactment of the reality of the Passion (p. 151). Because theology as knowledge is rightly understood as "the performance of the soul's return to God in the company of faith that it must refuse to be encyclopedic" – thus the open-ended character of the *Summa*. I am indepted to Carole Baker for this way of putting the matter.

skills into which the student is initiated, but those skills should habituate the student in a manner that they acquire power to do what otherwise they could not do. As a result students will be able to discover that knowledge, at least the knowledge associated with theology, requires that our lives be transformed. Such a transformation, however, is best understood retrospectively because the very virtues acquired in learning the story are necessary to understand what has happened to us. Thus the virtues require that we have become virtuous in order for us to recognize we have done so.

Education so understood happens through imitating a master. Yet the key to learning from a master is learning when it is appropriate to depart from what one has learned from the master. Innovation is necessary because no stone is the same nor is any significant story finished. In order to recognize the challenge, the difference this or that stone may present, the stone carver must learn the "grammar of the stone." Language is constitutive of not only the practice of stone carving, but any significant practice. Just as a master stone carver teaches his apprentice through the stories of the craft so any teacher must help the student learn how to say what they do. For the apprentice can only become a master by locating their lives in and through the narratives that have shaped their training.

To learn the language of stone carving is to learn to tell the stories constitutive of the trade. These stories make up the tradition of stone carving so that the skills of stone carving can be passed on from one generation to the next. Still, the tradition of stone carving – like any significant tradition – changes, requiring that those in the tradition be articulate in order to insure the changes remain faithful to the work of stone carving.

Yet the tradition of stone carving gains its purpose and intelligibility from other stories and traditions. How the tradition of stone carving fits within these larger narratives will require ongoing discussion and argument. For it may turn out that some practices and stories may distort the very character of stone carving. It is, moreover, quite possible for stone carving to be put to the service of quite perverse purposes and traditions. Which is but an indication that stone carving is not self-validating.[10]

[10] Those familiar with Wittgenstein I suspect have realized that the account I am giving draws on his example of "Slab" in *Philosophical Investigations*, translated by G.E.M. Anscombe (New York: Macmillan, 1953), pp. 19–21. This part of the *Investigations* has been commented on by Rush Rhees in his "Wittgenstein's Builders-Recapitulation" in *Wittgenstein and the Possibility of Discourse*, edited by D.Z. Phillips (Cambridge: Cambridge University Press, 1998) pp. 178–97. Rhees argues that Wittgenstein used "Slab" to show the connection between the use of language and what people are doing, but Wittgenstein was wrong if, as he seems to suggest, giving orders of one sort or another might be the entire language of a tribe. Rhees acknowledges it is possible to imagine a people with such a limited vocabulary yet "the trouble is to imagine a people who had a language at all and yet *never* spoke apart from times when they happened to be on this kind of building job." Rhees observes, "I do not think it could be speaking a language" (p. 182). In his *Ethics as*

This brings me to what I think we must learn from Alasdair MacIntyre if we are to ascertain what Vincent and Roger have taught us. Of course my account of what Roger and Vincent have to teach us has obviously been shaped by MacIntyre's Aristotelian understanding of the virtues. The virtues, according to MacIntyre, are dispositions to act in specific ways for definite reasons. The exercise of the virtues, however, is not only for the sake of the virtue, but also for enjoying the kind of life of which the virtues are constitutive. Therefore to understand how the life of virtue is also the best life means the virtues must be part of an ongoing tradition about the goods that constitute a life worth living.[11]

MacIntyre notes that there is an important analogy between the development of the capacity for right judgment about the good life and how capacities for right judgment are developed in more particular forms of activity with their specific standards of excellence. According to MacIntyre,

> Just as an apprenticeship in sculpture or architecture is required in order to recognize what excellent performance in these arts consists in, just as training in athletic skills is necessary to recognize adequately what excellence in athletic performance is, so a capacity for identifying and ordering the goods of the good life, the achievement of which involves the ordering of all these other sets of goods, requires a training of character in and into those excellences, a type of training whose point emerges only in the course of the training. Learning of this kind, as of other kinds, is what the uneducated, left to themselves, do not and cannot want: "those engaged in learning are not at play; learning is accompanied by pain" (*Politics* VIII, 1239a29).[12]

According to MacIntyre, Plato and Aristotle thought a *polis*, a politics, was necessary to provide the context for the disciplines necessary for the acquisition as well as the ordering of the virtues. Yet it was also the case, according to MacIntyre, that Plato and Aristotle recognized that no such *polis* was available. The Academy and the Lyceum were their attempt to develop philosophical schools that might discharge the function of the *polis*. Yet no school can do the work of the *polis*. MacIntyre argues that the same situation that faced Plato and Aristotle also faces us. As a result we try to substitute something called "education" for

Grammar: Changing the Postmodern Subject (Notre Dame: University of Notre Dame Press, 2001), Brad Kallenberg defends Wittgenstein against Rhees arguing that Wittgenstein's understanding of language achieves the nuance Rhees suggests is needed (p. 47).

11 Alasdair MacIntyre, *Whose Justice? Which Rationality?* (Notre Dame: University of Notre Dame Press, 1988), p. 109.

12 MacIntyre, *Whose Justice? Which Rationality?*, p. 110.

what only a tradition can do.[13] That is why stone carvers like Vincent and Roger are so important for MacIntyre. For as long as such people exist MacIntyre thinks we at least have some examples left of what a virtuous tradition entails.[14]

Yet MacIntyre also argues that in the absence of a *polis* it is not possible to provide an account of the "systematic forms of activity within which goods are unambiguously ordered and within which individuals occupy and move between well-defined roles that the standards of rational action directed toward the good and the best can be embodied."[15] Which means no matter how much effort we may as Christians put into education, the education that results, if it is not

13 For MacIntyre's most developed understanding of the role of "education" see his "Aquinas's Critique of Education: Against His Own Age, Against Ours," in *Philosophers on Education: Historical Perspectives*, edited by Amelie Rorty (London: Routledge, 1998), pp. 95–108. MacIntyre's remarks in this essay on the relation between philosophy and theology are particularly interesting given his insistence that philosophy must maintain an independence from theology. He does say, however, that philosophers do have to learn from theology the limitations of their mode of inquiry (p. 101), which has important implications for education given Aquinas's views. For according to MacIntyre given Aquinas's understanding of the aims of education to involve training in virtues to achieve the goods a good education cannot be supplied only by schools and universities. Rather cooperation is required between family, households, schools, and local political communities. This does *not*, however, mean that there must be a theological agreement between home, school, and political community, but rather an agreement is required concerning the practice of the virtues, an agreement that is independent of religious belief (pp. 105–6). One may wonder if this last conclusion is consistent with MacIntyre's understanding of the unity of the virtues. What is clear is that MacIntyre thinks Aquinas's understanding of education as formation in the virtues to acknowledge a good that is not chosen is at odds with education in America that "takes it for granted that there is no such thing as *the* human good, but that each individual must at some point choose for her or himself among a variety of different and rival conceptions of the good. A good education is then an education that prepares individuals for making such choices. And by that standard a Thomist education is a bad education" (p. 107).

14 MacIntyre, *Whose Justice? Which Rationality?*, p. 99. See for example MacIntyre's account of the "plain person" in his "Plain Persons and Moral Philosophy: Rules, Virtues, and Goods," in *The MacIntyre Reader*, edited by Kelvin Knight (Notre Dame: University of Notre Dame Press, 1998), pp. 136–52. MacIntyre argues that the "plain person" is a proto-Aristotelian because every human being lives out their life in a narrative form structured by a *telos*. He argues that even philosophical alternatives that reject such a view of the "plain person" are still informed by it. Kwame Anthony Appiah has recently argued that MacIntyre's understanding of the importance of narrative is not foreign to the kind of liberalism represented by John Stuart Mill, *The Ethics of Identity* (Princeton: Princeton University Press, 2005), pp. 22–3.

15 MacIntyre, *Whose Justice? Which Rationality?*, p. 141. These issues involve the vexed question of the unity of the virtues. In *Whose Justice? Which Rationality?* MacIntyre acknowledged he was wrong to criticize Aquinas's understanding of the unity of the virtues in *After Virtue* (p. x). For a good discussion of the significance of this change in MacIntyre's position see, Christopher Stephen Lutz, *Tradition in the Ethics of Alasdair MacIntyre: Relativism, Thomism, and Philosophy* (Lanham: Lexington Books, 2004), pp. 101–4.

shaped by the practices of the church, may reflect a quite different understanding of the world than that determined by the Gospel. We may think as Christian educators, for example, we are teaching the language of the Trinity, but if that language is divorced from the habits and practices necessary for work to be done by the church the language will seem at best "idealistic" and at worst useless to those whom we teach.

3. LEARNING THE GRAMMAR OF CHRIST

In his book, *The Nature of Doctrine: Religion and Theology in a Postliberal Age*, George Lindbeck helps us see the challenge before us by providing a typology of three theories of religion each of which entails an account of language. The cognitive-propositional type assumes that the language of doctrine corresponds in an unproblematic way with objective realities. The experimental-expressive type interprets religious speech as symbols correlative to and interpretations of feelings or attitudes characteristic of the human condition. A third approach, which has obviously informed the position I have taken in this chapter, Lindbeck calls the cultural-linguistic. From a cultural-linguistic perspective religious faith is understood to resemble a language correlative to a way of life. To be a Christian from a cultural-linguistic point of view is not like learning another language, but rather is to learn another language.[16]

Lindbeck observes that the great strength of those who represent the experimental-expressive type, who are usually associated with theological liberalism, is that they attempt to make religion experientially intelligible to those who do not share the faith.[17] That project usually assumes some account of epistemological foundationalism in order to

[16] George Lindbeck, *The Nature of Doctrine: Religion and Theology in a Postliberal Age* (Philadelphia: The Westminster Press, 1984), pp. 16–18. Lindbeck's book appeared four years before MacIntyre's, *Whose Justice? Which Rationality?*, so he could not have anticipated MacIntyre's extremely important account of translation. Lindbeck's case, I believe, can be strengthened by MacIntyre's argument that there is no such "language as English-as-such or Hebrew-as-such or Latin-as-such" (p. 373). Rather there is only Latin as written or spoken in the Rome of Cicero. Therefore MacIntyre does not deny that translation is possible, but he does deny that it is possible to translate a language in use (p. 376). To learn a language in use requires we learn to be speakers of a second first language (p. 375). I take it that what it means to be a Christian is to be committed to becoming an adequate speaker of a second first language called Christian – a language that in the learning teaches me how much I have to learn.

[17] Lindbeck, *The Nature of Doctrine*, p. 129. Paul De Hart has recently challenged Lindbeck's (and Frei's) attempt to draw a strong contrast between liberalism and postliberalism. In the process he provides a very useful contrast of Lindbeck's and Frei's agendas. De Hart's argument I think very successfully exposes the limits of Lindbeck's and Frei's typologies, but I think both Lindbeck and Frei rightly understood their work to be in discontinuity with most of the presumptions of liberal Protestantism. See Hart, *The Trial of Witnesses: The Rise and Decline of Postliberal Theology* (Oxford: Oxford University Press, 2006). That said, I have never had a stake in being a postliberal.

sustain an apologetic strategy aimed to show that religious language can be correlated with characteristics of the human condition that are allegedly universal. The task of the theologian, therefore, "is to identify the modern questions that must be addressed, and then to translate the Gospel answers into a currently understandable conceptuality."[18] The difficulty, however, is that if such a translation project is successful it is not clear why you need the language of faith at all.[19]

As an alternative Lindbeck suggests that the very idea of "translation" is a mistake. Rather what we need is a method that more closely resembles ancient catechetical practices. Instead of trying to describe the faith in new concepts, we should instead try to teach the language and practices of the faith. Lindbeck observes,

> This has been the primary way of transmitting the faith and winning converts for most religions down through the centuries. In the early days of the Christian church, for example, it was the gnostics, not the catholics, who were most inclined to redescribe the biblical materials in a new interpretive framework. Pagan converts to the catholic mainstream did not, for the most part, first understand the faith and then decide to become Christians; rather, the process was reversed: they first decided and then they understood. More precisely, they were first attracted by the Christian community and form of life. The reasons for attraction ranged from the noble to the ignoble and were as diverse as the individuals involved; but for whatever motives, they submitted themselves to prolonged catechetical instruction in which they practiced new modes of behavior and learned the stories of Israel and their fulfillment in Christ. Only after they had acquired proficiency in the alien Christian language and form of life were they deemed able intelligently and responsibly to profess the faith, to be baptized.[20]

Lindbeck notes that after Christianity became socially established this kind of catechetical process disappeared though similar results was obtained in diluted form through normal processes of maturation. This normalization is now part of the problem because people, at least people who inhabit the countries that once were in some general sense "Christian," know just enough "tag ends of religious language" to inoculate them from recognizing the transformation of life required to speak Christian. The grammar of people formed in this way is exemplified

18 Lindbeck, *The Nature of Doctrine*, p. 132.

19 I will not deal with the cognitive-propositional type because I do not think it necessary for the position I am trying to develop.

20 Lindbeck, *The Nature of Doctrine*, p. 132.

by statements, often heard in America, such as, "I believe Jesus is Lord, but that is just my personal opinion."

The problem, therefore, becomes that the unchurched, as well as many who are churched, may think of themselves in this time "after Christendom" as quite pious but their piety does no work. In Lindbeck's words, they are often "interested in translations of the Gospel into existential, depth-psychological, or liberationist language that articulates their latent Christianity," but the language so translated does no work analogous to the language Vincent and Roger had to learn in order to become carvers of stone.[21]

Just as Vincent and Roger had to learn the language of stone carving to carve stone, Christians must learn the language of faith if we are to carve and thus to be carved to be Christ for one another and the world. Vocabulary is everything. Few tasks are more important in our day than teaching the language of the faith. But as we saw in the case of Roger and Vincent the language must be constitutive of the work to be done. It is not as if the language is a means to do the work, but the language is the work to be done. What we say as Christians cannot be separated from the practices of a people called Church.

One of the ways Christians have tried to articulate the relation between what we say and what we do is by drawing on the tradition of the virtues. That we have done so should not be surprising because speech itself is habit. To learn to speak Christian, to learn to speak well as a Christian, is to be habituated. Thus we are told we must speak the truth in love. The love that we believe necessary to make our words true is not a subjective attitude, but rather is to be formed by the habits of the community necessary for the Church to be a true witness. That is the work our speech is to do. Part of the educational task of the Church requires some to be set aside, you can call them theologians if you desire, in order to ensure the words we use do not go on a holiday.

For some time, many, Christians and non-Christians alike, no longer believe that the words Christians use do any significant work. In such a situation some are tempted to think the task of the theologian is to develop theories of meaning to show that what Christians say makes some sense even though there is no work for the language to perform. In contrast I am suggesting the task of the theologian, who may or may not be a master carver but must at least know what it means to be a master carver, is to direct attention to those masters of the faith whose lives have been shaped by the grammar of Christ. Let us, for example, reflect on lives like Dorothy Day and Jean Vanier whose lives are unintelligible if Jesus is not the Lord.

I believe God, the master carver, is doing a new thing for his people in our time. The "new thing" is not unprecedented if we remember that the story of Israel is also our story. For I believe, as Lindbeck suggests, that the social and political power of the church is being "reduced," just as

[21] Lindbeck, *The Nature of Doctrine*, p. 133.

Israel was "reduced," so that what has been hidden might be revealed. For a church so "reduced" education is not some further activity the church needs to do beyond being church. For to be Christian will mean that you cannot avoid discovering that, as we say in Texas, you "talk different." I am convinced, moreover, that those who discover the difference our speech makes will also find their lives have been made happy. For they have been given good work to do in a world increasingly determined by the belief that there is no good work to do.

Not least among the good work Christians have been given is prayer. All Christian speech is to be tested by the one work we have been given as God's creatures. We call that work "liturgy," which is the work of prayer. And when we, like Vincent and Roger, learn the joy of the work we have been given our work will be sung. Indeed the language of the Christian, the stories that make us who we are, must be sung because the language of our faith is the very act of witnessing to the master who shared the gift: Father, Son, and Holy Spirit. Christian education begins and ends in the praise of God.[22]

22 No one has argued this as well as Julian Hartt in his book, *Theology and the Church in the University*, Foreword by Stanley Hauerwas (Eugene: Wipf and Stock, 2006). Hartt's book was first published in 1968.

8

Pro Ecclesia, Pro Texana: Schooling the Heart in the Heart of Texas

1. THE CHALLENGE OF THE PRESENT

I believe we live in dark times. By "we" I mean we Christians. We live in a country that I believe is quite literally out of control. Possessed by power unchecked, Americans think they can do what they want. After September 11, 2001, moreover, Americans seem ready to do anything to return the world to normalcy. By "normal," Americans mean they want to live in a world in which they feel safe no matter what the cost securing our safety imposes on the rest of the world. The American desire for security, to have our lives protected not only from the reality of death but also the recognition we will die, is clothed in the language of the highest ideals. America does not go to war in its own interest, but to make the world more democratic.[1] Americans believe that they are what anyone anywhere would want to be if they had our money and education. In short Americans believe that America is the world's first universal society. Americans' most benevolent ideal is that someday the whole world will be America.

1 The day after I wrote this sentence an editorial by Condoleezza Rice entitled "A 'Freedom Deficit' Haunts the Mideast," appeared in the *Durham Herald-Sun* (August 8, 2003, p. A-11) that explicitly confirmed my set of claims. While noting that America went to war in Iraq because Saddam Hussein's regime posed a threat to the security of the United States and the world, Rice argues that the goal is to "work with those in the Middle East who seek progress toward greater democracy, tolerance, prosperity and freedom." She then quotes one of Bush's speeches in which he says, "The world has a clear interest in the spread of democratic values, because stable and free nations do not breed ideologies of murder. They encourage the peaceful pursuit of a better life." It seems never to occur to Rice or Bush that many people might think that the United States represents a society that "breeds ideologies of murder." America, however, is so powerful that we can call our killing "war." It is also interesting to note that even in her justification of the war in terms of the self-interest of the United States, Rice notes that the security of the world is threatened. So America did not go to war strictly from self-interest, but because the security of the world demanded we go to war. One assumes she assumes that what is necessary for American security is also what is necessary for world security because America is the world.

I believe we live in dark times. By "we" I mean we Christians. We find ourselves in churches that are hardly distinguishable from Rotary Clubs. The church has accepted her bargain with America, allowing herself to become sequestered into the private. So sequestered, we are not even doing well in the so-called personal side of life. Our churches are torn apart by questions about sexual behavior when in fact our lives are dominated by greed. Indeed one of the most disturbing developments in our time is how lust has become a form of greed. So the church in a time of war accepts the devil's bargain to focus our lives on genitalia. As a result our sexual ethics becomes incoherent because Christians have forgotten that how our lives are formed by singleness and marriage is intelligible only if we remember that the church exists to offer the world an alternative to war.[2]

I believe we live in dark times. By "we" I mean we Christians. In particular I mean Christians who work in universities. If we have learned anything after September 11, 2001, it is that universities have abused our privileged position by doing little more than confirming for our students that the way things are is the way things have to be. September 11, 2001 is obviously an event not quickly absorbed or understood. The first response rightly must be one of silence.[3] Yet nowhere has the failure of the university been more apparent than in our inability to provide truthful descriptions for the sorrow that should grip our lives in response to September 11, 2001. "We are at war" are not words of appropriate sorrow. They are words necessary to make Americans feel safe in an unsafe world.[4]

If universities are about anything, they are about the careful use of words; but the response to September 11, 2001, surely suggests that the universities of America have failed to form those we graduate to care

2 See, for example, my essay, "Why Gays (as a Group) are Morally Superior to Christians (as a Group)," *Dispatches From the Front: Theological Engagements With the Secular* (Durham: Duke University Press, 1994), pp. 153–5. I was obviously having fun in the essay, but I think I am right that one of the difficulties with the arguments about gays in the church is the failure to see how such arguments are shaped by the accommodation of the church to our culture. If Christians really were prohibited from serving in the military as a group, would the "gay issue" look the same as it currently does? If Christians were not trusted by the military, would gays want to be part of Christian communities? Gays have enough problems. Why would they want to make their lives even more difficult by becoming Christian? Moreover, if the church was constituted by a discipline necessary to sustain a despised people, then the discipline of chastity might not appear so "outdated." In such a church to ask gays to live lives of chastity might not appear so "oppressive."

3 See, for example, the wonderful reflections of Rowan Williams on September 11, 2001 in his *Writing in the Dust: After September 11, 2001* (Grand Rapids: Eerdmans, 2002). See also *Dissent From the Homeland: Essays After September 11*, edited by Stanley Hauerwas and Frank Lentricchia (Durham: Duke University Press, 2003). Selections of Williams's reflections appear in this book.

4 See my "September 11, 2001: A Pacifist Response," in *Dissent From the Homeland*, pp. 181–95.

about word care.[5] Universities that claim to be shaped by Christian convictions, like their secular counterparts, seem to have produced not only students who are unable to recognize when they are serving powers foreign to the Gospel but even more discouraging, the same students in fact desire to aid the rule of those powers. That desire, moreover, is only enhanced by what students learn during their time at the university.

My litany is not meant to create despair. I certainly have no interest in making the world darker than it is. I realize some suspect my negative characterizations of American society are overdrawn and my characterizations of the church are too romantic. In effect I am accused of making the church look good by making American society look bad. I certainly hope that is not the case. If I am guilty of such a strategy, I would certainly be making a theological mistake. After all, for Christians despair is a sin. Moreover as apocalyptic people, Christians do not assume that the times in which they happen to live are more dark than other times when Christians have lived. For Christians to get in the game of "My time is worse than your time" can only be a sign of self-righteousness. Yet the darknesses do differ.

For Christians the discovery of the difference requires attention to that which makes us an apocalyptic people. In his important book, *Paul Among the Postliberals: Pauline Theology Beyond Christendom and Modernity*, Douglas Harink observes that:

> most simply stated, "apocalypse" is shorthand for Jesus Christ. In the New Testament, in particular for Paul, all apocalyptic reflection and hope come to this, that God has acted critically, decisively, and finally for Israel, all the peoples of the earth, and the entire cosmos, in the life, death, resurrection, and the coming again of Jesus, in such a way that God's purpose for Israel, all humanity, and all creation is critically, decisively, and finally disclosed and effected in the history of Jesus Christ.[6]

Harink notes that the language of apocalyptic puts the emphasis on God's action, which means that Christians cannot help but understand

[5] Dennis O'Brien calls attention to the universities beginning in monastic schools in order to remind us that for monks speaking and reading took place in the context of prayer and were "enveloped in a life of silence." O'Brien quotes Jeremy Driscoll's observation that in our day the monastic reverence toward words expressed in silence is simply incomprehensible. We think – and it is certainly true of most university cultures – the more words and images, the better, but "monks attempt to practice silence and be careful when they speak. They sing words which they reverence as the very word of God, and they let this word form some few images in their hearts." "The University: Before, After, and Beyond" (Unpublished Paper given as the Phi Beta Lecture at Holy Cross College, March 10, 2003).

[6] Douglas Harink, *Paul Among the Postliberals. Pauline Theology Beyond Christendom and Modernity* (Grand Rapids: Brazos Press, 2003), p. 68.

our existence as a conflict with enslaving powers from which we have been freed by God's action in Christ. Accordingly Christians believe what has occurred in Jesus Christ is cosmic, "unsurpassed and unsurpassable," revealing what was previously hidden.[7]

No small set of claims – claims moreover that meant that Christians had no choice but to develop a robust intellectual tradition. Thinking for Christians, however, was not a speculative enterprise; but as Robert Wilken contends, always reflected their attempt to understand what had happened in Christ. Accordingly Christian thought has always been governed by the facts of revelation, by the language and imagery of the Bible, and how "the life and worship of the Christian community gave Christian thinking a social dimension that was absent from ancient philosophy."[8]

This is but a reminder that Christians did not need the creation of universities to establish a Christian intellectual tradition. Indeed one might well ask that if one of the tasks of the Christian intellectual tradition is to help Christians discern how the darknesses differ, is the university as we know it not more of a hindrance than a help in such an endeavor? That is particularly the case in universities in America whose wealth seems to require us to educate our students to believe that they are the end of history. What alternative did the United States have but to go to war against terrorism? Just to the extent most students that graduate from the universities of America, whether they be Christian or not, think the answer to that question is "none," we have an indication that the American university, whether the university is Christian or not, serves the state.

The modern university and the modern state are by design mutually supportive projects.[9] For example, consider the legitimating story, a story giving legitimacy in numerous disciplines in the university, about the rise of the state. The state – that is, the peculiar institution developed over the last four centuries characterized by a centralized and abstract power exercised through a monopoly over physical coercion within a geographically defined territory – we are told was necessary to end the religious wars of Europe.[10] The only problem with this story, a story at

7 Harink, *Paul Among the Postliberals*, pp. 68–9.

8 Robert Wilken, *The Spirit of Early Christian Thought* (New Haven: Yale University Press, 2003), p. 3.

9 For example, that "freedom deficit" that Condoleezza Rice observes haunting the Middle East results in "a sense of hopelessness" which "provides a fertile ground for ideologies of hatred and persuades people to forsake university educations, careers and families and aspire instead to blow themselves up – taking as many innocent lives with them as possible." Rice simply cannot understand why someone who is receiving a university education could be so irrational as she takes "terrorists" to be. The task of the university is to produce rational lives well formed for the modern nation state, and its terrorism. In short universities ought to produce more people like Condoleezza Rice.

10 William Cavanaugh, *Theopolitical Imagination: Discovering the Liturgy as a Political Act in an Age of Global Consumerism* (London: T&T Clark, 2002), p. 10.

the heart of most defenses of liberal democracy, is that it is not true. As William Cavanaugh argues in his book, *Theopolitical Imagination*, the state as we know it began before the rise of the so-called religious wars. Indeed the states that were being born at that time of the so-called religious wars found it quite useful to play different religious loyalties off one another in order to concentrate power.[11] The legitimating story the state uses to justify its existence is the same story used to create something called "religion" that is now acceptable only if it is kept private.

The state so constituted now replaces the church as the exemplification of universal values.[12] Cavanaugh observes, "The rise of the modern state is marked by the triumph of the universal over the local in the sovereign state's usurpation of power from the Church, the nobility, guilds, clans, and towns."[13] We should not be surprised, therefore, that the sciences become the paradigm of knowledge in the modern university just to the extent that the various sciences characteristic of the modern university are able to repress their particular histories. Moreover the results the sciences promise, e.g. "soon we will cure cancer," results crucial for the support sciences receive from the state, can be used by the state to satisfy the desires of the populace so necessary for the legitimation of state power. The state's support of research to delay death now becomes the necessary condition to sustain the work of the university.

What, you may ask, does this highly contentious diatribe have to do with the schooling of the hearts of our students in the universities of America. At the very least it should make clear that American higher education is an extraordinarily successful system of moral formation. The loyalty college graduates have toward the state called America is remarkable. Of course I am well aware such loyalty is well formed before they come to the university; but through the education students receive through university, their loyalty to the state called America is made unquestioned just to the extent they learn "to be critical thinkers." Any society that produces "critical thinkers" must be superior to those societies that still require conformity. I believe few developments more

11 Cavanaugh, *Theopolitical Imagination*, pp. 20–31. Cavanaugh summarizes his argument noting "the rise of a centralized bureaucratic state *preceded* these wars and was based on the fifteenth-century assertion of civil dominance over the Church in France. At issue in these wars was not simply Catholic versus Protestant, transubstantiation versus spiritual presence. The Queen Mother who unleashed the massacre of St. Bartholomew's Day was not a religious zealot but a thoroughgoing *Politique* with a stake in stopping the nobility's challenge to royal pretensions toward absolute power" (pp. 29–30).

12 Of course the church never represented "universal values." The church represented people who were put in contact with one another through the Bishop. What Christians shared was not common "values" but a common Lord found in the meal of bread and wine.

13 Cavanaugh, *Theopolitical Imagination*, p. 99. For an analysis quite similar to Cavanaugh's see John Milbank, "Sovereignty, Empire, Capital, and Terror," *Dissent From the Homeland*, pp. 63–82.

determinatively confirm this analysis than the popularity of "ethics" in colleges and universities. This is a remark I must now try to explain.

2. WHY ETHICS MALFORMS THE HEART

I begin with a story about the development of ethics at Duke. A North Carolina philanthropist decided as one of his last great philanthropic acts to give Duke University 20 million dollars to develop a center for ethics. He wanted to do so because he was concerned that our society was losing our "Jewish-Christian" heritage. His trust company told him that to give the university that much money would be a mistake because "all they do is sit around and talk." So a modest three million dollars was given to the university to give us an opportunity to plan and develop the center. When I was told about these developments, I observed that such a center faced two obstacles: namely, that the two most distinguished ethicists at Duke, Alasdair MacIntyre and myself (not that I am in Alasdair's league) did not believe in ethics and we certainly did not believe in ethics centers.

Sure enough when they told Alasdair about these developments, the first thing he is alleged to have said is he was on the side of the trust. Then he asked whether anyone had observed a correlation between those that teach ethics and the quality of their lives. He suggested if the philanthropist really wanted to do something to enhance the moral character of Duke as a university, they should give the money to do something about the inequity of pay between those who clean our classrooms and those who teach in the same classrooms. Suffice it to say, his comments did not prevent the center from becoming a reality.

I want to be clear. I am not suggesting that little good may be done by such centers. I serve on the board of the center at Duke and I admire the people who head the center as well as many of the programs that the center develops. I even think some good may come from service learning, but I worry that the downside of such programs is to encourage undergraduates to believe they should take themselves seriously as moral agents. I assume that the most important lesson undergraduates should be taught is that they are not yet well enough formed to know what they should and should not want.[14]

[14] In a paper that as far as I know has never been published, MacIntyre observes that "there is a widespread conception among our students that to learn, to grow in knowledge and understanding, is to acquire means to implement desires and goals which the student had already, which the student brings to his or her education from outside it. Sometimes students are asked by their parents or by their advisors at the outset, 'What do you want to do?' And when they have produced some kind of stumbling answer to this, they are then advised as to what they should learn in order to achieve what it is they want. One's education is to be useful to one in reaching certain goals. Against this, I want to suggest that what education should be about is the transformation of students' conceptions of their goals. The desires, the needs, the goals that people bring to their education are in general going to be as corrupt as the

I am, moreover, extremely sympathetic with those who try to teach ethics to undergraduates. It is not their fault that they find themselves in an impossible position. That position is quite simply that they lack the authority to teach ethics in a manner that any serious teaching of ethics should be about, that is, to change lives. Because they lack the authority to change lives, too often they must teach in one form or the other what I call "the standard course in ethics." The standard course begins by helping the students understand the importance of the distinction between metaethics and normative ethics. Students are told this is a very important distinction because if they are not able to sustain some account of the status of the right or the good, then relativism is right around the corner and we will all go to hell in a hand basket.

After spending six weeks doing metaethics, the students cannot make up their minds whether they will be non-naturalist about the good or naturalist about the right. They are relieved to learn, however, that whatever metaethical position they think most defensible does not entail the normative alternative they think most defensible. The normative alternatives are usually identified as teleological or deontological. Basically that means you choose between Mill or Kant. After some weeks of discussing the weaknesses and strengths of these normative positions, most students discover they would like a little of each.

Finally the course begins analysis of cases, which piques the students' interests. So they are asked to imagine what they would do if they are among a group of students exploring a cave. They are on their way out of the cave, but the first one exiting the cave turns out to be the largest of the group and gets hopelessly stuck in the entrance. He or she cannot go forward or back. Whether the one stuck is a he or she will provide an opportunity for gender analysis. Suddenly the group notices the water is rising in the cave at an alarming rate. They are all going to drown except fatty who will only get his butt wet. They search the area that is still dry and discover a stick of dynamite and matches. Do they blow fatty out of the mouth of the cave to allow them to escape? The utilitarians argue greatest good for the greatest number so blow the big one up. The deontologists hold fast to "never do an evil that a good may accrue" and decide it is better to die than to kill fatty. Students love this kind of game because they understand such exercises are no threat to their lives.

---

culture that produced them. So they are going to have to be transformed as persons. Aristotle pointed out that what pleases and pains the virtuous person is very different from what pleases and pains the vicious person, and both again are different from what pleases the merely immature person. Morality thus is in a very important way educative of desire. And the desires that people bring to their education are ones which they are going to have to modify, or even abandon, if they are to acquire the intellectual and moral virtues. If we treat the students' desires as given, the students' original goals as given, we are in effect abdicating from the task of educating them into the intellectual and moral virtues" ("Values and Distinctive Characteristics of Teaching and Learning in Church-Related Colleges" (Unpublished Manuscript)). I do know that MacIntyre gave this lecture to those responsible for Methodist colleges and universities. He told me that what he had to say was not well received.

Indeed these kind of ethics courses, and I am willing to acknowledge that some courses may be more substantive, are designed to underwrite the presumption the students have prior to taking such courses. Students assume that ethics names that part of life in which you have to make up your own mind. The kind of course I have described legitimates that assumption by giving students names to describe the choices they are going to make anyway. Often such choices are said to be about the fundamental values that should guide our lives, which means students never entertain the thought that the very idea of "values" underwrites the presumption that when it comes to what we care about, it is finally up to us to decide what we "value."

Please note I am not trying to make anyone who has taught this kind of ethics course feel guilty. What choice do they have in the absence of any background of shared practices sufficient to sustain argument? Yet I think it would be better that such courses not be taught. They should not be taught because such courses hide from us and our students the moral debates we ought to have in America. Alasdair MacIntyre suggests that one of the tasks of the

> moral philosopher is to articulate the convictions of the society in which he or she lives so that these convictions may become available for rational scrutiny. This task is all the more urgent when a variety of conflicting and incompatible beliefs are held within the same community, either by rival groups who differ on key moral questions or by one and the same set of individuals who find within themselves competing moral allegiances.[15]

The ahistorical character of the ethics courses I have just described is the attempt to avoid MacIntyre's understanding of the task of the moral philosopher. It is important to note, moreover, that the abstract character of such ethics courses is not accidental but rather the outworking of the attempt of modern universities to be ahistorical institutions that can serve anyone anywhere. Of course in trying to serve anyone anywhere, it turns out that the universities turn out people educated to be willing agents of the modern state.

Moreover, this is not just a problem for courses in ethics but for most of the humanities in the modern university. Indeed I think one of the great moral crises confronting the university is the crisis in the humanities. In many ways the challenges represented by postmodernism and multiculturalism could not have come at a worse time. Such challenges only confirm the judgment of our colleagues in the sciences that the work done in the humanities is finally a matter of opinion. Anyone who has served on the Appointment, Promotion, and Tenure Committee of a

[15] Alasdair MacIntyre, "Is Patriotism a Virtue?" in *Theorizing Citizenship*, edited by Ronald Beiner (Albany: State University of New York Press, 1995), p. 209.

research university can testify to the difficulty those in the humanities have when we try to explain to our colleagues from the sciences why certain forms of research in the humanities are significant. I shall never forget in one of the meetings of the committee at Duke when a statistician with the best will in the world asked, "What is modernity?" A good question with many good answers, but where do you begin to answer that question if universities now produce highly educated people who have never encountered the notion of modernity prior to serving on the Appointment, Promotion, and Tenure Committee?

The crisis in the humanities is, of course, deeper than this example indicates. The humanities name disciplines determined by memory, thought, crucial for the articulation of the good community through time. Yet we live in a social order that is now trying to survive without memory. Accordingly, the work done in the humanities depends on normative commitments that the contemporary university cannot acknowledge because any such acknowledgment would betray the alleged neutrality of the universities.

Of course some of the humanities, such as history, try to avoid these challenges by pretending to be a social science. I suspect, however, the only difference between courses in ethics and, for example, history is that students assume historians know something the student does not, so they defer to the authority of the historian.[16] So history, as well as the social sciences, seem to have greater veridical status for students because in such courses you gain information otherwise unavailable.[17] That is why history courses are of greater moral significance than courses in ethics for most students in the university. In history courses students

[16] Disciplines in the university that continue to claim they are "objective" because they insist on a strict distinction between facts and values are also the disciplines that are most destructive for the moral training students should receive. The very notion of "information" is used to sustain the legitimacy of descriptions that should require further justification. "Information," however, legitimates the formation of students without acknowledging that the student is receiving a moral education. Wendell Berry observes, "Education is not properly an industry, and its proper use is not to serve industries, either by job-training or by industry-subsidized research. Its proper use is to enable citizens to live lives that are economically, politically, socially, and culturally responsible. This cannot be done by gathering or 'assessing' what we now call 'information' – which is to say facts without context and therefore without priority. A proper education enables young people to put their lives in order, which means knowing what things are more important than other things; it means putting first things first" (Wendell Berry, "Thoughts in the Presence of Fear," in *Dissent From the Homeland*, p. 41).

[17] I am well aware of the ongoing dispute among historians concerning the status of history, that is, whether history is one of the humanities or one of the social sciences. The increasing dominance in the social sciences of rational choice methodologies has seemed to force history increasingly to acknowledge it is a humanity. If I were a historian, I would consider that a very welcome development for history. The legitimating character of the social sciences for a capitalist order is nowhere better revealed than in the development of rational choice as the explanatory paradigm in the disciplines of economics, political science, sociology, and psychology.

allegedly gain the descriptions necessary to reinforce the assumption that what happened ("the facts") is inevitable. World War I was unavoidable and it is good "we" won. So history seems to be about truth, but as a result students conclude that war is always a possibility necessary to counter "bad guys." History, it turns out, is one of the most influential ways to teach ethics without having to defend that what you are doing is initiating students into discourses that underwrite the contemporary nation state.

In truth I suspect the best moral training that occurs in the contemporary university is in the sciences. At least in those disciplines the student is disciplined to acquire habits necessary to participate in ongoing research. I think "negative results are as good as positive results" is an impressive form of moral training. That the highest praise one mathematician can give another mathematician is that the work they do is "deep" is a lovely indication of the moral character of mathematics. In like manner the highest complement a physicist uses to describe the work of another physicist is that the work is "elegant." I think the aesthetic character of these judgments suggest that the moral formation the sciences require can teach us a great deal about how we should live in other aspects of our lives. The difficulty, of course, is the very language of "other aspects of our lives" means the disciplinary divisions of the contemporary university reflect as well as contribute to the fragmentary and compartmentalized character of modern life.

Therefore we should not try to school the hearts of our students by teaching "ethics" as a desperate attempt to supplement what we fear students do not get as part of their general education in the university. If the hearts of students are not formed by the work they do in all their classes in the university, then teaching ethics will not and cannot be of any help and in fact may do much harm. As MacIntyre contends:

> Insofar as education has moral import, it is not in and through the teaching of morality or values or religion or anything else as a separate and additional set of subjects; it is rather that there is a moral import in the whole structure of education, in everything that we teach, and that morality is not primarily about constraints upon how we pursue the various goals which we pursue, it is primarily about the nature of these goals themselves.[18]

3. "PRO ECCLESIA, PRO TEXANA"

I am aware that what I have had to say about "the schooling of the heart" has not exactly been an upbeat message. Surely I should have some suggestions to make about how universities like Baylor (who

[18] Alasdair MacIntyre, "Values and Distinctive Characteristics of Teaching and Learning in Church-Related Colleges," p. 2.

are after all Christian) should go about schooling the hearts of students. I do have some modest suggestions, but before making them I need to express a worry about the language of the "schooled heart." I confess when I first saw the title of the conference I thought the Baptists had finally given up and become Methodist. We Methodists are heart people. Baptists have no hearts at all. Instead Baptists have the Bible which they use as a club to beat one another into submission.

In this respect I am on the side of the Baptists. I am so because I think Jim Burtchaell is right in *The Dying of the Light* to see one of the reasons Protestants were not able to sustain the Christian character of their universities was because they were pietist. I am sure he is right about this which makes it all the more remarkable that, at least as far as I know, the many reviews and reactions to his book seldom discuss his argument concerning the role of pietism. Of course there were and are many kinds of pietism, but I think Burtchaell rightly identifies the movement with a stress on the all-sufficiency of scripture, that the laity should not be subject to the clergy, and with spontaneity as an alternative to liturgy.[19] I think, moreover, that Burtchaell is right to suspect that though pietism seemed to oppose rationalism, in fact the pietist critique of dogmatism, clericalism, legalism, and formalism well prepared the ground for rationalism. Certainly the name Immanuel Kant is enough to suggest that there is something to the connection between pietism and rationalism.[20]

One of the great deficiencies of pietism was the belief that the Christian intellectual tradition could be left behind. No more did Christians need to quarrel about the two natures of Christ. Moreover, pietists often had little use for the church. Christian doctrine as well as an overemphasis on the church from the perspective of pietism only leads to conflict, if not religious wars. Of course pietism did develop an intellectual tradition. It is called Protestant liberalism, which means Protestants became advocates of the universalism that the growth of the modern state found so useful.

Burtchaell argues that pietism in one form or the other was shared by most of the Protestant denominations that founded colleges and universities in America. As a result these denominations thought:

> that religious endeavors on campus should be focused upon the individual life of faith, as distinct from the shared labor of

[19] James Burtchaell, C.S.C., *The Dying of the Light: The Disengagement of Colleges and Universities From Their Christian Churches* (Grand Rapids: Eerdmans, 1998), p. 462. Thomas Howard substantiates Burtchaell's suggestions about the role of pietism in the formation of the modern German university in his *Protestant Theology and the Making of the Modern German University* (Oxford: Oxford University Press, 2006).

[20] See, for example, Kant's extremely interesting remarks in *The Conflict of the Faculties in Religion and Rational Theology*, translated and edited by Allen Wood and George Di Giovanni (Cambridge: Cambridge University Press, 1996), pp. 276–80.

> learning. Religion's move to the academic periphery was not so much the work of godless intellectuals as of pious educators who, since the onset of pietism, had seen religion as embodied so uniquely in the personal profession of faith that it could not be seen to have a stake in social learning.[21]

So the Christian character of the college or university was no longer thought to be found in the academic subjects of the university, except possibly the department of religion, but instead "had to live an eccentric existence in chapel, in volunteer service, and in clean living and all-around manhood."[22]

I fear the language of the "schooled heart" can reproduce this understanding of the relation of church and university. Hopefully Baptists are just too mean (and I mean that as a complement) to make the mistakes the Methodists have made. At least I would hope to save the Baptists from becoming Methodist, though I suspect given the current turmoil in Baptist life the so-called "Moderates" are well on their way to becoming Methodists. Soon Baptists will find themselves saying, like the Methodist Board of Higher Education, that the religious task of Baptist colleges and universities is to sensitize their students "to intellectual, moral, and value-centered issues ... to affirm a universal gospel for a universal community."[23] If Baptists are to avoid such drivel, then it becomes all the more important for the church as well as for Baylor that Baptists rediscover that they are unintelligible without the resources of the Christian tradition usually called catholic.

In fact I think Baylor is wonderfully positioned to school the hearts of students. Barry Harvey recently reminded me of a comment I made at Baylor several years ago that explains why I think Baylor is well positioned to be a research university in which Christian practice actually makes a difference for what is taught there.[24] I was, I believe at a conference at the Center of Church and State. (I should say I have never approved of the Baptist fetish about the separation of church and state. The separation usually means the state is free to do anything it wants to do and the church should keep its mouth shut.) I was given a cup of coffee with Baylor's shield so I discovered Baylor's motto is "Pro

[21] Burtchaell, *The Dying of the Light*, p. 842.

[22] Burtchaell, *The Dying of the Light*, p. 844.

[23] Quoted in Burtchaell, *The Dying of the Light*, p. 849.

[24] This is actually a true story. I have discovered that there exist stories about what I have said in this or that circumstance that are not true. For example, I have been introduced at least three times with a story that is not true. It seems I was in Cambridge walking across the Yard at Harvard trying to find my way to the library. I am alleged to have stopped an undergraduate and asked, "Can you tell me where the library is at." The student responded, "We do not end sentences with prepositions at Harvard." To which I responded, "Can you tell me where the library is at, asshole." I realize this is the kind of story that seems so true it should be true, but in fact it did not happen. Of course "did not happen" may be an inadequate way to understand "true."

Ecclesia, Pro Texana." I exclaimed, "What a great university. Your life is determined by the only ontological realities that count."

I feared Baylor might go the way of Harvard. Harvard's original motto was "Veritas: Christo et Ecclesia." I do not know when Harvard shortened the motto, but now "Veritas" is quite enough for Harvard. I noted I feared that Baylor might go the way of Harvard.[25] As soon as a university begins to talk about excellence, you can kiss Christianity goodbye. But I noted even if Baylor shortened its motto, you will still be in a better position than Harvard because you could still have "Texana" – at least, you would be in a better position if Texas names the radical tradition based on the confession of sin. The attempt to make truth qua truth the purpose of the university results in the failure of those at universities dedicated to the "search for truth" to acknowledge whose truths they serve because they think they serve no one's truth in particular.[26] The questions that are seldom asked at universities because we do not know how to answer them are: "What is the university for?" and "Who does it serve?"

What a wonderful thing it would be if Baylor could say it served Texas. At the very least, such service might offer some resistance to service to the nation state. Of course such service must be on guard if it is that of Texan dust storms and barbed wire because, as Bill Cavanaugh points out, in a world dominated by global markets the local and the particular can be prized because they have now become a novelty.[27] I am not suggesting that being a good Texan does not require knowledge that is not Texas's knowledge. Rather Texans should understand better what it means to be Texan after they have read Plato's *Republic.*

In *Goodbye to a River*, a book given me by Kyle Childress, as John Graves makes his way down the Brazos, he observes,

25 Curtis Freeman informs me that the motto of Wake Forest University is "Pro Humanitate."

26 I believe the most important book about the difference the church should make for the university is Dennis O'Brien's *The Idea of a Catholic University* (Chicago: University of Chicago Press, 2002). What makes O'Brien's book so significant is his insistence that what matters is truth—the truth that matters, moreover, is what O'Brien calls "signature." He argues that art most determinatively exhibits the character of truth that is signatured just to the extent that art works are "essentially historical insofar as they are connected to and express particular visions and historical placement" (p. 35). He argues this is true for all the knowledges of the university except the sciences. Even though I am not convinced he is right about the sciences, I am sure he is right to insist that the signatured character of truth means no truth is available abstracted from a tradition. In his Holy Cross Lecture he puts the argument he makes in his book succinctly, observing that humans may signature art, but we cannot signature life. "The shock of Christianity is the proclamation that there is one who can *signature* life itself, one who can appropriate chaos, waste, misery, sin and death. Jesus makes his Cross Holy by taking on all the destruction of mankind and without himself being destroyed. *He* can say 'I am the way, the truth, and the life.' "

27 Cavanaugh, *Theopolitical Imagination*, p. 111.

> The provincial who cultivates only his roots is in peril, potato-like, of becoming more root than plant. The man who cuts his roots away and denies that they were ever connected with him withers into half a man. ... It's not necessary to like being a Texan, or a Midwesterner, or a Jew, or an Andalusian, or a hybrid child of the international rich. It is, I think, necessary to know in that crystal chamber of the mind where one speaks straight to oneself that one is or was that thing, and for any understanding of the human condition it's probably necessary to know a little about what the thing consists of.[28]

Which is a reminder that Texans can only be Texans if we remember that "Pro Ecclesia" precedes "Pro Texana." The history of Texas, like all the histories of the world, is a bloody history. Such a history cannot and should not be denied nor should it be forgotten. Such a history threatens to entail further violence, however, if there is not a more determinative community that can acknowledge that such a history is ours without trying to justify such violence as necessary. We believe that community is called church, whose practice of forgiveness makes possible the truthful telling of the story of Texas.[29] The Christian story, like the story of Texas, is also a parochial story of a Jew who turned out to be the Son of God. That we believe the One called Jesus is the One who moves the sun and the stars makes the story of Jesus no less parochial.

But we also believe that any university shaped by the story of Christ is also a university that is peopled by those who would rather die than lie.[30] Such people, such parochial people, rightly expect they should hold themselves, their colleagues, and the students they teach to speak truthfully in the face of the lies that would dominate our lives. Schooled hearts require training by schooled speech, hopefully beautiful speech that makes possible the exposure of those powers that would have us kill in the name of "universal values."[31]

28 John Graves, *Goodbye to a River* (New York: Knopf, 2001), p. 145. I suppose it is not necessary to have fished Possum Kingdom Lake to appreciate Graves' book, but it has got to help. I caught the largest Brim ever trolling by those wonderful red rock cliffs.

29 See my "A Tale of Two Stories: On Being a Christian and a Texan," in my book, *Christian Existence Today: Essays on Church, World, and Living in Between* (Grand Rapids: Brazos Press, 2001), pp. 25–45.

30 For my reflections on truthfulness and lying see *Performing the Faith: Bonhoeffer and the Practice of Nonviolence* (Grand Rapids: Brazos Press, 2004).

31 Mary Margaret Nussbaum, in an article in *The New York Catholic Worker* (June–July, 2003) entitled "How to Sing Our Days," argues that few developments are more disastrous for our lives than the debasement of our language. She teaches high school English in New York. She describes the minds of her students as "full of ad copy and full of the cruel language of a culture that has falsely married beauty to cash and love to exploitation. ... Our own language has become windy and vague – full of important-sounding acronyms and prose fit to novel technologies. As a result our

So by all means I hope Baylor will be a university committed to schooling the heart, and, in particular, the heart that is the church. To so school the heart will require great drafts of courage made possible by the resources of the Christian tradition: to be Texan means the truth that is Texas must be shaped by the Gospel. The future of Baylor – a future committed to being a university at once Christian and a player in the world of research universities – will require a church exists that demands such a university exists. To trust that such a church exists is a risk, but such a risk is after all what it means to be Christian.

I believe we live in dark times. By "we" I mean we Christians. But I do not believe that there is nothing we can do. We can take the time God has given us to speak truthfully to one another. Such speech is hard and takes time. Yet Christians believe we have been given all the time in the world to take the time to do the work necessary to discover the difference between the false and the true – discoveries as wonderful as why the wings of butterflies are differently colored or why Dante's poetry burns with truth. I believe the university can be and sometimes is one of the institutions of God's time. As Christians who have the privilege of being called to do the work of the university, we must do our work with the confidence and joy that comes from having good work to do. If we do our work with joy, I do not think we will have to think about schooling hearts. Such hearts cannot help but be schooled by the wonderful world that is opened when we learn to see that all that is God's burning bright creation.

---

language is more capable of deception" (p. 7). Ms. Nussbaum notes that "One can't fight an impersonal and mechanized culture with android language or vagueness with vagueness. The great witnesses of peace in the last century – Mahatma Gandhi, Dorothy Day, Nelson Mandela – did not accept the dominant means of speech, action, or thought. As prophets, they saw a better way. As readers, they were given language to articulate their vision, knowing as Wendell Berry writes, that 'by their ignorance people enfranchise their exploiters' and that 'the only defense against the worst [language] is a knowledge of the best' " (p. 8). Accordingly Nussbaum directs us to poetry. The implications of Nussbaum's article for thinking about the way universities should school hearts I think is obvious. Universities have become far too "noisy." I blame the tenure process for some of the noise. Faculties are forced to say something before they can have anything to say. Surely we must find some way to recover the importance of silence. Without silence we will be devoid of the time it takes to see and hear the beautiful.

9

Christians and the So-called State (We Are In): A Meditation on Loyalty after September 11, 2001

The question of loyalty to the government of the United States, particularly after September 11, 2001, is not a theoretical issue for me.[1] For example, a friend wrote me in response to my critical appraisal of the American reaction to September 11, 2001, asking if my refusal to identify with the "war on terrorism" did not require me to disdain all "natural loyalties" that bind us together as human beings. Does my refusal to be "patriotic" mean I am indifferent to the gifts I have received through those that have sacrificed their lives in the wars that have made America such a great country? I had to reply that if "patriotism" is a "natural loyalty," then I certainly had to disavow being patriotic.[2]

So it seems I do not measure up to being appropriately loyal to America by those who identify themselves with the political right in American politics. But the left is not happy with me either. For example, Jeff Stout claims that "no theologian has done more to inflame Christian resentment of secular political culture" than I have.[3] Indeed I am a bit taken aback by Stout's assessment of my influence. He seems to think I have almost single-handedly convinced Christians in America to give up on democracy. I had no idea a theologian could have that kind of impact, particularly on other Christians.

1 I normally do not make myself the subject of the papers I write, but I found it hard to avoid the first person perspective given the subject of this chapter – that is, the question concerning loyalty to America. There is something right about those that challenge my understanding of Christianity because they think it betrays what I owe to America.

2 Stanley Hauerwas, "September 11, 2001: A Pacifist Response," in *Dissent From the Homeland: Essays After September 11*, edited by Stanley Hauerwas and Frank Lentricchia (Durham: Duke University Press, 2003), pp. 180–9.

3 Jeff Stout, *Democracy and Tradition* (Princeton: Princeton University Press, 2004), p. 140. For my response to Stout's very important book and his criticism of me, see "Postscript: A Response to Jeff Stout's *Democracy and Tradition*," in my *Performing the Faith: Bonhoeffer and the Practice of Nonviolence* (Grand Rapids: Brazos Press, 2004).

I am not only bemused but also confused by these assessments of my failure to support America. I am far too conventional to be thought to be outside the American mainstream. Taxes are taken out of my salary every month. I do not like the fact my money is used to support the Pentagon, but I do not know what to do about it. It is true I do not take national politics as seriously as I once did. I voted for Ralph Nader in the last two presidential elections. I continue to vote even though I am not all that convinced voting is a good idea. My friend and former student, Mike Baxter says, "Don't vote – it only encourages them." Yet I was raised a yellow-dog democrat in Texas and voting is a hard habit to break.

I also have the problem that I am, at least according to some, a "success." For example I have been elected to the American Academy of Arts and Sciences. In the literature welcoming me to the Academy, I was informed that the Academy was founded in 1780 by a small group of scholar-patriots led by John Adams. They founded the Academy even before the Revolutionary War had ended, believing that the new republic would have need for new knowledge and ideas. Accordingly, they adopted as the purpose of the Academy: "To cultivate every art and science which may tend to advance the interest, honor, dignity, and happiness of a free, independent, and virtuous people." That I am now a member of the Academy must surely mean I am or should become a good American. To be anything else would make it appear that I am not above biting the hand that feeds me. In truth I do not want to bite the hand that feeds me, but I do not think that means I have to lick the same hand.

The problem is complicated for me because I am a pacifist. For pacifists, questions of allegiance to the nation are not as urgent as questions concerning the implications of our commitment to nonviolence for our relation to those closest to us. Commenting on the work of John Howard Yoder, Grady Scott Davis observes that Yoder's account of Christian nonviolence asks us to forsake "goods attendant" not only for our own lives but for those whom we love. Davis notes that this seems to run contrary to right reason, but he commends Yoder for "his willingness to embrace this conclusion." According to Davis, Yoder rightly does not try to argue that his pacifism meets the commonsense meaning of justice and right reason. Rather Yoder argues that Jesus initiated a revolution, an "'original revolution,' in which the participants acknowledge God's call by giving themselves over to His providential will." Such a giving over was made possible because Yoder believed that through the life, death, and resurrection of Jesus, God instituted a new politics. In Yoder's own words, Jesus gave his followers

> a new way to deal with offenders – by forgiving them. He gave them a new way to deal with violence – by suffering. He gave them a new way to deal with money – by sharing it. . . .

> He gave them a new way to deal with a corrupt society – by building a new order, not smashing the old.[4]

I believe Yoder's understanding of the politics that pacifism requires offers a constructive way to understand how Christians can and should serve our neighbors – including the neighbor who may be our spouse and children – in the world as we find it, that is, a world that seems to assume that violence is unavoidable if we are to care for ourselves and one another. The challenge before those committed to Christian nonviolence, however, is not peculiar to them because they are pacifist. Rather, pacifism represents the tension between church and world that is inherent in Christian practice. Nowhere is that tension better seen than in the account Augustine gives in *The City of God* of the relation between the city of God and the city of man. That I call attention to Augustine may seem quite odd, given the assumption by many that he represents the defense of the Christian use of violence. But I hope to convince you that Augustine shares more with John Howard Yoder than is recognized.

In order to make the connection between Augustine and Yoder, I will use Robert Wilken's account of Augustine's understanding of the Christian responsibility for the earthly city in his book, *The Spirit of Early Christian Thought*. I do so because Wilken certainly cannot be counted as someone tempted to identify with Christian nonviolence; but his careful display of Augustine's understanding of the two cities and their relation I believe not only to be the "real" Augustine, but also I hope to show Wilken's account of Augustine helps Christians discern our peculiar situation in America.

Wilken argues if we are rightly to understand Augustine, we must begin by noting that though Augustine never identifies the city of God with the church, it is nonetheless the case that for Augustine the church must be a "community that occupies space and exists in time, an ordered, purposeful gathering of human beings with a distinctive way of life, institutions, laws, beliefs, memory, and form of worship."[5] If you lose this sense of the church in Augustine it is too easy to turn Augustine into an apologist for the liberal regimes that provide a place for the church only to the extent the church is willing to accept its relegation to the "private."

Wilken argues that in order to understand the relation between the two cities, we must see the significance of Augustine's contention that peace is the end for the city of man as well as the city of God. "The peace for which the city of God yearns is a 'perfectly ordered and harmonious fellowship in the enjoyment of God.'"[6] Such a peace is possible for the church because the church is constituted by right worship, that is, where

4 Grady Scott Davis, *Warcraft and the Fragility of Virtue: An Essay in Aristotelian Ethics* (Moscow, ID: University of Idaho Press, 1992), p. 40. The quote from Yoder is from *The Original Revolution* (Scottdale, PA: Herald Press, 1977), p. 29.

5 Robert Wilken, *The Spirit of Early Christian Thought* (New Haven: Yale University Press, 2003), p. 191.

6 Wilken, *The Spirit of Early Christian Thought*, p. 195.

true sacrifices are made to the One alone worthy of such sacrifices. Accordingly the greatest gift the church gives to the worlds in which she finds herself is a glimpse of what the peace of God looks like. Without the church, Augustine doubts whether the politics of the city of man even deserves the description "politics." Augustine says,

> It is we ourselves – we, his City – who are his best, his most glorious sacrifice. The mystic symbol of this sacrifice we celebrate in our oblations, familiar to the faithful. ... It follows that justice is found where God, the one supreme God, rules an obedient City according to his grace, forbidding sacrifice to any being save himself alone; and where in consequence the soul rules the body in all men who belong to this City and obey God, and the reason faithfully rules the vices in a lawful system of subordination; so that just as the individual righteous man lives on the basis of faith which is active in love, so the association, or people, of righteous men lives on the same basis of faith, active in love, the love with which a man loves God as God ought to be loved, and loves his neighbor as himself. But where this justice does not exist, there is certainly no "association of men united by a common sense of right and by a community of interest." Therefore there is no commonwealth; for where there is no "people," there is no "weal of the people."[7]

Peace, the *telos* of any city, is not to be had short of the true worship of the true God. Yet Wilken quite rightly calls our attention to Augustine's contention that Christians must try to achieve the peace of the city of man, imperfect as it is. Augustine goes so far as to suggest that the Christian may find he must take on the office of the judge. The office of the judge, moreover, may require the torture of innocent people in order to determine guilt or innocence.[8] Wilken notes that the fact that Augustine could consider that Christians might be judges, a thought Origen could not even entertain, may well have depended on Constantine's legalization of Christianity. Yet whatever advantages may have come to the church through the Constantinian settlement, those advantages did not tempt Augustine to be any less insistent that the only true peace to be found in this life would be found in the church.[9]

7 Augustine, *The City of God*, translated by Henry Bettenson (Harmondsworth: Penguin Books, 1977), pp. 889–90.

8 Augustine, *The City of God*, p. 860. For Wilken's discussion of Augustine's account of the judge see *The Spirit of Early Christian Thought*, pp. 198–9.

9 Much is made of Augustine's use of the "power of the state" to suppress the Donatists, but in fact he opposed any use of capital punishment against the Donatists. In his biography of Augustine, Gary Wills calls attention to Augustine's letters to the Christian tribune, Marcellinus, which counseled patience in dealing with the Donatists (Gary Wills, *Saint Augustine* (New York: Viking, 1999), pp. 99–126).

Accordingly, Wilken's account of Augustine's understanding of the relation between the two cities is quite different than that made so prominent by Reinhold Niebuhr. Niebuhr argued that in this time before the end time – when we cannot distinguish between the cities given their mixed character – Christians must take up the work of the earthly city in order to achieve the lesser good.[10] Yet what a Niebuhrian account ignores is Augustine's view that the church provides the context for Christian discernment about the Christian role in the earthly cities. To be sure, citizens of the city of God must "make use of earthly and temporal things," but it is equally true that "the customs and practices of society can be embraced as long as they do not misshape the souls of the faithful or detract them from their ultimate goal of fellowship with God and with one another."[11]

Augustine says the Heavenly City, the City on Pilgrimage in this world, calls out citizens from all nations and so collects a society of aliens speaking all languages. Accordingly she takes no account of any differences in customs, laws, and institutions by which earthly peace is achieved and preserved. She does not annul or abolish any of these customs or institutions just to the extent they provide for earthly peace unless (and this is the "unless" that Niebuhrian interpreters of Augustine so often ignore) these institutions are a hindrance "to the religion which teaches that the one supreme and true God is to be worshipped."[12] Wilken observes that Augustine supports this unexpected sentence a few paragraphs later by citing Exodus 22:20, "Whoever sacrifices to any god save to the Lord alone will be destroyed."

Augustine does not "solve" the problem of how Christians are to negotiate their divided loyalties. Rather Augustine creates the problem of how Christians are to negotiate the worlds in which we find ourselves. Yet Augustine does provide an account of how such a negotiation is to be undertaken. He does so, according to Wilken, not, as if often assumed, by offering a theory of political life. Rather Augustine:

> shows that God can never be relegated to the periphery of a society's life. That is why the book (*The City of God*) discusses two cities. He wants to draw a contrast between the life of the city of god, a life that is centered on God and genuinely social, and life that is centered on itself. Augustine

10 Niebuhr's most developed account of Augustine's significance is his essay "Augustine's Political Realism," included in his book *Christian Realism and Political Problems* (New York: Charles Scribner's Sons, 1953), pp. 119–247. Niebuhr argues that Augustine's realism can escape cynicism because he recognized "that the corruption of human freedom may make a behavior pattern universal without making it normative" (p. 130). That is, though self-love dominates the earthly city (and the church), it is still possible to achieve relative justice made possible by the demand of love.

11 Wilken, *The Spirit of Early Christian Thought*, p. 203.

12 Augustine, *The City of God*, p. 878.

> wished to redefine the realm of the public to make place for the spiritual, for God. As Rowan Williams, the Archbishop of Canterbury, has observed, *The City of God* is a book about the "optimal form of corporate human life" in light of its "last end." In Augustine's view, "it is life outside the Christian community which fails to be truly public, authentically political. The opposition is not between public and private, church and world, but between political virtue and political vice. At the end of the day, it is the secular order that will be shown to be 'atomistic' in its foundations." A society that has no place for God will disintegrate into an amoral aggregate of competing, self-aggrandizing interests that are destructive of the commonweal. In the end it will be enveloped in darkness.[13]

But what does all this have to do with the question of divided allegiance for Christians in that state called the United States? At the very least it reminds Christians that we have a divided allegiance. For surely one of the great betrayals of Christians in America to America is confusing America with the Kingdom of God. Christians have done so because we assume that America is a democracy and democracies are less coercive than other forms of political organization. Allegedly democracies are the limited form of government that some claim is incipiently present in Augustine's understanding of the two cities. So Christians now assume that democracies can ask us to make sacrifices that are unproblematic because they are uncoerced sacrifices. I do not think you need to be a pacifist to think there are problems about such an assumption. Augustine gives you all you need to recognize that the sacrificial system called democracy remains for Christians problematic just to the extent we fail to recognize that America names a sacrificial system.

In an article entitled "Is Patriotism a Virtue?" Alasdair MacIntyre observes that there is a deep tension between the dominant account of morality in our culture and patriotism.[14] In order to act morally we believe the agent must as far as possible assume a position abstracted from all social particularity and partiality. My way to put this understanding of morality is to point out that we believe you should have no story except the story you choose when you had no story. We call this "freedom." The primary expression of such freedom is to be found in the assumption that we should not be held responsible for decisions we made when we did not know what we were doing. The only problem with this view of the moral life is it makes marriage and the having of children unintelligible. How could you ever know what you were doing when you promised life-long monogamous fidelity? Moreover, you will never get the children you want.

13 Wilken, *The Spirit of Early Christian Thought*, p. 208.
14 Alasdair MacIntyre, "Is Patriotism a Virtue?" in *Theorizing Citizenship*, edited by Ronald Beiner (Albany: State University of New York Press, 1995), pp. 209–28.

According to MacIntyre, patriotism is constituted by an alternative moral perspective. Patriotism "requires me to regard such contingent social facts as where I was born and what government that ruled over that place at that time, who my parents were and so on, as deciding for me the question of what virtuous action is – at least insofar as it is the virtue of patriotism that is in question. Hence, the moral standpoint and the patriotic standpoint are systematically incompatible."[15] It is, therefore, the central contention of a morality of patriotism that a crucial dimension of my ability to live well is lost "if I do not understand the enacted narrative of my own individual life as embedded in the history of my country."[16]

MacIntyre observes that liberal social orders, such as the United States, cannot help but regard patriotism so understood as morally problematic. Liberal social orders and the corresponding accounts of moral rationality require me to assume that I act morally not as a parent, farmer, or American, but only when the principles of my action can be justified by my assumed status as a rational agent qua rational agent. America names that peculiar country in which the cause of America, understood in the language of patriotism, and the cause of morality, understood in liberal terms, came to be identified. MacIntyre observes that the history of this identification could not help but be the history of confusion and incoherence. "For a morality of particularist ties and solidarities has been conflated with a morality of universal, impersonal, and impartial principles in a way that can never be carried through without incoherence."[17]

15 MacIntyre, "Is Patriotism a Virtue?", p. 212.

16 MacIntyre, "Is Patriotism a Virtue?", p. 224. MacIntyre's analysis of the tension between liberal cosmopolitanism and patriotism has deep implications for how one understands the duty to care for refugees. The best account I know of the challenges refugees present to liberal polities is Luke Bretherton, "The Duty of Care to Refugees, Christian Cosmopolitanism, and the Hollowing of Bare Life," *Studies in Christian Ethics*, 19, 1 (2006), pp. 39–61. Bretherton, in a manner similar to MacIntyre, argues that liberal internationalists cannot provide a coherent account of why the claims of refugees should be privileged vis-à-vis other demands. They are unable to do so because liberalism cannot account for how a particular loyalty must be understood as having a *telos* toward a common good Christians understand as fulfilled in communion with God. Accordingly, he contrasts Christian cosmopolitanism, which he understands as a movement, "via differentiation and development through history, to an eschatological fulfillment of creation," with "the rationalist cosmopolitans whose Platonic protological teleology posits a return to an undifferentiated 'humanity' which is unable to incorporate the fulfillment of humanity through differentiation into particular societies of persons that involve differences of languages, kinship and territoriality" (p. 48). He then provides an argument, using Agamben's account of "bare life" to describe the character of the refugee, stating that Christians in their local contexts have an obligation to welcome the refugee while recognizing that no single polity can be responsible for all refugees. Bretherton does not say how a polity might distinguish between its obligation to different populations of refugees, but surely such discrimination comes by way of historical narrative, e.g. America clearly has an obligation to receive refugees who have suffered because of our imperial ambition.

17 MacIntyre, "Is Patriotism a Virtue?", p. 228. For a confirmation of MacIntyre's analysis see Edmund Morgan's, "Inventing the 'Liberal Republic' Mind," *New York*

More troubling (at least for me) than incoherence is such a conflation of patriotism and liberal universalism cannot help but result in violence – a violence all the more virulent because our violence allegedly is not self-interested, but rather perpetrated in the name of ideals allegedly all people share. Young people in American armed forces may think they are serving in the military as part of their obligations to their families and local communities; but in fact those parochial loyalties are being used in the interest of an empire that lacks the means to acknowledge it is just that, an empire. The conflict in the former Yugoslavia was fueled by hatreds harbored for centuries, but at least people in Yugoslavia did not kill one another in the name of a universal cause.

The ongoing war in Iraq is an obvious example of American arrogance cloaked in the pretensions of a universal cause. In many ways it would be a moral advance to attack Iraq because America needs and wants its oil. But Americans cannot go to war out of self-interest. We can only go to war for American ideals of freedom and democracy which makes it all the more difficult to conduct war in accordance with just war commitments. The higher the ideals invoked to justify a war, the more difficult it is to keep war limited. For example, now that Iraq has been defeated, we think "we," that is, Americans, must make Iraq a democracy.[18] On what possible grounds can that assumption be justified? What could it possibly mean for Iraq to institutionalize a separation between church and state? Islam has no idea it is a church or a religion. To ask an Islamic society to "privatize" religion is to ask Muslims to be something else than Muslims.

The incoherence MacIntyre suggests is at the heart of the American project makes it impossible for Christians to be American patriots. Christians, certainly Catholic Christians, cannot and do not believe that America represents what is truly universal.[19] The Christian word for universal is catholic. Moreover the universal church is not constituted by ideals such as freedom, but rather for Christians universal

---

Review of Books, LIII, 18 (November 16, 2006), pp. 30–2. Morgan's article is a review of Robert Kagan's, *Dangerous Nation* which is a description (and defense?) of American foreign policy as an exercise in "universalistic nationalism."

18 I had written this paper before I received the 2002 Witherspoon Lecture of John Alden Williams: "Can a State be Virtuous? Muslim Political Theories Then and Now." I should like to think his lecture helps us see what a hopeless task confronts those who would try to make Iraq a "democratic state." There simply is no basis in Islam for the modern notion of the "state." It would be interesting to compare and contrast Augustine's understanding of the two cities with al Farabi's account of "erring cities."

19 Political liberalism is not the primary engine that drives the universalist train. Capitalism is the most determinative practice that materially embodies the liberal drive to destroy what from a liberal point of view cannot help but appear as parochial. The American dollar is, therefore, the most determinative form of the universal. For a prescient analysis of the conflict between capitalism and Catholicism see Michael Budde, *The Two Churches: Catholicism and Capitalism in the World System* (Durham: Duke University Press, 1992).

names the connection across time and space between real people united by a common story. The office of the church that holds the particular responsibility for sustaining our unity is called "bishop." That office, moreover, is only intelligible to the extent the bishop helps diverse Eucharistic assemblies to share their stories with one another so that the church becomes the one mighty prayer for the world. Indeed, it is my view that the reason our world thinks it has no alternative to war is the disunity between Christians.

Patriotism – at least MacIntyre's understanding of patriotism – can only be a possibility for Christians if we are determined by a more parochial loyalty than our loyalty to country or people. Christians by being Christian are not asked to deny being Ugandan, Texan or, even American. However, what it means to be Ugandan Christian and what it means to be an American Christian present quite different challenges. How those challenges are negotiated, though, requires that a church exists that is at once more parochial and, thereby, more determinative than what it might mean to be Ugandan or American. Christians in Uganda and America rightly want to be of service as a Ugandan or an American. But you have an indication that such service is in tension with our being Christian if it means being American takes priority to the unity forged between American Christians and Ugandan Christians by the church.

The forging of such connections is peace. That is why I find it odd for pacifists to be criticized for being politically irresponsible or disloyal. To be committed to Christian nonviolence should not prevent those so committed from trying, even in America, to make our relations with one another more just. I think, however, the way Christians committed to nonviolence as well as Christians not so committed can best serve this land called America is by refusing to be recruits for the furtherance of American ideals. Let us rather be parochial people. For the only way we will be saved from the temptations to serve the universal ideologies of the empire is through the concrete relations which make our actual lives possible. The lives of the people who worship at Holy Family Episcopal Church in Chapel Hill, North Carolina, have first claim on me. Whatever loyalty that abstraction called the United States may have will need to be tested by the effect it has on what I owe to those that worship at Holy Family and how what I owe to them puts me in contact with Christians around the world.

Finally I need to return to the criticism made by those on the left and right concerning my alleged failure to support America. I teach and work in a very secular university. I try to be as good a citizen as I can be in the life of the university. I serve on university committees, which means I often work with those who think theology is just a step above witchcraft. Indeed in the current university witchcraft often is thought to be more interesting and respectable than Christianity. Yet I continue to think universities should and do provide the space and time for the rational deliberations necessary to explore the convictions that shape our lives. The kind of analysis MacIntyre provides of the incoherence of the moral and political ethos of America is the kind of work I believe the university can and should make possible. I should like to think that I am serving my Christian and non-Christian neighbors, neighbors who are American, through my work in the university. I try to remember, however, that honest craftsmen and women are probably doing more important work for the common good.

I suspect calling attention to my service in the university will not satisfy those who think I am not loyal to America or that I fail to work to make America a more just society. They may be right about that, but at least such a judgment is not about me but about how you understand the role and importance of the university as an institution for the furtherance of our common good. I think the work of the university is crucial for any attempt to live in peace with one another and how such peace is constitutive for any justice worth having. I confess I worry that the university too often is willing to sell itself to the interest of the State Department and the Pentagon, but at the very least the university is constituted by commitments that make it possible to criticize such sell-outs.

I have often used the trope of being a Texan to distance myself from the desire for the universal so characteristic of our time. I am well aware that the "Texas" to which I appeal is imaginary, but there are still places in Texas where you can eat a chicken-fried steak. Eating chicken-fried steaks may not be a sufficient form of resistance against the lure of the universal, but you have to start somewhere. To be a Christian is to be trained to care for one another through the building up of a common life by engaging in the time-consuming and time-creating work of the everyday. The work of the university is often pretentious, promising more than it can deliver. But I also think the university can be an institution that not only helps us live at peace with ourselves and one another, but also is peace. My commitment to the work of the university may not satisfy those who think I am not sufficiently grateful for what I have been given. All I can say is I am doing what I have been given in the hope I may be able to give back in some small measure the gifts I have received from those that call themselves Americans.

10
Democratic Time: Lessons Learned from Yoder and Wolin

1. STOUT ON DEMOCRACY

Though the subject for this session is "Christianity and Radical Democracy," I think it disingenuous not to acknowledge that I am still thinking about the issues raised by Stout with the publication of *Democracy and Tradition*.[1] In my first response to Stout I thanked him for forcing me to revisit some of the early and, I hope, continuing influences on me that determine my understanding of how Christians should negotiate this allegedly democratic society.[2] Often gestures of gratitude toward one's critics are made to dismiss the criticism by showing the critics do not understand or may even be so ill educated they are not able to grasp the position they critique.

For example, in his recent book, *Lying: An Augustinian Theology of Duplicity*, Paul Griffiths praises Newman, and the Victorians in general, for the sharpness of their polemics. Newman responds to Kingsley's anti-Catholic polemics by observing he did not think Kingsley's misunderstanding was due to malice, but rather was the result of Kingsley's "intellectual build. He appears to be so constituted as to have no notion of what goes on in minds very different from his own, and moreover to be stone-blind to his ignorance."[3] I report Newman's judgment to say that is certainly not how I regard the criticism made by Stout of my work. Indeed I am in debt to Stout, because he has forced me to revisit

1 Jeffrey Stout, *Democracy and Tradition* (Princeton: Princeton University Press, 2004).

2 Stanley Hauerwas, *Performing the Faith: Bonhoeffer and the Practice of Nonviolence* (Grand Rapids: Brazos Press, 2004), pp. 215–41.

3 Paul Griffiths, *Lying: An Augustinian Theology of Duplicity* (Grand Rapids: Brazos Press, 2004), p. 200. Griffiths is certainly right to praise the Victorians for knowing that disagreements are important, requiring sharp rhetorical habits. See, for example, David Newsome's wonderful book, *The Parting of Friends: The Wilberforces and Henry Manning* (Grand Rapids: Eerdmans, 1993) for confirmation of the Victorians' "sharp rhetorical habits." For example Newsome observes that the conversion of Henry Wilberforce to Catholicism "may have saved his soul from perdition, but it certainly did nothing to sweeten his temper or to improve his manners" (p. 361).

judgments I had made in the past which I now understand I did not make sufficiently articulate for others and, most important, for me to understand what I think.

Accordingly I am extremely grateful to have this opportunity to explore how Christians should understand their relation to "radical democracy." In *Democracy and Tradition* Stout challenges me to join the struggle to make America more democratic. He thinks I have confused liberal political theory with democratic practice in a manner that allows me to disdain the struggles for justice, for democracy, in American society.[4] Indeed he fears that the many ministers who have been influenced by me will shape their congregations in a manner that makes the church the enemy of democracy.

Stout may well be right that I have conflated liberal theory with democratic practice, but if that is the case I have had good reason to do so because that is what many liberals have done. As I will argue below I think Sheldon Wolin is right to interpret liberalism as the attempt to avoid the challenge of democratic politics, but it is nevertheless the case that liberal presuppositions have dominated accounts as well as justifications of democracy in recent theory. Of course the difficulty begins with what or how democracy is understood. I take it that is why we are trying to explore what and how we should understand radical democracy.

In order to clarify my take on radical democracy I will simply try to draw out some lessons I have learned from Yoder and Wolin. Before doing so, however, I want to raise some questions about Stout's understanding of the democracy I am alleged to have convinced Christians to give up. Stout says his focus is on democracy in America; yet it is not clear to me what he means by democracy or how democracy and America are interrelated.[5] At times he sounds – particularly when he is talking about community – like a radical democrat, though he seldom references current theorists identified with that alternative. He, rightly I think, says we cannot call the mode of government in America democratic given the corporate influence on legislation,[6] but it remains unclear to me what Stout understands to be the alternative.

Stout's favorite way of describing democracy is that it is "practice of giving and asking for reasons."[7] Such a claim I assume is equivalent to his admittedly aphoristic and paradoxical statement that "pragmatism is democratic traditionalism," that is, that pragmatism names the space

4 Charlie Collier has pointed out to me that Stout's request that I do Christian theology in a manner compatible with if not a handmaid to democracy could be reversed. I could claim that Stout's political theory is not Christian theology and is therefore incompatible with my ecclesiology, so Stout needs to do theology. This is a way to suggest that Stout's criticism of me sometimes seems to ask me to be something else than a theologian.

5 Stout, *Democracy and Tradition*, p. 15.

6 Stout, *Democracy and Tradition*, p. 305.

7 Stout, *Democracy and Tradition*, p. 6.

that combines rebellion against hierarchy with a love of virtue.[8] Therefore democracy does not seem to name a form of government for Stout, but rather "is a culture in its own right."[9] Accordingly he insists that the ideal of democratic individuality is not complete independence but rather the interlocking virtues of courage and self-trust that allow citizens to resist conformity.[10] Indeed Stout insists the democratic critics of democracy must temper their criticism with generosity. Generosity is required in order to show that the critic is open to having their indictment indicted.[11]

It remains unclear to me, however, how Stout understands the role of "the people" and democracy. He worries "under circumstances like ours" whether "the people can summon the spiritual wherewithal, the moral fiber, to act on behalf of democracy before democracy gives way."[12] However, in response to Eliot's "Anglophilia and Traditionalism," which Stout criticizes for looking away from his own people to find hope and value in some other place and time," Stout confesses that his "democratic wager is that the grounds for this-worldly hope and the evils we need to resist are both to be found among the people."[13] I am not suggesting that Stout cannot consistently hold these judgments about the role of "the people" in democracies, but I would like to know more about how he understands who the people are and what role they should play in his democracy.

8 Stout, *Democracy and Tradition*, p. 13.
9 Stout, *Democracy and Tradition*, p. 195.
10 Stout, *Democracy and Tradition*, p. 293.
11 Stout, *Democracy and Tradition*, p. 60.
12 Stout, *Democracy and Tradition*, p. 23. On page 24 Stout provides a list of the pathologies he fears is now characteristic of those who are citizens. Among the pathologies mentioned is that citizens have ceased to "trust ourselves to be competent initiators of action" and have "withdrawn from politics into docility, apathy, or despair." I think he is right to call attention to this characteristic of our time, but I do not think he provides a significant account of why our lives are so determined. If Stout provided such an account I think he would have to deal with the subversion of politics by capitalism. Sheldon Wolin points out that the achievement of liberal capitalist societies was to "perfect" the Marxist idea by showing how administration could supersede politics without resorting to repression. Wolin observes, "the economy of opposition is the solution to the political problem created for capitalism by the historical evidence that saw democracy emerge contemporaneously with capitalism. Capitalism depended upon the consumer who, concurrently, was being installed as citizen in the democratic imaginary. The problem was to avoid alienating the former without provoking the latter into becoming a self-conscious demos fired by populist resentments. The solution was to present both cultures as centered on free choice. The sovereign citizen and the sovereign consumer alike would 'choose' between options, albeit ones that had never formulated. A miracle of transubstantiation was then accomplished. Popular sovereignty was absorbed into economic impotence and consumer sovereignty into political impotence" (*Politics and Vision* (Expanded Edition) (Princeton: Princeton University Press, 2004), pp. 575–6). Wolin's analysis of how and why we no longer trust ourselves is, I think, the kind of challenge Stout must address
13 Stout, *Democracy and Tradition*, p. 57.

Early in *Democracy and Tradition* Stout says democracy as a "strictly political referent is a form of government in which the adult members of the society being governed all have some share in electing rulers and are free to speak their minds in a wide-ranging discussion that rulers are bound to take seriously."[14] Public deliberations are essential to this form of government, requiring people's representatives to deliberate on behalf of their constituency and the judgments of their constituencies. Such a context is the link between democracy in its strictly political form and democracy as a cultural phenomenon.

Stout's argument in *Democracy and Tradition* rightly, I think, avoids associating democracy with governmental institutions, but I am not quite sure what he means above by the "strictly political referent."[15] For example, Stout criticizes me for failing to provide an account of justice, which he says is crucial if the struggle against terrorism is to be rightly conducted. He observes that the language of justice is necessary to explain "why we have just cause to bear arms against terrorists, why our armed forces should not be firing at civilians, and why we should not be supporting regimes that depend on us to thwart the democratic aspirations of their own people."[16] I worry that the "we" in this sentence may legitimate the assumption about power that accepts the status quo.

I wonder if that "we" is what Stout means by a "civic nation?" Drawing on the work of David Hollinger, Stout reminds us that three formidable constituencies – a business elite, those with diaspora identities, and middle Americans – that constitute America are all members of a "civic nation."[17] Yet Stout also maintains that it is a grave mistake to believe a nation like America could become a community in the communitarian sense.[18]

What is not clear to me is how Stout understands the democracy fostered in his neighborhood is connected with, depends on, or is a manifestation of what he takes to be the "civic nations." I do not ask this question as a disguised criticism but rather because I think it is a question that challenges anyone, myself included, who advocates some form of "radical democracy."

I think this question is also at the heart of Stout's chapter on "Democratic Norms and Terrorism." I found his discussion of the unavoidability as well as the limits of "dirty hands" illuminating, but I wonder if Stout needs this account to sustain his advocacy of democracy. He

[14] Stout, *Democracy and Tradition*, p. 4.

[15] One way to put the question I am raising is to ask Stout what he makes of Wolin's refusal to describe democracy as a form of government. See Wolin, *Politics and Vision*, p. 602.

[16] Stout, *Democracy and Tradition*, p. 160.

[17] Stout, *Democracy and Tradition*, p. 297.

[18] Stout, *Democracy and Tradition*, p. 303. This is a point made by MacIntyre who disavows being a communitarian exactly because in the world that inhabits us a call for community too often becomes a form of state power.

tells us that heads of state hold office that burdens them with unique responsibilities. They must protect "the people" even if such protection gives them dirty hands. Such rulers "are unlike the rest of us in being officially responsible for the exercise of coercive power on behalf of the people's survival and well-being."[19] Rulers are going to do what rulers have to do. I simply do not see why we need to give rulers legitimating accounts (even accounts as carefully qualified as the one Stout gives) for doing what they say they have to do for our survival. More to the point, I do not see how those accounts are required if you believe, as Stout seems to do, that democracy is meant to disrupt those who rule and act in the name of serving "the people."[20] If democratic theory provides accounts that legitimate the ruling powers, then the subversive thrust of democratic practice is in danger of functioning in a purely ideological manner.[21]

I need to be clear, however, that the issues raised by Stout in his chapter on "dirty hands" are also issues that I cannot avoid. In a review of *Performing the Faith*, Terry Tilley asks, "How are we to think about structures and officers of the churches? What can we say about the diversity of offices, tasks, and witnesses within our churches? Do not some of our leaders have 'dirty hands' in running the churches?"[22] If, as I maintain, the church is an alternative politics, such questions cannot be avoided. This means that questions of how the churches are governed are at the heart of how Christians should understand their witness to the world. But that is what I take to be the center of Yoder's "politics" and in particular, how he taught us to see how the acknowledgment of the sinfulness of the church is crucial for understanding the "politics of the church." So it is to Yoder I now turn.[23]

19 Stout, *Democracy and Tradition*, p. 190.

20 Another set of problems with Stout's account of democracy involves his understanding of how democracy came into being. He observes that "modern democracy was in some sense a revolutionary break with the past" (p. 201). In particular he claims that "democracy came into the modern world opposing the representatives of a feudal and theocratic past" (p. 225). I think neither of these claims would be accepted by most historians or political theorists. At the very least Stout owes us some account of why A.D. Lindsay's understanding of the role of the Puritan congregation for the formation of democracy is wrong. See A.D. Lindsay, *The Modern Democratic State* (New York: Oxford University Press, 1962).

21 I owe this way of putting the matter to Alex Sider. Alex also observes that disruptions inherent to democratic practice are themselves a *de facto* acknowledgment of the right to rule.

22 Terrence Tilley, "Faith-Based Initiatives: Review of *Performing the Faith*," *Commonweal* (September, 2004), p. 31.

23 As influenced by C.B. MacPherson, I have always been reticent to recommend democracy qua democracy because I was doubtful I knew what I was recommending. See MacPherson's *The Real World of Democracy* (New York: The Oxford University Press, 1966). I also learned from MacPherson that discussion of democracy cannot be separated from capitalist subversions of democracy.

2. YODER ON CHURCH AND DEMOCRACY

In his essay, "The Christian Case for Democracy," Yoder observes that it "did not occur to the early Christians to ask whether the empire was or was not the best form of government."[24] It is equally the case that in many parts of the world the call for democracy is not a self-evident given. So to ask "What is the best form of government?" is a Constantinian question, that is, it presupposes that the one asking the question is in an "established" social posture that presumes a position of power. Yoder suggests that the "paradigmatic ethical agent" capable of asking the question of what is the best form of government is "assumed to be free, adult, healthy, male (as even our generic pronouns testify), and owner of property, and able to earn."[25]

Yoder's disavowal of the question of what form of government is best does not mean that he thinks we live politically in a world in which all cats are gray. Christians can and should distinguish between different societal and governmental alternatives, but they must do so without assuming they need a theory of legitimacy to discern the difference between political societies. That Christians refuse to speculate about what form of government may be best does not mean they must abandon all attempts to discern between better and worse forms of societies.

Nonviolence obviously plays a role in discernment in the evaluation of governments, but according to Yoder the most basic issue facing Christians is not that of war, but rather the social assumptions that lead Christians to assume the necessity of war. He observes that no Christian accepts war because they like it or think war is a good thing, but

[24] John Howard Yoder, *The Priestly Kingdom: Social Ethics as Gospel* (Notre Dame: University of Notre Dame Press, 1984), p. 154.

[25] Yoder, *The Priestly Kingdom*, p. 154. Yoder's generalization about the agent capable of asking the question of what form of government is the best is just that, a generalization. He would certainly be ready to acknowledge that the call for democratic forms of life might come from the dispossessed. In *Democracy Matters* (New York: Penguin Books, 2004) Cornel West identifies Constantinianism as the problem besetting "Christian America." According to West, when Christians become Constantinians, they rob Christianity of the "prophetic fervor of Jesus and the apocalyptic fire of that Jew-turned-Christian named Paul" (p. 107). No doubt Yoder would be in agreement with West's criticism of the effect of Constantinianism, but he might well distance himself from West's identification of Rauschenbusch as a representative of "prophetic Christianity." No doubt Yoder shares Rauschenbusch's critique of capitalism but Rauschenbusch's blessing of democracy as *the* form of Christian government would appear to Yoder as a Constantinianism of the left. West, however, is quite clear that he "speaks as a Christian whose commitment to democracy is very deep but whose Christian convictions are even deeper" (p. 171). In a very important chapter, "Christ the Hope of the World" in *The Original Revolution* (Eugene, OR: Wipf and Stock, 1998), Yoder develops an account of neo, neo-neo, neo-not-neo-Constantinianism that helps us see how Constantinianism can emigrate into diverse forms from some developments in Latin American liberation theology to outright secular formations (pp. 132–54).

"because they assume that the church is called to run society in collaboration with the state."[26]

Therefore Yoder praises Reinhold Niebuhr for criticizing the pacifism of the peace churches in the 1920s and 1930s. The assumption that people have the capacity to make the world come out right or that an insightful minority could make the world good by coercively outlawing war through the technique of minority control was not faithful to the Gospel. But that does not mean that Christians can take a pessimistic stance toward the world. "It is the business of the church to change the world, not only by changing individuals but also by being a different kind of human community in the midst of the world."[27]

If I have any complaint against Stout's characterization of me in *Democracy and Tradition*, it is that he fails to credit this emphasis in my own work that I learned from Yoder. The oft made charge that Yoder (or Hauerwas) is a sectarian simply fails to take seriously Yoder's emphasis that the church should be a community that models for the world what the world can be. That I refuse to provide an account of legitimacy for the state may seem to be irresponsible to some is but an indication that such critics, at least as far as I am concerned, are not being "realistic." A refusal to develop accounts of legitimacy, moreover, does not mean that discriminating judgments cannot be made by Christians about the limits and possibilities of the societies in which they find themselves. Such judgments, however, should not ever prevent Christians from becoming missionaries in societies that they might well regard as politically oppressive.

Yoder thinks it quite important that civil freedoms such as speech, press, and assembly arose out of religious agitation. It is another matter that these freedoms became in a secular translation "inalienable rights" that may create problems for Christians. Moreover Yoder, drawing on A.D. Lindsay's work, thinks it significant that the Puritan conviction that because God's word must be heard there must be freedom to preach, print, and read, became the model for secular town meetings. This is not

26 John Howard Yoder, "The Unique Role of the Historic Peace Churches," *Brethren Life and Thought*, 14 (Summer, 1969), p. 136. Yoder often made this point, but it is interesting how seldom critics of Yoder's "pacifism" "get it." I am indebted to Charlie Collier for finding this article in *Brethren Life and Thought*. Critics of Yoder seldom do the reading necessary to sustain their criticisms of him. I suppose they may be excused for failing to do so because John's essays are scattered in a wide range of journals and books, but often critics do not even read with care Yoder's materials that are widely available.

27 Yoder, "The Unique Role of the Historic Peace Churches," p. 147. Yoder explicitly rejects the spiritualistic and theocratic alternatives for understanding the place of the church in the world. The church "is to *be* a new society. We cannot say that the gospel does not have social expression if we have any meetings at all, because if we meet that is already a social expression of the gospel, and it is going to change the neighbors ... Neither biblically nor historically is the choice between personal obedience and social impact a choice at all. Each is permissible, each is possible, only with the other" ("The Unique Role of the Historic Peace Churches," p. 149).

without significance for Christians. Problems may be created when those meetings are justified by the assumption that the individual is reliable, but that is a problem that Christians are glad to have.[28]

Yoder even suggests that Christians committed to nonviolence, particularly those who are rurally and evangelically oriented, are not fully honest about the ways they are also happy in the world. They may criticize the "wild-eyed Quakers" for assuming that Christians can change the world by joining the United Nations, but they must recognize that their pride in their clean fence rows, the lack of weeds in their corn, that their fields have less erosion, and that they have discovered the importance of crop rotation is coupled with the tendency of peace people "to migrate to democratic parts of the world, away from totalitarian parts of it. If we (the peace churches) took it really seriously, this would mean that we *do* see a difference between a better society and a worse society, and that we would all rather live in a better one."[29]

Some may think Yoder's observation concerning the need of peace churches to give an account of why they prefer to live in societies described as democratic is inconsistent with his claim in *The Christian Witness to the State* that the "Christian witness does not provide any foundations for government, either practically or philosophically, but that the Christian rather accepts the powers that be and speaks to them in a corrective way."[30] In my early essay on Yoder, "The Nonresistant Church: The Theological Ethics of John Howard Yoder" (the essay Stout likes), I criticized Yoder for not providing a theory of legitimacy by which states can be judged.[31] Yet I came to think Yoder was right to insist that: "The state does not need to be theoretically justified in order to exist; it does exist. Whether our speaking to the state presupposes that we must have a theory of why the state exists will depend on the nature and ground of our critique."[32] Not only is Yoder's insistence that "the state" does not need legitimacy true to the New Testament's understanding of the powers, but his position realistically provides the concrete way to make a political difference. In other words his refusal to provide a "theory of legitimacy" is but the other side of his admirable historicism.

28 John Howard Yoder, "Response of an Amateur Historian and a Religious Citizen," *Journal of Law and Religion*, 416 (1989), p. 415. In this essay Yoder does not explain what he means by identifying himself as a "religious citizen." I confess I am not quite sure how he would understand what it would mean to be a "religious citizen." I suspect John would say that it depends on what you mean by "citizen."

29 Yoder, "The Unique Role of the Historic Peace Churches," p. 147.

30 John Howard Yoder, *The Christian Witness to the State* (Scottdale, PA: Herald Press, 2002), p. 41.

31 Stanley Hauerwas, *Vision and Virtue: Essays in Christian Ethical Reflection* (Notre Dame: University of Notre Dame Press, 1981), pp. 213–21.

32 Yoder, *The Christian Witness to the State*, p. 78.

Yoder does not provide a theory of legitimacy, but he remains Pauline in acknowledging that governmental authority is God's instrument in a process which will lead to its own defeat.[33] In this time between the two aeons in which the reign of Christ channels violence, turns violence against itself, to preserve as much as possible of the order necessary for human society, Christians are subject to that order. Accordingly Christians do not ask governments to be nonresistant, but they can ask that those in power be just, care for the orphans and widows, and use the least violent means possible to secure order.[34] Christians can do so because they recognize that "government" is "by no means only the sword," making it possible for Christians not only to witness to the state but also to participate in government.[35]

I realize that talk of "two aeons" for those concerned with politics may sound at best fanciful, but I believe that such talk is crucial not only for understanding Yoder but also for understanding how the church and Christians serve any politics in which we find ourselves. At the heart of Yoder's understanding of politics is time, an apocalyptic time that means in a world that too often assumes we do not have time to be political Christians refuse to be hurried. Accordingly Christians do not believe that history is just one damn thing after another.[36]

That is why Yoder recommends that Christians "should be more relaxed and less compulsive about running the world" and make use of what is given us; that is, we should learn how to make fruitful use of the self-justification language of rulers who always claim to be our benefactors.[37] Democracies, at least as theories of state power, are best understood not as the rule of the people, but rather as "a most realistic way of exercising vigilant supervision over the authority entrusted to a few."[38] In the name of democracy we are still ruled by an elite whose decisions are not the result of a democratic process; but the reasons elites

33 Yoder, *The Christian Witness to the State*, p. 12. Yoder quite rightly rejects the view that such a thing as anarchy exists (p. 39). There are, of course, varying forms of governments from tyranny to constitutional democracy, but Yoder refuses to accept those that would justify any order on grounds that without such order anarchy will reign. Those that would justify "democracy" as the happy alternative between totalitarianism and anarchy need to attend to Yoder's refusal to accept such abstractions.

34 Yoder, *The Christian Witness to the State*, p. 42.

35 Yoder, *The Priestly Kingdom*, p. 165.

36 Alex Sider raises an extremely interesting criticism of this claim by pointing out that apocalyptic means having something hidden revealed. What is revealed may be about time but it is, at least for Yoder, "the Lamb that was slain is now worthy to receive honor . . . ." Accordingly Alex wonders if the point about time is not that we have all the time in the world, but "with the Resurrection time ceases to be a first principle." The question then becomes how to combine the refusal to make time a first principle with the sense of urgency in the New Testament and that with democratic practice. He notes his view requires "extended exposition." That is no doubt true, but I think the form that exposition should take is to show how Yoder's understanding of patience is possible only because of what has been revealed in the Resurrection.

37 Yoder, *The Priestly Kingdom*, p. 158.

38 Yoder, *The Christian Witness to the State*, p. 19.

give for the decisions they make may provide the means for those subject to those decisions to hold their rulers to account.[39] Democracies, particularly, if they are understood not as majority rule but as an arrangement for minority leverage can be a form of government Christians rightly prefer.[40]

The question must still be pressed, however, whether Yoder can be read as an advocate of "radical democracy." In a review of Stout's *Democracy and Tradition*, Rom Coles argues that Yoder's understanding of the church and in particular, Christian tradition, has the marks of radical democracy.[41] Coles thinks Yoder's understanding of the sinfulness of the church that requires a stance of constant reformation to be an exemplification of the kind of practice required by radical democracy. In particular Coles commends Yoder's understanding of tradition in which wholesome growth is not so much understood to be like branches from a tree but rather more like a vine. The kind of "looping back" to test current practices by the Lordship of Christ means Christian tradition is best understood as "a story of constant interruptions of organic growth in favor of pruning and a new chance for the roots."[42]

Equally important is Yoder's understanding of the "hermeneutics of peoplehood" in which agents of the community bear the responsibility to maintain an open process for the interpretation of scripture. Such a process is what is required for a community to discover judgments in common. Indeed the agents of memory, of direction, of linguistic self-consciousness, and of order and due process are the gifts a community needs to "loop back" and discover what is required if the church is to be faithful to Christ.[43] For Yoder, moreover, such agents do not necessarily come from within the church. In fact agents of the Enlightenment have taught and continue to teach the church crucial lessons about religious liberty. From Yoder's perspective it is unfortunate that critics of Christianity had to assume an anti-church stance in order to critique the Protestant dependence on governments to accomplish church reforms. As a result of this unfortunate development the contributions Christians should have made for the development of democracies were undercut.[44]

Coles, I think, is right to point to these aspects of Yoder's understanding of the church as indicators of how Yoder's understanding of the

39 Yoder's understanding of Christian political responsibility requires continuing discernment because the Christian must "speak in terms of available, or at least conceivable, alternatives." In an odd way this makes Yoder a very "realistic" political alternative just to the extent the Christian never asks the state to eliminate all evil, but rather to combat one visible sin at a time (*The Christian Witness to the State*, p. 38).

40 Yoder, *The Priestly Kingdom*, p. 167.

41 Romand Coles, "Democracy, Theology, and the Question of Excess: A Review of Jeffrey Stout's *Democracy and Tradition*," *Modern Theology*, 21, 2 (April 2005), pp. 301–22.

42 Yoder, *The Priestly Kingdom*, p. 69.

43 Yoder, *The Priestly Kingdom*, pp. 15–45.

44 Yoder, *The Priestly Kingdom*, p. 23.

church may well parallel what some mean when they commend radical democracy. Yoder's insistence that the church has the time to care for and listen to the "weakest" member is equally important for appreciating how the church might embody democratic habits. Yoder, moreover, would have no reason to object to such parallels, for as he makes clear in his essay "The Christian Case for Democracy," analogies can be drawn between the practices of the church and practices of social organizations that do not follow Jesus.[45]

Stout may well object, however, that Coles' attempt to make Yoder a representative of radical democracy fails to see that Yoder is not doing political theory nor is he describing any real politics. Rather Yoder is doing ecclesiology. However, Yoder has no reason (at least if he is right that the difference between church and world is not an ontological difference but rather a difference between agents) to think when he does ecclesiology he is not also reflecting on politics.[46] The difference between what is possible for Christians and those who do not follow Christ is that which is a duty for Christians is but a possibility for those who are not Christian. As Yoder puts it,

> the difference between Christian ethics for Christians and a Christian ethic for the state is therefore due to duality not of realms or levels, but of responses. Where God speaks to the reconciled and committed believers, the command to "be minded as it befits someone who is in Christ (Phil. 2) takes into consideration all the possibilities of the Holy Spirit and the church. When God's will is communicated to man or men in their rebellion, neither God nor His ultimate will changes, but His current demands take into account the nonbelief of the addressee (just as any truly *personal* communication encounters the addressee where he is) and therefore stay within other limits of possibility.[47]

45 Yoder, *The Priestly Kingdom*, pp. 160–6. My hunch is that Yoder in this essay, which in some ways he must have learned from Barth's attempt to develop analogies from Christian doctrine to political life, was exploring a different way from Barth to suggest how Christians might make a political witness than the middle-axiom approach he took in *The Christian Witness to the State*. The strength of Yoder's "generalizations" in contrast to Barth's analogies is that Yoder discovers analogies from the actual practices of the Christian community rather than from Barth's rather forced analogies from doctrines. Yet Yoder shares Barth's fundamental commitment to a Christological understanding of governing authority.

46 Yoder, *The Christian Witness to the State*, pp. 24–5. Particularly important for Yoder's understanding of politics is his *Body Politics* (Nashville: Discipleship Resources, 1989). Yoder always insisted that the boundaries between church and world were permeable.

47 Yoder, *The Christian Witness to the State*, p. 32. Earlier in *The Christian Witness to the State* Yoder argued that the Christian is always to address those who do not follow Jesus on the basis of the Gospel. For example Christians might address a statesman who is engaged in an activity that they think reprehensible with the presumption that if the statesman repented they would see that their office was

Coles rightly observes that Yoder's pacifism constitutes a vulnerable politics not only because it is a politics that demands a sense of what it means to follow Jesus, but also because Yoder refuses to let the church "be assimilated into what he takes to be even the most admirable currents of civic nationalism." Rather Yoder pursues "the local piece-meal approach of reciprocal translation" that Coles thinks Stout desires. Such a stand requires that Christians *must* cultivate a vulnerability in the face of contingency if they are to fulfill not only the Christian but also the democratic promise.

Of course there is still the question whether Yoder's church exists, but that very question presupposes that the unfaithful church cannot be the church. However, as I suggested above, at the heart of Yoder's understanding of the church is the confession of sin.[48] The "body politics" constitutive of the church must exist, for how else will the church have the means to confess her sinfulness.[49] The practices that constitute that body will be more or less present in this church and in that time than in other churches and other times; but just to the extent they can hold the church that exists to account, they serve not as some never realized ideal but rather as an ever present reality.

In his review of Stout, Coles suggests that Sheldon Wolin – whom Coles characterizes as "one of the most profound radical democratic theorists of the past several decades" – offers a political vision that resonates with Yoderian themes. That Coles so identifies Wolin is important for the case I am trying to make. The suggestion of Coles that Wolin's understanding of politics may resonate with Yoder's understanding of how the church must conduct her life reminded me that I had read Wolin before I read Yoder. This has led me to wonder if one of the reasons I found Yoder so compelling is he offered me an account of ecclesial existence I thought required if Wolin's criticisms of liberalism were correct. That is the thought I now want to explore.

3. WOLIN'S LESSONS

Coles observes that Wolin values many American exemplifications of radical democracy that Stout embraces – the abolitionists, the civil rights movement, feminist struggles, grassroots organizations formed against exploitive corporate-state power. Yet Coles also thinks Wolin's

incompatible with being a Christian. Yoder, however, argues that it is "improper" to begin with this conclusion or to impose this logic on the statesman before beginning the conversation. Yoder suggest, for example, that to ask a French intelligence officer in Algeria not to torture on the basis of the Geneva Convention does not cease to be the Gospel simply because he is addressed in terms of his present options (p. 25). This respect for the one addressed in Yoder is a correlate of what it means to be nonviolent.

48 In this respect the contemporary theologian who most resembles Yoder is Rowan Williams.

49 John Howard Yoder, *Body Politics: Five Practices of the Christian Community Before the Watching World* (Nashville: Discipleship Resources, 1989).

understanding of history pulls him toward a more insurgent stance than Stout seems to embrace. I think that is right; but to understand why it is so requires a return to the way Wolin tells the story of the development of political theory. Indeed I fear that the Expanded Edition of *Politics and Vision* may tempt some to read the new materials without reading or rereading the chapters that constituted the first edition. The new chapters added to the edition are so interesting, dramatic, and filled with the insights about our everyday reality that one has come to expect of Wolin (insights such as how the postmodern economy has begun to appear as a variant of totalitarianism) that one can forget those judgments and insights are possible because of Wolin's extraordinary erudition as well as how he tells the story of the nature and development of political theory.

Wolin credits Plato with the discovery of "the political," that is, he taught those who would come after him to think of political society as a coherent and interconnected whole.[50] By doing so Plato exercised the power of the imagination that is absolutely crucial for the political theorist. Through the use of exaggeration and extravagance Plato, as well as those who followed him, helped us see what might otherwise go unseen.[51] Yet Plato represents an ambiguous beginning for Wolin just to the extent Plato discovered politics as the form of rule necessary for the management of public affairs for the community, Plato also regretted the turbulence of Athenian democracy.[52] As a result, Wolin argues, Plato failed to establish an adequate understanding of the relationship of the *political* and *politics*, that is, how to gain the knowledge we need to act wisely in a context of conflict, ambiguity, and change.[53] When all is said and done, it is Wolin's judgment that Plato finally desired to defeat the contingent and incomplete art called politics through philosophy. Yet according to Wolin "the concluding note of Plato's political science is not of an unlimited arrogance that man can fashion a polity untouched by time, but of a heroism chastened by the foreknowledge of eventual defeat. It is, in Shelley's words, 'Eternity warning Time'."[54]

Time, however, is exactly what Christians brought to politics. They did so, moreover, at a time when the possibility of politics was in danger of being lost, at a time when the politics of the Greeks, a politics dependent on the polis for its intelligibility, was subsumed into empire. The polis required according to Wolin a kind of "nervous intensity" in contrast to later Stoicism, "which leisurely, and without the sense of compelling urgency, contemplated political life as it was acted out amidst a setting as spacious as the universe itself."[55] In the empire people

50 Wolin, *Politics and Vision*, pp. 30–1.
51 Wolin, *Politics and Vision*, pp. 18–19.
52 Wolin, *Politics and Vision*, pp. 38–9. Whether Wolin is right about Plato is not crucial for how I understand the importance of his setting up the problem.
53 Wolin, *Politics and Vision*, p. 40.
54 Wolin, *Politics and Vision*, p. 62.
55 Wolin, *Politics and Vision*, p. 66.

no longer had a sense of common involvement, which meant that political loyalty was centered in a common reverence for power.[56] As a result of these changes a politics of interest was created, a politics that inevitably results in bureaucracy. In our day these bureaucratic developments are underwritten by social science to make the way things are seem to be the only way things can be. It fell to Christianity to revivify political thought not by what Christians had to say about politics, but by what Christians had to say about their own lives. How Christians struggled to order their lives as well as how they came to understand that order provided a new source for ideas in political thought. Wolin observes:

> Christianity succeeded where the Hellenistic and late classical philosophies had failed, because it put forward a new and powerful ideal of community which recalled men to a life of meaningful participation. Although the nature of this community contrasted sharply with classical ideals, although its ultimate purpose lay beyond historical time and space, it contained, nevertheless, ideals of solidarity and membership that were to leave a lasting imprint, and not always for good, on the Western tradition of political thought.[57]

Wolin notes that Christians could entertain doubts about political obligation because they were members of an alternative politics. In other words, Christians mistakenly equated politics with power and then attributed to the church a more positive form of politics as an alternative to the politics of the world. As a result the church too often failed to acknowledge the power exercised in the church on its members. Equally troubling was the tendency of the church after Constantine to use secular power to support orthodoxy.

According to Wolin, however, the great gift of Christianity, associated in particular with Augustine, was quite literally the gift of time. Prior to Christianity time had been conceived in classical terms of cycles. In contrast for the Christian such an understanding of time could lead only to despair. "Christianity broke the closed circle, substituting a conception

[56] Wolin, *Politics and Vision*, p. 69.

[57] Wolin, *Politics and Vision*, p. 87. In his discussion of Augustine Wolin observes that Augustine's account of the two cities displayed a new temporal dimension for the political order, but "the new time-dimension was both unpolitical and anti-political: unpolitical in that the vital moments of meaning in time, such as Creation, Incarnation, and Redemption, lacked any essential connection with political matters; and anti-political in that political society was implicated in a series of historical events heading towards a final consummation which would mark the end of politics" (p. 112). Wolin, I think, rightly sees that Augustine thought the most fundamental needs of man no human society could satisfy, but Wolin sometimes seems to suggest that Christianity, and, in particular, the hope in the kingdom of God puts Christianity on the side of an "other worldliness," that was and is no doubt often present, but I think can be a mischaracterization of the Christian hope in the coming Kingdom.

of time as a series of irreversible movements extending along a line of progressive development. History was thus transformed into a drama of deliverance, enacted under the shadow of an apocalypse that would end historical time and, for the elect, bring a halt to suffering."[58] Wolin notes that this new time-dimension could be unpolitical and even anti-political in some forms of Christianity, but it is nonetheless the case the Christian encounter with politics revitalized a tradition of political thought.[59]

It is against this background, I think, we can appreciate Wolin's concern with recent developments in political theory and practice. For Wolin the development of political liberalism looks very much like the attempt to deny contingency – a denial that often is associated with empire – that is the heart of the political. The effect of liberal theorists such as Hobbes and Locke (an effect to be sure they might well not have welcomed) is to subject politics to the economics of interest – or perhaps better, to subject politics to economic presumptions derived from capitalism. Wolin's last chapter in the first edition of *Politics and Vision*, "The Age of Organization and the Sublimation of Politics," was his attempt to help us see how the fear of politics, a fear he finds at the heart of the liberal theorist, has resulted in a rationalism embodied in the modern corporation.

In the new edition of *Politics and Vision* the chapters on "Liberalism and the Politics of Rationalism," and "Liberal Justice and Political Democracy" are further reflections Wolin began in his analysis of the modern organization which includes the modern state. For Wolin, therefore, Rawls becomes the exemplification of the end of politics. Of course Rawls's declared purpose in writing *A Theory of Justice* was to further the interest of a democratic society; but Wolin argues that Rawls lacked any conception of politics, political power, or the role of the citizen.[60] That Rawls represents for Wolin the denial of politics is a correlate of Rawls's ahistorical account of political life.[61] From Wolin's point of view Rawls is the final outworking of the contractarian tradition which

[58] Wolin, *Politics and Vision*, p. 112. It is fascinating that Wolin's primary source for this understanding of time is Oscar Cullmann's *Christ and Time* as well as *The State in the New Testament*. Moreover Cullmann was one of John Howard Yoder's teachers. I am not trying to argue that Wolin sounds a lot like Yoder because they both learned from Cullmann, but rather to indicate that we should not be surprised that at least on some of these matters they strike some of the same notes. I must observe, however, that I do not think Wolin's characterizations of the cyclic character of time he attributes to the Greeks does justice to the variety of Greek thought. Wolin and Yoder drew on the scholarship of the day that made generalizations about Greek and Hebrew thought that are now problematic. For a critique of Yoder's use of this contrast, see Stanley Hauerwas and Alex Sider, "Introduction" to John Howard Yoder's *Preface to Theology: Christology and Theological Method* (Grand Rapids: Brazos Press, 2002), pp. 9–29.

[59] Wolin, *Politics and Vision*, p. 125. Wolin's account of Calvin repeats this theme because he thinks Calvin, in contrast to Machiavelli and Hobbes, understood that the power of a community if it is not repressive requires active membership (p. 171).

[60] Wolin, *Politics and Vision*, p. 538.

[61] Sheldon Wolin *The Presence of the Past: Essays on the State and the Constitution* (Baltimore: Johns Hopkins University Press, 1989), pp. 142–3.

was from the beginning the attempt to deny history, particularity, and difference.[62]

Such a politics, a politics without memory, is "the precise definition of the media-constituted politics which forms such an essential element in the structure of megastate power and of the structure of passivity which sustains it."[63] In the "Preface to the Expanded Edition" of *Politics and Vision* Wolin describes his evolution as a theorist as "the journey from liberalism to democracy."[64] Wolin rightly, I think, thought liberalism served at certain times as an expression of democratic hope, but the ahistorical character of liberalism failed to acknowledge we come into this world with a "birthright."[65] Birthright politics, historical politics, is composed of ambiguous historical moments, deep ambiguities, that require interpretative modes of understanding that make us able to reconnect past and present experience and in the process reconstitute our politics.[66] But memory, it turns out, is exactly what liberal arrangements are meant to repress.

The politics of memory cannot help but disrupt liberal politics, at least the kind of liberalism exemplified by Rawls, if for no other reason than that democratic politics is not first and foremost (as liberal theory seems to be) concerned with questions of legitimacy of state power. From Wolin's perspective, those who care about a political life of participation – that is, who desire to originate or foster cooperative action with others – must abjure current forms of state power. "The result of state-centeredness is a politics in which at one extreme are the experts struggling to be scientific and rational while at the other is a politics of mass irrationality, of manipulated images, controlled information, single-issue fanaticism, and pervasive fear."[67]

Wolin, therefore, recommends rather than accepting a conception of democracy that makes it indistinguishable from constitutions necessary for state power, we should accept the charge that "democracy is inherently unstable, inclined toward anarchy, and identified with

62 Wolin observes that "Civic forgetfulness is the tribute that the political unconscious pays to the power of the forgotten. A civic celebration organizes forgetfulness so as to ward off the return of the repressed, which, though overcome or rejected, is still perceived as threatening" (*The Presence of the Past*, p. 83). I think it is not a stretch to interpret Wolin's account of Rawls as a contemporary form of Stoicism correlative to the politics of empire.

63 Wolin, *The Presence of the Past*, p. 184.

64 Wolin, *Politics and Vision*, p. XV.

65 Wolin's chapter "Contract and Birthright" in *The Presence of the Past* is his classic statement of this contrast (pp. 137–50). Wolin observes "the birthright that we have made over to our Jacobs is our politicalness. By politicalness I mean our capacity for developing into beings who know and value what it means to participate in and be responsible for the care and improvement of our common and collective life. To be political is not identical with being part of government or being associated with a political party. These are structured roles, and typically they are highly bureaucratized. For these reason, they are opposed to the authentically political" (p. 139).

66 Wolin, *The Presence of the Past*, p. 111.

67 Wolin, *The Presence of the Past*, p. 149.

revolution. ... This democracy might be summed up as the idea and practice of rational disorganization."[68] Wolin makes this recommendation because he is convinced that democracy in the late modern world cannot be a complete political system, but rather democracy can only succeed temporarily as a witness to a political mode of existence that exists through memory.[69] I think it is not unreasonable to suggest that radical democracy is Wolin's name for the kind of interruption he thinks the church represented in the Roman Empire.[70]

Wolin does not believe our situation is at all hopeless. Indeed he thinks we have time to draw on our ability to tend to one another when we are sick or when the garden needs weeding. To so tend requires the development of skills through which our tending is tempered by "a concern for objects whose nature requires that they be treated as historical and biographical beings. The beings are such as to need regular attention from someone who is concerned about their well-being and sensitive to their needs."[71] Such tending politically should direct our attention to practices constituted by habits of competence and skill that are routinely required if things that matter to us are to be taken care of.

If that is "radical democracy," then I think I can claim to be a radical democrat. Indeed I should like to think that the attention and reflection I have developed concerning the place of those called the mentally handicapped represents my most determinative political reflections. A community that has the time and can take the time, the patience, to be constituted by practices represented by those "slower" than most of us is a community that may provide an alternative to the politics of speed that currently shapes our lives.

4. RETURNING TO STOUT

Stout may well object that I have made my identification with radical democracy far too easy by concentrating on Wolin's criticism of liberalism and his alternative understanding of radical democracy as the

68 Sheldon Wolin, "Norm and Form: The Constitutionalizing of Democracy," in *Athenian Political Thought and the Reconstruction of American Democracy*, edited by Peter Euben, John Wallach, and Josiah Ober (Ithaca: Cornell University Press, 1994), p. 37.

69 Wolin, "Norm and Form: The Constitutionalizing of Democracy," pp. 54–5.

70 Wolin suggests that democracy should best be understood as about forms rather than *a* form of constitution. That is, democracy names a response to felt grievances of needs on the part of those whose main preoccupation – an occupation that demands time and energy – is to scratch out a decent existence. Small scale is the only scale commensurate with the kind of power democracy is capable of mobilizing. "The power of democratic politics lies in the multiplicity of modern sites disposed among local governments and institutions under local control (schools, community health services, police and fire protection, recreational, cultural institutions, property taxes) and in the ingenuity of ordinary people in inventing temporary forms to meet their needs" (*Politics and Visions*, p. 603). I cannot help but think such an account of politics would be very appealing to Yoder.

71 Wolin, *The Presence of the Past*, p. 89.

recovery of a genuine politics. No doubt he would want to raise questions about Wolin's understanding of how we have got to where we have got as well as the adequacy of Wolin's account of where we are. I am obviously quite persuaded by the overall analysis Wolin provides. That I am so persuaded may be because his analysis seems to suggest my kind of Christianity and church are politically significant. If that is so, I am not sure that is a failure. But at least I hope I have made clear why I think John Howard Yoder supplies us with an account of a politics that is not only hopeful but hopefully is not only for Christians but will prove attractive for anyone.[72]

[72] I am indebted to Jonathan Tran, Charlie Collier, and Alex Sider for their criticisms of this paper.

11

The State of the Secular: Theology, Prayer, and the University

No movement that aspires to more than mere belief or inconsequential talk in public can remain indifferent to state power in a secular world.

Talal Asad[1]

1. SOMEWHERE BETWEEN NOTRE DAME AND DUKE

I am honored to be asked by the Catholic Theological Society to address you on the topic, "Dangers and Promise in the Encounter of Theology and the Secular Intellectual World." I am also aware I am in a precarious position. I am, after all, a "sectarian, fideistic, tribalist," or at least I have been so described by James Gustafson in an address to the Catholic Theological Society in 1984.[2] More recently Gustafson has identified me, along with Peter Ochs and John Milbank, as a representative of a "rejection-strategy" against secular learning and, in particular, the sciences.[3] In his book, *Democracy and Tradition*, Jeff Stout seems to

1 Talal Asad, *Formations of the Secular: Christianity, Islam, Modernity* (Stanford: Stanford University Press, 2003), p. 200.

2 Gustafson's address was published as "The Sectarian Temptation: Reflections on Theology, the Church, and the University," in the *Proceedings of the Catholic Theological Society*, 40 (1985), pp. 83–94. For my response see the "Introduction" to my book, *Christian Existence Today: Essays on Church, World, and Living in Between* (Grand Rapids: Brazos Press, 2001), pp. 1–19. *Christian Existence Today* was originally published in 1988. For a good discussion of Gustafson's criticism and my response see Gavin D'Costa, *Theology in the Public Square: Church, Academy, and Nation* (Oxford: Blackwell Publishing, 2005), pp. 77–87.

3 James Gustafson, *An Examined Faith: The Grace of Self-Doubt* (Minneapolis: Fortress Press, 2004), pp. 37–44. Gustafson bases his case on the description given to the series, "Radical Traditions: Theology in a Postcritical Key," that Peter Ochs and I edit. Gustafson is quite critical of our disavowal of "modernist" reading habits, but it seems odd for him to criticize us for rejecting secular intellectual sources because it was exactly those sources that taught us to be critical of "modernism." I also find it quite odd that Gustafson, who criticizes us for not exercising appropriate scholarly care toward those we criticize, has no difficulty criticizing Peter and me without reading what we write.

support Gustafson's charge by suggesting that I have rejected "liberalism" as a "secularist ideology that masks a discriminatory program for policing what religious people can say in public."[4]

This makes it all the more remarkable that you have asked me to address you and, in particular, on this topic. Of course you may have done so in an anthropological mode, that is, you simply want to confirm by observation that I am a "sectarian, fidiestic, tribalist" who assumes that the "secular" must be rejected in the name of theology. If, however, this is an anthropological exercise you must be careful because anthropologists have become so sensitive about the ethical issues raised by their study of "the other" they now spend most of their time studying other anthropologists.

I am, moreover, aware that I am at the Catholic Theological Society. Will what I have to say about the "secular intellectual world" confirm the opinion many of you may have that I do not have an adequate account of "the natural?" Is my refusal to begin Christian ethics with a robust account of natural law a failure to understand that grace does not destroy nature but rather grace perfects and completes nature? Or do my doubts about natural theology in *With the Grain of the Universe* suggest that I must disavow what we may learn about God from other sources?[5] I mention these matters because they bear on the argument I will develop below: namely, that the identification of natural law with secular reason in the attempt to insure a common moral discourse can result in a failure to recognize the challenge presented by the development of the modern state.[6]

4 Jeffrey Stout, *Democracy and Tradition* (Princeton: Princeton University Press, 2004), p. 76. I confess when I read this sentence in Stout's book I was a bit surprised because I could not remember using "secular" as a description of "liberalism." Stout quite rightly notes that Rawls, for example, particularly after *Political Liberalism* insists that his account of public reason is not equivalent to secular reason and secular values. In particular see Rawls, "The Idea of Public Reason Revisited," in *The Law of Peoples* (Cambridge: Harvard University Press, 1999), pp. 143, 148. But I cannot find anywhere where I suggested that Rawls's account of reason is secular. "Secular" is not a word I often use. I did, however, discover in a footnote in *Dispatches From the Front: Theological Engagements with the Secular* (Durham: Duke University Press, 1994) that I had disavowed having any "theory" of the secular. Yet in the same footnote I commended Milbank's account of the secular which may have given Stout the impression I think liberalism to be a "secular ideology." In spite of my commendation of Milbank's account, an account I continue to find instructive, I remain hesitant to underwrite Weberian accounts of the "secular." As I hope this paper makes clear, secular as a description is primarily an account of modern political arrangements.

5 Stanley Hauerwas, *With the Grain of the Universe: The Church's Witness and Natural Theology* (Grand Rapids: Brazos Press, 2001).

6 John Howard Yoder observed that "the notion of 'nature' in medieval Catholic thought was not the modern one of knowing how to talk with outsiders. The medieval concept of natural law was developed in a world where there were no non-Christians present in the neighborhood, and no non-theists in the known world that needing to be convinced ... it (natural law) was to distinguish the things that everyone (including Christians) need to obey from those elements of divine moral guidance from Scripture which can be left to the Hebrews" (*The Priestly Kingdom: Social Ethics as Gospel* (Notre Dame: University of Notre Dame Press, 2001), p. 42).

I do not, of course, believe that I have an inadequate account of the "natural," natural law, or natural theology. Some may doubt whether I have developed a robust constructive account of natural law, but I have often argued that at the very least we can discover what it means to be a creature through negative results.[7] My difficulty with natural law is not whether or not such a law is constitutive of our existence. Rather my difficulty is with the presumption of some defenders of natural law that natural law is rational in contrast to revelation. In other words, my criticism of the attempt to make natural law a rational bedrock for ethics reflects my doubts in general about the foundationalist epistemological enterprise.[8]

My refusal to "do" epistemology I learned from philosophers such as Wittgenstein, Anscombe, and MacIntyre. That I have tried to do theology in a manner that reflects what I learned from them makes the charge that I "reject" what can be learned from "secular sources" seem quite odd to me. Some, of course, may question whether Wittgenstein, Anscombe, and MacIntyre are secular thinkers. Anscombe and MacIntyre are Roman Catholics, but MacIntyre insists that his philosophy does not in any way depend on his theological convictions.[9]

7 See, for example, my chapter, "Natural Law, Tragedy, and Theological Ethics," in my book, *Truthfulness and Tragedy: Further Investigations into Christian Ethics* (Notre Dame: University of Notre Dame Press, 1977), pp. 57–70. I would argue the case quite differently today, but that essay made clear I did not think it possible to ever leave natural law behind. By "negative results" I mean that we discover how we have gone wrong from the reasons we have given to hide from ourselves how we have gone wrong. See my essays, "A Story-Formed Community: Reflections on Watership Down," in *A Community of Character: Toward a Constructive Christian Social Ethics* (Notre Dame: University of Notre Dame Press, 1981), pp. 9–35 and "The Truth About God: The Decalogue as Condition for Truthful Speech," in *Sanctify Them in the Truth: Holiness Exemplified* (Nashville: Abingdon, 1998), pp. 37–9.

8 See, for example, my *The Peaceable Kingdom: A Primer in Christian Ethics* (Notre Dame: University of Notre Dame Press, 1983), pp. 64–71. In a recent dissertation written at the University of Virginia entitled *Agency and Practical Reason: The Critique of Modern Moral Theory from Anscombe and Hauerwas*, Mark Ryan puts the matter well noting that I refuse to dichotomize reason and revelation, seeing "no need to negate (abstract from) the particular and history-like character of scriptural revelation in order to be rational. Rather abstractions like 'nature' should be considered short-hand reminders that help us retell the story of how and why God created the universe – they are, that is, pragmatic tools that help the community reconstitute the larger narrative. Abstract concepts like 'nature' and 'grace,' by their nature, 'require narrative display for their intelligibility' " (p. 150).

9 In response to a question whether his more recent philosophical positions conceal a reassertion of Christianity, MacIntyre says, "It is false, both biographically and with respect to the structure of my beliefs. What I now believe philosophically I came to believe very largely before I reacknowledged the truth of Catholic Christianity. And I was only able to respond to the teachings of the Church because I had already learned from Aristotelianism both the nature of the mistakes involved in my earlier rejection of Christianity, and how to understand aright the relation of philosophical argument to theological inquiry. My philosophy, like many other Aristotelians, is theistic; but it is as secular in its content as any other" (*The MacIntyre Reader*, edited by Kelvin Knight (Notre Dame: University of Notre Dame Press, 1998), pp. 265–6). I must

No philosopher, moreover, has been more important to me than Aristotle. Of course it may be a mistake to identify Aristotle as a representative of a "secular intellectual world." To say that Aristotle represents the secular is no more informative than the claim he was a pagan. I assume both designations mean he was not a Christian. He obviously was not a Christian, but then that turns out not to be very interesting.

Which raises the complex problem of what "secular" might mean in the description "secular intellectual world." As much as possible I hope only to touch on the controversies surrounding the secularization thesis in order to address the assigned topic. In general I do think that the process of differentiation for the development of modern societies is extremely important for understanding the world in which we live, but I have no idea if it is helpful to call that process "secularization" because the developments associated with a rationalized and differentiated society means such social orders are no longer enchanted.[10] It is by no means clear, moreover, why Christians would have a stake in an "enchanted world." As Charles Taylor observes the "secular" is itself a Christian term used to designate:

---

confess that I am not sure what MacIntyre means by describing the content of his philosophy as secular. I assume he means that his philosophical arguments in no way assume "theism" as necessary for their validity. In his early book, *Secularization and Moral Change* (Oxford: Oxford University Press, 1967), MacIntyre used "secularization" to mean transition from beliefs, activities, and institutions presuming beliefs of a Christian kind to beliefs, activities, and institutions of an atheistic kind (pp. 7–8). MacIntyre argues in *Secularization and Moral Change* that the secularization of English society was not due to the decline of religion, but rather lay in the development of urbanization and institutionalization that made Christianity unintelligible to itself. As he puts it, "Christianity when confronted with the secular life of the post-Industrial Revolution society has in fact found it impossible to lend meaning to life or to enable people to understand and find justification for living out its characteristic forms. It is rather that Christianity has been shaped and reshaped by the forces of modern secular life. Thus insofar as the claims of Christianity are themselves social, so far the claims of Christianity are impugned by the actual history of modern society" (p. 66). Accordingly, Christianity has found it no longer valuable to incarnate itself in social life and to give them justification they would otherwise lack. MacIntyre's analysis obviously draws upon his Marxism – a Marxism that continues to inform his (and my) work and in particular the argument of this chapter.

10 For an extremely clear and informative account of the debate surrounding the secularization theories see Christian Smith's "Introduction" to the volume he edited, *The Secular Revolution: Power, Interests, and Conflict in the Secularization of American Public Life* (Berkeley: University of California Press, 2003), pp. 1–96. Smith argues quite convincingly that "secularization" was not an inevitable process, but rather the determined result of elites who wished to free themselves and the world in which they found themselves from religious authority. Clearly the often made claim that secularization means a decline of religious belief seems empirically false, but the "belief" that continues to flourish may not recognize that it has been secularized just to the extent it is now "belief." Saba Mahmood explains, "to say that a society is secular does not mean that 'religion' is banished from its politics, law, and forms of association. Rather, religion is admitted into these domains on the condition that it take particular forms; when it departs from these forms it confronts a set of regulatory barriers. The banning of the veil as the proper form of attire for

> the time of ordinary historical succession, which the human race lives through the Fall and the Parousia. This time was interwoven with higher times, different modes of what is sometimes called "eternity," the time of Ideas, or of the Origin, or of God. Human beings were seen as living in all these times, but certain acts, or lives, or institutions, or social forms could be seen as more thoroughly directed, towards one or another. Government was more "in the saeculum" by contrast with the Church, for instance. The state was the "secular arm." A similar point could be expressed by contrasting the "temporal" and the "spiritual" or, in another context, ordinary parish clergy, ministering to people who were very much embedded in the world and history, were called "secular" to distinguish them from the religious orders or "regular clergy."[11]

In short, Christians created a differentiated world, to be sure one quite different than the one in which we now live, but nonetheless a world that bears some relation to its origin in Christianity.

John Milbank's famous line, "once, there was no 'secular',"[12] has led some to attribute to him a completely negative judgment about the "secular." But Milbank quite clearly assumes Taylor is right to remind us that there is a meaning of the secular that Christians think is intrinsic to our understanding of God. The "secular" Milbank thinks once did not exist, the secular he thinks has had such disastrous consequences, is one he associates with the displacement of the Christian secular by a quite different secular in service to modern state power.[13] As will become clear I am sympathetic with many of Milbank's criticisms of the "new science of politics," but I believe Christians have no reason to mourn the loss of Constantinianism. Indeed that loss has made it possible for Christians to reclaim theology as a free science in service to a free church.

---

girls and women in Turkey and France is a case in point" ("Feminist Theory, Embodiment, and the Docile Agent: Some Reflections on Egyptian Islamic Revival," *Cultural Anthropology*, 16, 2 (2001), p. 226). Of course one of the "forms" is that each tradition must understand itself as a "religion."

11 Charles Taylor, "Modes of Secularism," in *Secularism and its Critics*, edited by Rajeev Bhargava (Delhi: Oxford University Press, 1998), p. 32. Robert Marcus argues that only Christianity could produce an understanding of the "secular" by which he means what Christians can share with non-Christians (*Christianity and the Secular* (Notre Dame: University of Notre Dame Press, 2006), p. 6). I regret Marcus's book was available to me only after I finished this paper. I am grateful, however, that he ends his book suggesting the positions I (and Yoder) hold Augustine might well support.

12 John Milbank, *Theology and Social Theory*, Second Edition (Oxford: Blackwell Publishing, 2006), p. 9.

13 Milbank provides a wonderfully clear account of the difference between the Christian secular and the secular of the modern in his "The Gift of Ruling: Secularization and Political Authority," *New Blackfriars*, 85, 996 (March 2004), pp. 212–38. Milbank argues against Pierre Manent that the church never assumed the secular was not open to the Christian shaping seeking to infuse secular practices of warfare,

By secular I mean the name given to that time, and the correlative politics, in which time is no longer, as Taylor suggests, interwoven with a higher time. I will try to show how such a time has been given a form of inevitability by the development of the modern state. The agent of legitimation of such a time and politics, however, has been the university and, in particular, the knowledges that constitute the curriculums of the university. That universities are formed to legitimate secular state power I think is true irrespective of whether the university is Christian or secular. Indeed I think that Christian theology may be more freely practiced in secular institutions. I loved teaching at the University of Notre Dame but I now realize I am more free to be a theologian at Duke, a very secular institution, than I was at Notre Dame. No one at Duke imagines that theology is a crucial subject for the future of the university or the society the university serves. At Notre Dame I was part of a mini-Constantinian establishment which made it hard to avoid the thought that theology was the critical discipline for the future of civilization – a very constraining assumption.

At least at Duke I am not part of a Constantinian project that is Christian, but that does not mean Duke does not represent a form of Constantinianism: a remark I must now try to explain by suggesting how the secular in our time has assumed a Constantinian form. By developing that claim I hope to show how the danger presented by the secular intellectual disciplines in the modern university lies in their power to produce and reproduce the knowledges that make the way things are seem inevitable. That is not a problem, moreover, only for non-theological disciplines, because I hope to show that theology in modernity is also a secular discipline. So the danger is not "out there" in the secular disciplines but is internal to theology itself. Just to the extent theology allowed itself to be one discipline among the disciplines we lost the resource necessary to challenge the legitimating function of secular knowledges in service to the state.

2. THE SECULAR AS STATE FORMATION

What could I possibly mean by suggesting that the secular has become a form of Constantinianism in modernity? To answer that question I will draw on the work of John Howard Yoder, Charles Taylor, Talal Asad, and Gavin D'Costa. By putting them into conversation I hope to show the secular names an account of time crucial for the legitimation of the modern state. Just to the extent Christians have confused our time, church time, with state time we have failed to provide an alternative to a world, and the knowledges that are constitutive of that world, which is increasingly unable to make sense of itself.

---

punishment, and trade with the exercise of mercy and forbearance (p. 216). Milbank thinks the development of modern secularization was the result of the theological failure to maintain that all existence is borrowed, that is, a gift. As a result a positivist and formulist theology of divine power invented liberalism – a secular lacking any extra-human or extra-natural norm.

In an extremely important but unfortunately overlooked essay, "Christ, the Hope of the World," John Howard Yoder develops a fascinating account of different forms of Constantinianism that suggests how the secular has now become a form of Constantinianism. For many the very mention of "Constantinianism" is reason not to take Yoder seriously on the presumption that he is wrong to condemn Constantine's favoring of Christianity. Yoder, however, is quite well aware of the historical complexities that surrounded the legalization of Christianity in the Roman Empire.[14] For Yoder the primary challenge Constantinianism presented for Christians was theological. Under the spell of Constantine, Christians begin to lose their eschatological conviction that we simultaneously live in two times. To live in two times does not mean, as is often put, that Christians live between times, but rather that we live in two times that can be distinguished only if there is a church whose life is governed by the reality of the new age. For the world to know that the world's time is not the church's time requires that how Christians live and think will be distinctive.[15]

These eschatological convictions constitute a politics exemplified, Yoder argues, by the presumption throughout the New Testament that the political task of the church was first and foremost to faithfully witness to the reality of the Lordship of Christ. Through such faithfulness the church understood her role, a deceptively difficult role, to be nothing less than to call the powers to modesty. Modesty requires, however, that Christians resist the temptation to legitimate the structures the New Testament identifies as the "powers."[16] Such powers do not need legitimating. Rather in order to be and remain modest these structures require a people capable of saying "no" when those who rule do so in a manner that goes beyond the limited task they have been given.[17]

[14] For a good critique of the language of declension to describe Constantine's support of the church see Daniel Williams, "Constantine and the 'Fall' of the Church," in *Christian Origins: Theology, Rhetoric, and Community*, edited by Lewis Ayers and Gareth Jones (London: Routledge, 1998), pp. 117–36. Williams points out that Denny Weaver's claim that Christians in the post-Constantinian church thought it more important to preserve the empire than to live by the teachings of Jesus is a "fantastic generalization." The sermons of Augustine on I John are sufficient to show Weaver is deeply mistaken (p. 122).

[15] John Howard Yoder, *The Christian Witness to the State* (Scottdale, PA: Herald Press, 2002), pp. 8–13.

[16] John Howard Yoder, "Christ, the Hope of the World," in his *The Original Revolution*, with a new Foreword by Mark Thiessen Nation (Scottdale, PA: Herald Press, 2003), p. 141. The summary of Yoder's account of the various forms of Constantinianism can be found on pp. 141–5 of *The Original Revolution*.

[17] The oft made criticism that Yoder justifies leaving the state to its own devices ignores Yoder's argument that the "church knows why the state exists – knows, in fact, better than the state itself – and this understanding provides both the justification for her speaking and the standards which she will apply in evaluating the way in which the authorities exercise their function" (*The Christian Witness to the State* (Newton, KS: Faith and Life Press, 1964), p. 16).

Constantinianism is the name Yoder gives to the time when Christians confused the time inaugurated by the resurrection of Jesus with the time of the old age. The identification of the church with the world means that the eschatological character of the Gospel is now domesticated in the interest of promoting an ethic that is workable for anyone.[18] Of course the Christian ethic is one Christians rightly think anyone can live by being redeemed, but Christians confused that understanding of the universal ethic with the presumption that the Christian way of life is open to anyone even if they are not a member of the church.

Yoder, however, commends the Constantinianism of Rome just to the extent the identification of the church with the Roman Empire gave expression to the appropriate Christian conviction that the God Christians worship is the God of all people. Accordingly the Roman church could think of herself as a servant of all humankind.[19] However, with the breakup of the Roman Empire a new phase of unity of the church and world developed, a neo-Constantinianism, in which the church understood herself no longer to be a servant of all people but was now concerned with maintaining the unity of a particular society.

The political revolutions that swept the world from 1776 to 1848 inaugurated a "secularization" in which the identification of the church with a particular society could no longer be taken for granted. Yoder notes this development could take quite diverse forms exemplified by the contrast between America and Sweden. In America there was a legal separation between church and state, but the people remained convinced there exists a close connection between church and society. In Sweden the secularization process took the form of state support of the church without the popular support of the people. Different though they are, these arrangements have in common the secularization of the Constantinian dream that the church can give her blessing to the nation in a manner that church and government mutually support one another.

Yoder calls this stage neo-neo-Constantinianism to indicate that this development represents the further weakening of the church in relation to the world just to the extent the church becomes subservient to *a* state. Soon some thinkers came forward, however, explicitly opposed

[18] John Howard Yoder, *The Christian Witness to the State* (Newton, KS: Faith and Life Press, 1964), p. 28. That Christian ethics is for Christians does not mean that Christians believe that how they live is not a possibility for anyone. Rather it means that the possibility to live as a disciple of Christ requires the work of the Holy Spirit, but that work is not restricted to the church.

[19] Of course that is not quite true just to the extent that Christians now thought it more important to kill the barbarians rather than convert them. Yoder observes that "Constantine did not really rule the entire world, which means it was necessary to write off any enemies to the north, east, and south to say nothing of the rest of the world" (*The Original Revolution*, p. 149). Yoder notes, however, that the church even in the Middle Ages still was able to take a critical stance toward those in power. "The ecclesiastical hierarchy had a power base and a self-understanding which enabled independent moral judgment. An emperor or a prince could really be forced to listen by the ban or interdict" (*The Original Revolution*, p. 150).

to any religious support of culture or state. In response religious thinkers, anxious that the church not lose her influence, argued that Christians must make common cause with "secular" governments preferring structured neutrality to any religious preference the nation might choose. They often did so appealing to natural law grounds as a basis to secure a common morality to legitimate government coercion. Yoder calls the alliance of the church with post-religious secularism neo-neo-neo-Constantinianism.

This brings us to the present in which the church tries to apply the habits of Constantinianism to the future. Convinced that the future is to be identified with some particular cause or system, Christians seek to take sides with the new before the old order collapses. Thus Christians identify with political revolutions in the hope they will be on the winning side of history. Yoder calls the attempt to approve an order before it exists, neo-neo-neo-neo-Constantinianism. This last development makes explicit what all these efforts to defend the cause of the church before the bar of secular reason have in common: that the true meaning of history, the locus of salvation, is in the cosmos and only in the church to the extent the church's identity is absorbed by the wider world.[20] Constantinianism is, therefore, to be identified by the convictions that the meaning of history lies outside the church whose agent is now the state. The eschatological tension between the two aeons is subordinated to a progressive view of history for which the only time available is that produced by state agency.

Yoder's narrative, a narrative that obviously begs for detailed development and qualification, has the great virtue of helping us see that how Christians understand and evaluate the development of the secular, and in particular the secular state, depends on their ecclesiology. His account, moreover, of the mutations of Constantinianism suggests that it may well be that the most determinative forms of Constantinianism in our day are secular just to the extent that secular ideologies now legitimate state formation. The habits that now constitute the secular imagination are so imbedded in how Christians understand the world we no longer have the ability to recognize the power they have over us.[21]

20 For Yoder "the ultimate meaning of history is to be found in the work of the church. The victory of the Lamb through His death seals the victory of the church" (*The Original Revolution: Essays on Christian Pacifism* (Scottdale, PA: Herald Press, 2003), p. 64). Therefore Yoder claims in *The Christian Witness to the State*, "the church is not fundamentally a source of moral stimulus to encourage the development of a better society – though a faithful church should also have this effect – it is for the sake of the church's own work that society continues to function" (p. 13).

21 Asad observes, "because the secular is so much part of our modern life, it is not easy to grasp it directly. I think it is best pursued through its shadows, as it were" (*Formations of the Secular*, p. 16). See, for example, Asad's account of the unstable character of "the religious" and "the secular" in *Power of the Secular Modern: Talal Asad and His Interlocutors*, edited by David Scott and Charles Horschkind (Stanford: Stanford University Press, 2006), pp. 297–9. For an even more complex, and I should say compelling, account of the ambiguous relation between secularization and

That power, I think, is exemplified by the assumption that time qua time names a duration that precedes the Gospel. As a result time is ontologically presumed to name the ground on which the Christian narrative of redemption occurs. Yet, as Jonathan Tran argues, Christians "conceptualize time through the narrative called 'Gospel;' for Christians 'time' is another way of saying 'the story goes this way.' There is no time qua time – no past, present, future as such – but rather temporal existence emanating from our narratival habits. We talk about past, present, future because our lives as stories are timeful; in other words, our stories become stories as they unfold within the larger story of God's redemption of all things."[22] Secular names the displacement of that story by the story of the state.[23]

Taylor provides an account of the secular that substantiates this understanding of the secular as a form of Constantinianism. Drawing on Benedict Anderson's account of the development of the modern nation-state as an "imagined community," Taylor argues that the inescapability of secularism "flows from the nature of the modern state. More particularly the nature of the democratic state."[24] According to Taylor there are two important features to this modern imaginary. The first involves a shift from a hierarchical mediated society to a horizontally understood society in which citizens are assumed to have direct access to those in power. Thus people conceive of themselves as participating directly in nationwide discussions as well as entering contractual relations in market economies on an equal footing.[25]

The second crucial feature of the modern imaginary, in contrast to the pre-modern state, is that an attempt to legitimate trans-local entities is no longer thought to require grounding in anything higher than common action in secular time. Taylor associates this development with social contract theories of the political which create the fiction that a people can be created out of a state of nature in which an appeal to a founding moment is no longer thought necessary. Now the "idea is invoked that a

---

the religious tradition that has allegedly been left behind see Vincent Pecora, *Secularization and Cultural Criticism: Religion, Nation, and Modernity* (Chicago: University of Chicago Press, 2006). Pecora quite forcefully argues against static and totalizing concepts of secularization by showing how advocates of secularization cannot, nor should they want to, rid themselves of various religious a prioris.

22 Jonathan Tran, "In the Far Country: Time, Eternity, and Memory After the Vietnam War" (Ph.D. Dissertation, Duke University, Durham, NC, 2006), p. 4.

23 Bruce Lincoln provides an illuminating account of what he characterizes as the "unresolved tension between the secularizing character of the modern state, and the potentially religious character of the nation," in his *Holy Terrors: Thinking about Religion After September 11* (Chicago: University of Chicago Press, 2003), p. 63.

24 Taylor, "The Secular Imperative," p. 38.

25 Taylor, "The Secular Imperative," pp. 39–40. Taylor observes that these modes of imagined direct access are linked to modern equality and individualism through creating uniformity. Once the necessity of mediation is reduced the individual has a growing self-consciousness as an individual. But to be an individual does not mean ceasing to belong, but rather "imagining one-self as belonging to ever wider and more impersonal entities: the state, the movement, the community of humankind" (p. 40).

people, or as it was also called at the time, a 'nation', can exist prior to and independently of its political Constitution, so that this people can give itself its own Constitution by its own free action in secular time."[26]

Talal Asad, commenting on Taylor's account of the development of the modern state, observes that such states have to make citizenship the primary principle of identity in order to transcend the differences of class, gender, and religion by replacing conflicting perspectives with a unifying experience. According to Asad,

> in an important sense, this transcendent mediation is secularism. Secularism is not simply an intellectual answer to a question about enduring social peace and toleration. It is an enactment by which a political medium (representation of citizenship) redefines and transcends particular and differentiating practices of the self that are articulated through class, gender, and religion.[27]

Asad argues that the secular state enacts a quite particular understanding of time. Such states depend on a homogenized time so that state bureaucracies and market dealings can be administered efficiently. Through homogeneous time speed and direction can be plotted with the precision necessary to legitimate the state as the guarantor of services.[28] Given this view of time what it means to be human is to be a

> self-conscious maker of History (in which calendrical time provides a measure and direction for human events) and as the unshakable foundation of universally valid knowledge about nature and society. The human agent is now responsible – answerable – not only for acts he or she has performed or refrained from performing. Responsibility is now held for

[26] Taylor, "The Secular Imperative," p. 41.

[27] Talal Asad, *Formations of the Secular*, p. 5. Asad argues that " 'the secular' should not be thought of as the space in which real human life gradually emancipates itself from the controlling power of 'religion' and thus achieves the latter's relocation. It is this assumption that allows us to think of religion as 'infecting' the secular domain or as replicating within it the structure of theological concepts. The concept of 'the secular' today is part of a doctrine called secularism. Secularism doesn't simply insist that religious practice and belief be confined to a space where they cannot threaten political stability or the liberties of 'free-thinking' citizens. Secularism builds on a particular conception of the world ('natural' and 'social') and of the problems generated by that world" (pp. 191–2). In like manner William Connolly argues that Kant's rational religion shares much with the "dogmatic" ecclesiology it sought to displace in his *Why I Am Not a Secularist* (Minneapolis: University of Minnesota Press, 1999), p. 32.

[28] Asad, *Formations of the Secular*, p. 5. In a response to Connolly's article, "Europe: A Minor Tradition," in *Power of the Secular Modern*, Asad observes in *Formations*, "I stressed that people, even in modern societies, live in multiple temporalities, and that a central aspect of secularism as a commanding doctrine is precisely its attempt to transcend such pluralities through the homogenous time of capital" (p. 223).

> events he or she was unaware of – or falsely conscious of... Chance is not considered to be tamable. The world is disenchanted.[29]

A political ethic peculiar to this sense of space and time is also required. Such an ethic, which Taylor thinks exemplified by Rawls's understanding of the necessity of overlapping consensus, does not try to exhaust the common identity by which people are held together.[30] But a distinction is required between private and public reason that demands that "religion" be placed in the former because the secular is identified by the public.[31] Accordingly Taylor argues that Rawls's account of overlapping consensus represents, in spite of Rawls's disavowal of secularism, a commitment to an independent ethic of autonomy that has

29 Asad, *Formations of the Secular*, pp. 192–3. For an account of how such a view of agency must be questioned in order to understand an Islamic women's movement in Egypt see Saba Mahmood, *Politics of Piety: The Islamic Revival and the Feminist Subject* (Princeton: Princeton University Press, 2005). It is often assumed that liberal accounts of agency are incompatible with the need of the modern democratic state to create a common identity through encouraging the growth of patriotism. Yet Taylor suggests that the willingness to sacrifice oneself for the state is made all the more powerful just to the extent the citizen is said to make such a commitment freely ("Modes of Secularization," p. 44). Asad's use of "disenchanted" does not mean he accepts Weber's understanding of secularization. Rather he understands, as the quote above suggests, secularism itself is a form of enchantment. In like manner, those who appeal to the staying power of religion to counter the thesis that religion will disappear given the development of secular societies fail to see that the "religion" that seems so vital has been transformed by the secular. Milbank notes that the "recrudescence of intolerant religion, this is not a problem that liberalism can resolve, but rather a problem that liberalism tends to engender" ("The Gifts of Ruling," p. 235). For a compelling account of the secular as not so much the refusal of theology and liturgy but rather as a parasitical and perverse reformulation liturgy see Eugene McCarraher, "The Enchantment of Mammon: Notes Toward a Theological History of Capitalism," *Modern Theology*, 21, 3 (July, 2005), pp. 429–61. McCarraher observes that a theological critique of "disenchantment" can avoid crude opposition between secular and sacred by suggesting those who claim to disenchant matter – goods by shifting faith in divine power to the transforming property of commodities (p. 450).

30 Taylor, "The Secular Imperative," pp. 48–53.

31 Asad, *Formations of the Secular*, p. 8. William Connolly puts this well in his "Europe: A Minor Tradition," noting that "the inner connection between Christianity and Europe today is not that all Christians demand common belief in Christianity as a condition of citizenship – though too many still do; rather it resides in the demand, growing out of the Christian Enlightenment, to disconnect the expression of religious belief from participation in embodied practices, so that it becomes possible to imagine a world in which everyone is a citizen because religious belief is relegated to the private realm and the interior of the self" (*Powers of the Secular Modern*, p. 78). Saba Mahmood argues, "contrary to the normative understanding of secularism today, its force seems to reside not in neutralizing the space of politics from religion but in producing a particular kind of religious subject who is compatible with the rationality and exercise of liberal political rule. In the current moment of empire, this aspect of secularism is most evident in the ambitious campaign the U.S. government has undertaken to reform and reshape Islam" ("Secularism, Hermeneutics, and Empire: Theopolitics of Islamic Reformation," *Political Culture*, 18, 2, p. 323).

no place for religious convictions.[32] Yet Taylor also suggests that Rawls's conception of overlapping consensus properly modified, that is, freed from Rawls's underlying justifications, is the best alternative we have.[33]

Jeffrey Stout's account of secular reason seems to be exactly the kind of modification of secular reason Taylor suggests we need. According to Stout the mark of secularization is "the fact that participants in a given discursive practice are not in a position to take for granted that their interlocutors are making the same assumptions they are."[34] Stout's understanding of public reason, therefore, seems more capacious than Rawls's "Proviso," but given Taylor's and Asad's account of the secular, it is hard to avoid the conclusion that even Stout's modest understanding of secular reason can slide inexorably towards service to the state. For example Stout says that he invites his readers to adopt the point of view of a citizen who is

> someone who accepts some measure of responsibility for the condition of society and, in particular, for the political arrangements it makes for itself. To adopt this point of view is to participate in a living moral tradition of one's people, understood as a civic nation. It is the task of public philosophy, as I understand it, to articulate the ethical inheritance of the people for the people while subjecting it to critical scrutiny.[35]

32 Taylor argues that the origin of the modern notion of secularism was to find an alternative to the wars of religion. Some rules of peace needed to be found. Two primary strategies were developed. The first was a common ground strategy in which an ethic of peaceful coexistence was maintained based on doctrines common to all Christians. The common ground strategy was still theistic. The second strategy was to develop an independent ethic abstracted from all religious beliefs. Rawls, Taylor believes, remains wedded to the second strategy ("The Secular Imperative," pp. 33–4 and 51). It is not clear to me if Taylor has accepted the mistaken narrative that the rise of the secular state was necessary to save us from the religious wars, but even if he has I think he is right to see the secular as a correlative of modern state formation. For the critique of the myth of the state as savior see William Cavanaugh, *Theopolitical Imagination* (London: T&T Clark, 2002).

33 Taylor, "The Secular Imperative," pp. 49–53.

34 Stout, *Democracy and Tradition*, p. 97.

35 Stout, *Democracy and Tradition*, p. 5. Stout's focus on the civic nation I think is the reason the problem of "dirty-hands" is so important to him. Thus his claim that "holders of high office are in some respects unique. They are unlike the rest of us in being officially responsible for the exercise of coercive power on behalf of the people's survival and well-being. By virtue of their office they have powers and responsibilities the rest of us do not have. Their responsibilities can give rise to hard choices. These choices invite them to exercise power in ways that leave their hands dirty" (p. 190). This may be true, but it is unclear to me why Stout thinks such considerations are the first order of business for explicating "democratic norms" unless you think that democracy names state formation. To be sure, Stout may not mean by citizen what Rawls means – suggesting that the citizen should think of themselves as a legislator or judge, but Stout's appeal to citizenship nonetheless indicates that his account of reason is in the interest of civic formation. Rawls's account of citizenship as legislator or judge can be found in "The Idea of Public Reason Revisited," in *The Law of Peoples*, pp. 135 and 168.

(Stout, to be sure, does not recommend "we become preoccupied with our identities as members of a civic nation."[36] I am moreover very sympathetic with his stress on the importance of reason giving as constitutive of the kind of conversations he thinks crucial to democratic life. Stout's account in principle does not require that Christians (or other traditions) abandon their self-understanding in order to participate in Stout's democracy. Which is to say that there are possibilities in Stout's account that are not yet fully worked out.)

If Taylor and Asad are right that the secular is the necessary legitimating discourse for the development of the modern state then, as odd as it may seem, I think, given Yoder's account of the mutations of Constantinianism, we can now see that Rawls and, possibly, Stout represent a form of Constantinianism. That they do so, moreover, is extremely important if we are to understand the promise and dangers of secular intellectual disciplines. Putting Yoder, Taylor, and Asad in conversation hopefully helps us see that the secular, even a secular that seems as innocent as Stout's, asks Christians to subordinate our understanding of the way things are in the interest of a "peace" that serves the nation.

Of course even if I am right that the secular has become Constantinian in modernity it may well be asked, why is this such a problem? It is a problem, I think not only for those who think Constantinianism is a strategy that results in the invisibility of the church, but also for those who think some form of Constantinianism is inevitable if not desirable. When the secular becomes Constantinian the church cannot help but be politically marginalized and relegated to the private and, as a result, assumes the state's time is the church's time. Asad is surely right when he says, "If secularism as a doctrine requires the distinction between private reason and public principle, it also demands the placing of the 'religious' in the former by 'the secular.' "[37]

Even more troubling, when the secular becomes Constantinian, Christians, long schooled by Constantinian habits, can forget we live in two times. All time is assumed to be homogenized; that is, all we know is the time that is but deviation. That there might be another time determined by a reality other than secular time is as unthinkable as the belief in miracles. As a result, Christians begin to think we must live impatiently because we do not have the time to live justly or nonviolently in a world with no time but secular time. The problem, quite simply, is that secular time results in the attempt to secure peace without eschatology.[38]

36 Stout, *Democracy and Tradition*, p. 297.

37 Asad, *Formations of the Secular*, p. 8.

38 Thus Yoder argues, " 'Peace' is not an accurate description of what has generally happened to nonresistant Christians throughout history, nor of the way the conscientious objector is treated in most countries today. Not does Christian pacifism guarantee a warless world. 'Peace' describes the pacifist goal, the goal in the light of which he acts, the character of his actions, the ultimate divine certainty which lets his position make sense; it does not describe the external appearance or observable results of his behavior. This is what is meant by eschatology: a hope which, defying

Universities, whether private or public, have been the crucial institutions for developing the knowledges to legitimate this understanding of the secular.[39] In effect the state and the university reflect the symbiotic relationship that once pertained between the university and the church. In the Middle Ages the university was used to produce clerks for church and state. Now the university is expected to produce people educated to serve the bureaucracies of modernity in which it is assumed the state is crucial for an ordered world. That the university serves this function should not surprise us given the fact that the modern university and the modern state developed together.[40]

The disciplines that constitute the knowledges that shape the curriculums of the modern university, moreover, reflect the presumptions of homogenized time described by Asad. Accordingly the account of the world produced and reproduced by those disciplines make it impossible for us to consider another time than secular time exists. How disciplines such as history, political science, English literature, economics, the various sciences serve to make the time of the modern state seem inevitable would require detailed display, but I do not think it hard to see how the very divisions in our curriculums function to produce the kind of intelligence necessary to sustain the "secular."

For example, why is it assumed that Dante is literature rather than an essential text in theology? Wendell Berry is reported to have said, "Not only should we not read the Bible as literature; we shouldn't even read literature as 'literature.' " That we read literature as literature might be an appropriate division of labor for a community to enhance memory, but too often distinctions between literature and theology reflect the homogeneous time Asad identifies. Dante becomes literature in the interest of creating a discipline that does not require the church exist as an alternative to the state.

---

present frustration, defines a present position in terms of the yet unseen goal which gives it meaning" (*The Original Revolution*, p. 53). For Yoder the problem of defending nonviolence as a secular alternative, that is, to be for peace without eschatology, is that a peace without eschatology invites its obverse – war without limit.

39 If this needs confirmation, C. John Sommerville has provided it in his article, "The Exhaustion of Secularism," *The Chronicle of Higher Education*, LII, 40 (June 9, 2006), pp. B6–B7. Sommerville's book, *The Decline of the Secular University* (New York: Oxford University Press, 2006) develops his arguments for the inclusion of religion in the university. Unfortunately, from my perspective, Sommerville's account of religion reproduces the presupposition of Protestant liberalism. Thus religion is about "ultimate concerns" (p. 48).

40 In *Seeing Like a State: How Certain Schemes to Improve the Human Condition Have Failed* (New Haven: Yale University Press, 1998), James Scott argues that the modernist ambition to refashion social habits through reason often exemplified by scientific abstraction is inherently a statist enterprise. Moreover, such an enterprise presumes a break must be made from the past insofar as it is assumed that rational thought and scientific laws can take nothing for granted if a single answer is to be given to every empirical question (p. 93). Scott substantiates these claims by concrete studies from city planning, third-world development, and agriculture.

I believe the same kind of analysis works to explain the character of the social sciences in the modern university.[41] History interestingly enough is seldom taught so that students learn that the discipline of history has a history.[42] The ideological character of history and the social sciences is seldom brought to the students' attention. For example, the triumph of rational choice methodologies in the social sciences now underwrites accounts of efficiency necessary to legitimate the "expert" in the interest of making politics but an extension of economic rationality.[43]

Please note I am not suggesting that there is not much to be learned from the disciplines as currently practiced in the university. Yet Constantinianism, even secular Constantinianism and the intellectual formations shaped by its understanding of time, tempts Christians to believe that the way things are is the way things have to be. There is no question that if we are to be faithful to the task of theology we must know what is represented by "the secular intellectual world." We must know that world for no other reason than it is so good at producing critiques of itself.[44] But we must also rediscover how theology itself can recover from its secularization if we are to serve the church as well as make a contribution to the secular world.

41 Sheldon Wolin observes that "most of the intellectual disciplines that study society, such as economics, political science, social psychology, and (more ambivalently) sociology have become or always were antihistorical in outlook; when they were not, they were reductionist, that is they sought to translate historical categories into social scientific ones and to replace narrative by demonstration. In response, historians have tried to find legitimacy in a post-mnemonic society by borrowing the methods and categories of the social sciences" (*The Presence of the Past: Essays on the State and the Constitution* (Baltimore: Johns Hopkins University Press, 1989), p. 33). Robert Pogue Harrison makes a similar point in his extraordinary book, *Forests: The Shadow of Civilization* (Chicago: University of Chicago Press, 1992). Harrison, in his chapter on the Enlightenment, notes that the post-Christian era is broadly defined here in terms of "historical detachment from the past. The new Cartesian distinction between the *res cogitans*, of the thinking self, and the *res extensa*, or embodied substance, set up the terms for the objectivity of science and the abstraction from history, location, nature, and culture" (p. 107).

42 The nationalistic character of the discipline of history has, however, been recently challenged by Thomas Bender. See his "No Borders: Beyond the Nation State," *Chronicle of Higher Education* (April 7, 2006), pp. B6-4-B8.

43 Wolin rightly sees the development of rational choice accounts of political behavior as the extension of the liberal political paradigms designed ironically to take the politics out of politics. See his *Politics and Vision*, Expanded Edition (Princeton: Princeton University Press, 2004), pp. 570–5. Wolin notes "the conception of theory that informs the academic study of politics has come to reflect the highly bureaucratized character of contemporary governance and of a politics in which corporate influences and state action are inextricably mixed. It represents the desperate effort of a modernist politics – elitist, science-inspired, rationalistic in an economistic vein – struggling to 'govern' an amorphous, unanchored citizenry that is unable to express its unsurveyed self except fitfully in anxiety, fear, anger, and irritation, a citizenry that is still attached to democracy, if tenuously and only sentimentally, but increasingly dependent on electronic media for its very con-/instruction" (pp. 574–5).

44 The kind of critique like that represented by Michel Foucault in his *The Order of Things: An Archaeology of the Human Sciences* (New York: Routledge, 1991) and *Society Must be Defended* (New York: Picador, 2003).

3. PRAYER AS A FORM OF RESISTANCE

I am not suggesting that the modern university or the knowledges characteristic of the university are explicitly subservient to the secular state. Obviously many universities and disciplines within the university assume a stance of indifference or take a quite critical position toward the secular state. I am, however, suggesting that the structure of the knowledges, even knowledges shaped in opposition to the state, are structured in a manner to reproduce secular habits about time necessary to justify and legitimate state formation. By "structure" I mean that they reproduce the practices of the secular and in the process makes invisible to Christians the alternative that we should be in a world that denies there is any other world.

In his extremely important book, *Theology in the Public Square: Church, Academy, and Nation*, Gavin D'Costa argues that the modern university, and the Christian university in particular, has been secularized.[45] He associates secularization with the loss of any connection between worship and the practices of everyday life exemplified by the triumph of money.[46] The latter development, D'Costa thinks, explains the loss of any attempt to maintain a coherent relation between different disciplines. Without any common understanding of the good or the true the university becomes subject to what sells.[47]

D'Costa agrees with Phillip Gleason and James Burtchaell's account of the loss of Christian identity by universities in Britain and America, but his primary interest is what has happened to theology. Influenced by Leclercq's analysis in *The Love of Learning and the Desire for God*, D'Costa argues that the shift of theology from the cathedral schools to the university may have prepared the way for the separation of theology from those practices that are essential for the work of theology. The division of knowledge represented by the University of Paris was the beginning of the fragmentation of theological knowledge which made theology ill-prepared to confront the challenges of the world created by the Reformation and the development of the natural sciences in the seventeenth century.[48]

45 Gavin D'Costa, *Theology in the Public Square: Church, Academy, and Nation.*

46 The relation of time and money was a consistent theme in the work of Peter Maurin. In his "In the Light of History" Maurin under the heading of "1600-Banker" observed, "Before Calvin people were not allowed to lend money at interest. John Calvin decided to legalize lending at interest in spite of the teaching of the Prophets of Israel and the Fathers of the church. Protestant countries tried to keep up with John Calvin and money-lending at interest became the general practice. And money ceased to be a means of exchange and began to be a means to make money. So people lent money on time and began to think of time in terms of money and said to each other, 'Time is money' " (*Easy Essays* (Chicago: Franciscan Herald Press, [1961] 1977), pp. 78–83). Maurin attributed the working out of "time is money" to the "Totalitarian Economists," Smith and Ricardo, who thought that everybody should try to sell what he has to the highest bidder.

47 D'Costa, *Theology in the Public Square*, pp. 2–3.

48 D'Costa, *Theology in the Public Square*, pp. 15–18.

Drawing on the work of Hans Frei, D'Costa argues that theology was subjected to the "great reversal," that is, the only way to make sense of scripture was and is to make the biblical story fit into the presupposition of the secular world.[49] The site of that transformation was the University of Berlin in which, under the direction of Schleiermacher, theology became a university subject because it was assumed, like law and medicine, that theology was necessary for the training of agents of the state who just happened to be ministers. Frei observes as a result "ministerial training was under the complete control of state authority, which delegated it to an educational institution whose basic intellectual and educational assumptions might well be completely at variance with those of the institution for the service of which the students were to be trained."[50]

D'Costa acknowledges that the genealogy of theology he develops is extremely complicated, but he draws two main conclusions from it. First, that institutionalized theology characteristic of the modern university bears the marks of the secularization process just to the extent that theology was transformed into a discipline acceptable to the Enlightenment university. Secondly, the significance of this transformation of theology means the very character of the university must be rethought. The subservience of the university to market economies and bureaucratic state formations designed to serve the market have resulted in a crisis in the humanities which only compounds the fragile status of theology.[51]

D'Costa's genealogy of what he calls "the Babylonian Captivity of theology" is, I believe, a correlative of the Constantinian identification of the church with the world. That is why his recommendation for the renewal of theology has a distinct anti-Constantinian form. For D'Costa suggests that if theology is to escape from captivity to the secular, that if

49 The institutionalization of the "great reversal" is the separation of the study of the Bible from theology. Much good has come from the historical/critical study of the Bible, but too often the disciplinary division between scripture and theology has hidden how that division makes the study of the Bible mirror (and legitimate) the liberal state. Jon Levenson has clearly seen this in his book, *The Old Testament, The Hebrew Bible, and Historical Criticism* (Louisville: Westminster/John Knox, 1993), pp. 106–26.

50 Hans Frei, *Types of Christian Theology*, edited by George Hunsinger and William Placher (New Haven: Yale University Press, 1992), pp. 101–2. Frei quotes the German constitutional historian, Rudolf Huber, concerning the paradoxical character of the achievement of freedom of education in Germany who observed that "the century which achieved freedom of education, research and doctrine created at the same time the greatest extreme in state direction and administration of school organization. But one can note the identical duality of nineteenth-century institutions in almost all areas; the epoch of the individual's highest freedom from the state was simultaneously the epoch of statism's greatest efficiency" (p. 100).

51 Of course we need to remember that the "humanities" are a modern invention that was a response to the "felt need for some secular substitute for the religion-based moral education that had heretofore been a central ideological charge of institutions of higher education" (Steven Marcus, "Humanities from Classics to Cultural Studies: Notes Toward the History of an Idea," *Daedalus*, 135, 2 (Spring, 2006), p. 16).

theology is to reclaim time not determined by the market and the state, it can do so only if theologians "learn to pray as part of their vocation as theologians."[52] According to D'Costa theology can be done with intellectual rigor only in the context of a love affair with God and God's community, the church. And the one cultivated habit of the greatest lovers, that is, the best theologians of the church, is prayer.[53] In particular he calls attention to the 1990 document, "Instruction on the Ecclesial Vocation of the Theologian, from the Congregation for the Doctrine of the Faith", which said:

> Since the object of theology is the Truth which is the living God and His plan for salvation revealed in Jesus Christ, the theologian is called to deepen his own life of faith and continuously unite his scientific research with prayer. In this way, he will become more open to the "supernatural sense of faith" upon which he depends, and it will appear to him as a sure rule for guiding his reflections and helping him assess the correctness of his conclusions.[54]

Prayer, moreover, presupposes a time that cannot help but challenge secular time. Prayer takes place in liturgical time and thereby challenges the presumption that there exists no other time but the time of historical succession. To pray means there is another time known through liturgical repetition that is made possible and necessary by the reality of the Kingdom of God. Accordingly, liturgical time is the necessary condition for the redescription of the world to challenge the presumption of secular disciplines that are aimed to make us believe the way things are is the way things have to be.[55]

D'Costa rejects any presumption that this account of theology makes theology unique among the disciplines of the university. For theology, like other disciplines, requires that students "inhabit" a tradition of inquiry "characterized by various dogmas and practices that facilitate a structured and disciplined co-habitation with the object of study, appropriate to that object."[56] Secondly, theology like other disciplines depends on "virtuoso" lives, that is, skilled and able practitioners whose heart and intellect have made possible extensions of the discipline not otherwise possible.[57]

D'Costa's argument for the recovery of prayer for theology is not a pious gesture, but rather his attempt to name the condition necessary for

52 D'Costa, *Theology in the Public Square*, p. 112.
53 D'Costa, *Theology in the Public Square*, pp. 112–14.
54 Quoted by D'Costa, *Theology and the Public Square*, p. 115.
55 I was only able to make this observation because of Randi Rashkover's remarkable account of Rosenzweig in her book, *Revelation and Theopolitics: Barth, Rosenzweig, and the Politics of Praise* (London: T&T Clark, 2005) pp. 100–6.
56 D'Costa, *Theology in the Public Square*, p. 117.
57 D'Costa, *Theology in the Public Square*, p. 123.

theology to be recognized as knowledge.[58] To recover prayer as the heart of theology involves a massive metaphysical claim that has extraordinary political implications. Sam Wells, for example, in a wonderful essay describing his ministry at St. Elizabeth's, Norwich, makes clear the difference prayer makes politically. St. Elizabeth's was a poor church on an English estate, but they both became part of a renewal grant sponsored by the government entitled "New Deal for Communities." Wells notes that the starkest difference between church meetings and New Deal meetings is that church meetings started with prayer. Wells observes:

> For church regulars saying a prayer at the start of a meeting may have become a habit. Given scant consideration. But at a New Deal meeting, sensing something curiously missing which one has elsewhere taken for granted one becomes slowly aware that this gathering is taking upon itself an enormous task – and is seeking to perform it in its own strength alone. How awesome is the sight! The spectacles that discern this are those given by the habit of corporate prayer.[59]

The significance of prayer for making it possible for St. Elizabeth's parish to sustain work in the New Deal initiative provides a helpful analogy for D'Costa's understanding of the recovery of prayer for theology. St. Elizabeth's habitual formation in prayer made participation in the New Deal program possible. Those from St. Elizabeth's did not have to take over the New Deal but rather brought creative energy to the New Deal that would have otherwise been absent. In like manner, a theology shaped by prayer has no reason to deny the importance of the university disciplines that comprise its curriculum, but a theology shaped by prayer can engage non-theological disciplines to illuminate their possibilities and limitations.

D'Costa is, of course, well aware that his understanding of the inseparability of prayer and theology may make it even more unlikely that theology can be acknowledged as a legitimate subject in the university. Yet he suggests that theologians, if they can reclaim the time presupposed by prayer, the time constitutive of the theologian's work, may find they occupy the discipline capable of integrating the seemingly

[58] In an extremely important article, "The 'Naked' University: What if Theology is Knowledge, Not Belief?" *Theology Today*, 62 (January, 2006), John Stoner argues that "if the university wants to preserve or, in some instances, recover its claim to be the seat of reason, it must again treat theology as an authentic form of knowledge, constituted by reasoning about God" (p. 525).

[59] Sam Wells, "No Abiding Inner City: A New Deal for the Church," in *Faithfulness and Fortitude: In Conversations with Stanley Hauerwas* (Edinburgh: T&T Clark, 2000), pp. 136–7. For a parallel story of the role of prayer in community organizing in which prayer made all the difference for the organization see Mark Warren, *Dry Bones Rattling: Community Building to Revitalize America* (Princeton: Princeton University Press, 2001), pp. 117–18.

unconnected disciplines that constitute the university. "Put bluntly," D'Costa argues,

> the purpose of the university is to find love at the heart of all things, for love is the cause of the world. This does not mean that the study of atoms is going to show that love rather than neutrons and protons is to be found. Rather, once the atomic structure has been explicated the question of how such ordering analogically facilitates the possibilities of love, harmony, beauty, and truth is vital, and is another way of recognizing the ethical and methodological dimensions of the disciplines.[60]

I do not believe what D'Costa is proposing is utopian, but it does place the responsibility on those of us who are theologians to do theology as if it mattered. Moreover, in a world we no longer control we are free to do theology freely. At the very least this should mean the disciplinary divisions that invite theologians to say, "I cannot comment on X or Y because scripture is not my field" must come to an end.[61] Indeed the attempt to make theology "objective" through the transformation of theology into a historical discipline must be seen for what it is, namely, a way to separate theology from its sources which is the praise of God. Of course none of us are capable of knowing all we need to know to do the work of theology, but we must not forget that we know all we need to know to make the work of theology compelling – we know "God is whoever raised Jesus from the dead, having before raised Israel from Egypt."[62]

D'Costa's call, therefore, for theology to rediscover prayer as the center of its life is anything but a call for theology to retreat from engagement with secular disciplines. Indeed, it is clear, he rightly thinks theology has much to learn from secular disciplines including religious studies and the sciences. Yet if theology is to be a subject capable of engaging as well as challenging the presuppositions of the disciplines that constitute the knowledges of the modern university, D'Costa rightly thinks we must recover the practice of theology as prayer. Which quite simply means that theology only makes sense as a discipline of the church.

As a discipline of the church it may well mean that how Christians do history, literature, politics, economics, physics, biology – or even whether those will be recognizable disciplines for a theological perspective – may

60 D'Costa, *Theology in the Public Square*, p. 190. For a similar argument dealing with Darwinism see Michael Hanby, "Reclaiming Creation in a Darwinian World," *Theology Today*, 62 (January, 2006), pp. 476–83.

61 In a yet unpublished paper, "The Ethics of Doing Theology: Towards the Recovery of a Withering Practice," Bernd Wannenwetsch argues that the theologian betrays their subject just to the extent they have allowed the discipline of theology to become theological disciplines.

62 Robert Jenson, *Systematic Theology: The Triune God, I* (New York: Oxford University Press, 1997), p. 63.

be different than how those disciplines are recognized or practiced by those who are not shaped by a life of prayer.[63] What is clear, however, is if theologians learn again to do their work as prayer we may at least make clear to the world, a world shaped by the presupposition of the secular state, that what we believe is not "mere belief."[64]

63 Linell Cady argues that the inability of the liberal academy to understand radical Islamic views of the United States is the result of the myopia created by the disciplinary divisions of the modern university. Because theology has been relegated to divinity schools, disciplines in arts and sciences, such as philosophy, history, and political science have failed to engage the cultural dimensions of religious convictions. See Cady's "Categories, Conflicts, and Conundrums: Ethics and the Religious/Secular Divide," in *War and Border Crossings: Ethics When Cultures Clash*, edited by Peter French and Jason Short (Lanham: Rowman & Littlefield, 2005) pp. 153–4. Put more directly the problem we now confront is that representatives of secular disciplines have become so stupid about what they do not believe they cannot begin to understand strong religious traditions.

64 Dennis O'Brien, in a wonderful response to this paper, suggests his understanding of history as drama, in contrast to history as cyclical, linear, or fragmentary time, is quite close to my understanding of eschatological time. (O'Brien develops this understanding of history in his soon to be published book, *The Catholic Church Losing Its Voice*.) Cyclical time is antithetical to the Christian understanding of history, linear time devalues the past, and fragmentary time (deconstructionist) can make no sense of the Christian claim that the calling of Israel and the life of Jesus determines the very meaning of time. In contrast to these alternatives O'Brien argues history as drama, precisely because it presumes an author who creates individual characters in an ensemble, is able to honor the uniqueness of the past, and honors what may come to be of greatest significance. O'Brien observes this understanding of history is closer to the deconstructionist because the characters in the drama are conscious they are in the midst of history and there is no purchase outside the Christian's claiming something happened in history that makes a difference for how one plays one's part in the history we have been given. Christians, with deconstructionists, believe its Truth is submersed in the historical, but they differ from the deconstructionist because they believe there is a world-play.

As a result O'Brien suggests that Christian theology does not fit the modern university's understanding shaped by an ahistorical epistemology. The sense of being in an Authored World-Play – and there can be no World-Play without an Author – means when Christians "speak Christian" they do not stand outside the play but "on the boards." Moreover they know the play is a comedy and that is why they can pray.

O'Brien concludes, observing that the voice of the modern university is secular in the clear sense because it can make no sense of an Authored World-Play. As a result too often Mother Nature, the Great Gene Cyclic history of Progress, is substituted for the Author. Which leads to the second sense of the secular i.e., that if there is no Author then we must become self-authoring. Unfortunately self-authoring without an Author ends in destruction.

O'Brien's understanding of history as drama is quite similar to Samuel Wells's account in *Improvisation: The Drama of Christian Ethics* (Grand Rapids: Brazos Press, 2004). Wells's account is informed by Von Balthasar's expansive theological vision. Wells suggests that the play has five acts: creation, Israel, Jesus, church, eschaton. I am sure there are five acts but the acts, as Wells implicitly suggests, are at once sequential but interpenetrable. Apocalyptic is the name that suggests how each of the acts is not complete in itself which means the characters must always be ready to be surprised. That the drama is apocalyptic is also the reason the deconstructionist narrative shares much with the Christian story.

12

To Love God, the Poor, and Learning: Lessons Learned from Saint Gregory of Nazianzus

It is the poor who tells us what the *polis* is.

Oscar Romero[1]

1. THE POOR AND THE UNIVERSITY

"Woe is me," wrote Gregory of Nazianzus when he was delayed from leaving Constantinople to return to Nazianzus and retirement.[2] Exactly my sentiments when faced with the task of writing on Gregory of Nazianzus. I am without eloquence yet I must write about the most eloquent theologian in the Christian tradition, Gregory of Nazianzus. My plight is even more deplorable. I am not a scholar or the son of a scholar. Even less can I count myself a patristic scholar. Alas, I am but a theologian, which means I live in fear that someday someone will say in response to a paper such as this, "You really do not know what you are talking about, do you?" To which I can only reply, "Of course, I do not know what I am talking about because it is my duty to talk of God." A self-justifying response that may indicate that theologians live in a permanent state of self-deception.

That I am in such a woeful state is the fault of Fred Norris. He told me I would be a natural for writing on Gregory of Nazianzus. So I have read the Orations of Gregory of Nazianzus that Fred told me I should read. I have also read the extraordinary scholarly work on Gregory by Fred Norris, John McGunkin, and Susan Holman. But my reading has only made me aware of my inadequacy. At best I can be no more than a

1 Quoted in Susan Holman, *The Hungry are Dying: Beggars and Bishops in Roman Cappadocia* (Oxford: Oxford University Press, 2001), p. 107.

2 Letter 182 in *The Fathers Speak: St. Basil the Great, St. Gregory of Nazianzus, St. Gregory of Nyssa*, selected letters translated by Georges Barrois (Crestwood, NY: St. Vladimir's Seminary Press, 1986), p. 71.

reporter of their work. I can only ask you not to judge me harshly for I am only doing what Fred Norris asked me to do.

I must now report, however, that this opening gambit exemplifies the rhetorical device known as the "Southern con," that is, the feigned incompetence to secure your listener's sympathy. As far as I know the scholarly study necessary to trace the origin and development of the "Southern con" has not been done, but I suspect we, that is those of us lucky to be born Southern, learned to use it on the Yankees who assumed if you talked with a drawl you must be stupid. It is a great advantage for your enemy to assume you are not all that bright.

My use of the "Southern con," however, is meant to pay homage to Gregory who, McGuckin observes, often disparaged "rhetoric" as "superficial decoration and verbosity." Yet McGuckin notes if we look closely we will see that Gregory is "merely using a carefully crafted rhetorical device to persuade his audience to lay aside their resistance to the craft he is employing to convince them of his argument's merit."[3] It turns out the Greeks must have had roots in the South.

The only problem is that this time the con happens to be true. God only knows what I am doing writing a paper on Gregory of Nazianzus and, in particular, his Oration, "On Love for the Poor."[4] It has been years since I originally read Gregory of Nazianzus. As a Wesleyan I have always held the Capadocians in high regard – *theosis*, we Methodists believe, was but an early anticipation of Wesley's understanding of perfection. Moreover reading Gregory again reminded me how deeply I admire Gregory's theology and style. Yet it remains true I have nothing new to say about Gregory's theology and, in particular, Oration 14, "On Love for the Poor."

But I do want to put Gregory's reflections on poverty, and in particular lepers, to show why Christians have a stake in sustaining the work of the university. You may well wonder what lepers have to do with universities, but I take it that Fred Norris's life work has been to make unlikely connections. After all Norris is a self-declared Anabaptist who has spent his life trying to teach anti-Catholic Protestants why they cannot make sense of their ecclesial practices unless they attend to the theologians that did their work in the wake of the Constantinian settlement.[5] I lack Norris's erudition, but like him I want to be a free-church Catholic who refuses to leave behind the institutions of Christendom, institutions like the university, simply because they too often are in service to Caesar rather than the poor.

3 John McGuckin, *Saint Gregory of Nazianzus: An Intellectual Biography* (Crestwood, NY: St. Vladimir's Seminary Press, 2001), p. 41.

4 St. Gregory of Nazianzus, "On Love for the Poor," in *Select Orations*, translated by Martha Vinson (Washington, DC: Catholic University of America Press, 2003), pp. 39–71. All references to "On Love for the Poor" will appear in the text using the usual format of the number of the Oration followed by the paragraph number.

5 For Norris's self-description as an Anabaptist see his *The Apostolic Faith: Protestants and Roman Catholics* (Collegeville, MN: The Liturgical Press, 1992), p. xiii. Not to be missed is his wonderful account of his family and the religious background they represented.

Universities, moreover, are institutions that depend on as well as serve wealth. Gregory of Nazianzus was able to develop his remarkable rhetorical skills because he came from a family of wealth and power. Gregory's years in Athens made him one of the most educated persons of his time, but his rhetorical power was used to serve the poor.[6] So it is not impossible for there to be a connection between the university and the poor, a connection that I hope to show Gregory's life and work not only exemplifies but also can help us to rethink as Christians what we ought to be about as people committed to love learning and the poor. That connection, moreover, entails a politics that I need first to make explicit.

2. GREGORY THE PHILOSOPHICAL RHETORICIAN

According to Fred Norris Gregory of Nazianzus "was a philosophical rhetorician."[7] Norris's description has the advantage of making clear that Gregory, though he desired to be a monk, could not avoid being drawn into the rough and tumble world in which Christians began to create an alternative political reality. To be a "philosophical rhetorician" was to take on the task, a political task, of establishing a Christian commonwealth through speech. It is only against that background that we can appropriately appreciate the significance of Gregory's great Oration, "On Love for the Poor."

Gregory was indebted to Hellenic culture for his rhetorical skill. Gregory thought Christians must use the resources and gifts of Hellenism to sustain the work of the church. But his commitment to Hellenism was always disciplined by his Christian convictions. Gregory was in fact baptized in Athens, but he knew, according to McGuckin, that his baptism meant that he was radically committed to Christian disciplines that might create tensions with his intellectual ambitions.[8] Yet under the influence of Prohaeresios, Gregory stood in the tradition of Origen, believing that there could be no disparity between the works of the Logos and the best developments of human culture.[9]

McGuckin, however, reminds us that Gregory's commitment to literature and learning was but a correlative of his desire to live as an

[6] Prior to going to Athens Gregory had studied at Caesarea Maritima which McGuckin describes as "the closest thing in the fourth century to a Christian university town" (pp. 36–7). Gregory's decision to study in Athens and to study rhetoric seems not to have pleased his mother because Athens, according to McGuckin, was widely known for its devotion to the gods and even excelled Rome in its devotion to pagan cults (p. 48). Gregory, however, unlike Basil loved Athens and excelled not only in his study of the Bible but the Hellenistic classics. His father basically forced him to leave Athens by cutting off his money.

[7] Frederick Norris, "Introduction," *Faith Gives Fullness to Reasoning: The Five Theological Orations of Gregory Nazianzen*, translated by Lionel Wickham and Frederick Williams (Leiden: E.J. Brill, 1991), p. 25.

[8] McGuckin, p. 55.

[9] McGuckin, p. 61.

ascetic. For Gregory to live as an ascetic was not in tension with his learning because he understood the discipline of thought to be one of the forms asceticism must take. Gregory did not follow the pattern of the idle rich, but rather he was "someone who wanted to follow the demands of intellect in a serious spiritual quest. The tools of his ascesis were books, enquiring conversation, and reflection in simple solitude. He is certainly an early and serious witness to the physical asceticism of vigils, and simplicity of lifestyle, and in this followed the intellectual tradition of simplicity of lifestyle as advocated by his intellectual hero Origen."[10]

In the Hellenistic world to become a philosopher was to be identified with a way of life and politics. Gregory wanted to be a rhetor but he understood that vocation to be a contribution to the establishment of a Christian polis.[11] Like the Hellenistic polis the city Gregory served was a city of words. According to Brian Daley, S.J. the Hellenistic city was one:

> supported by the power of words, of rhetoric, and embodying what might be called a philosophy... Basil and the two Gregories sought to move the heart by the incantation of words, cunningly arranged, and by the power of the imagination to elicit new resolve for action; they invited their hearers to enter into and know themselves, by what Pierre Hadot has called an ancient variety of "spiritual exercises," as well as to reflect on the universal characteristics of human nature; their aim was not simply to promote a way of living successfully in the city, but of living well – of realizing human excellence

10 McGuckin, p. 97. McGuckin notes that as the son of a very wealthy landowning bishop, Gregory spent much of his career reflecting on the moral value of wealth. He came to the conclusion that the only attitude one could take toward wealth was to assume that material goods are only temporary. As we shall see in Oration 14 he realizes, in McGuckin's words, that "only almsgiving can restore to a human being that condition of freedom that humanity lost in the ancient fall from grace, since it renders us liberal in the image of God rather than cramped in cupidity which is the mark of oppression" (pp. 152–3).

11 Gregory was a rhetor, but he had no use for rhetoric to secure personal power. With his usual candor, in a letter to Gregory of Nyssa, Gregory of Nazianzus accuses Nyssa of desiring glory by pushing away scripture for pagan literature. "You have taken in hand dried-up, insipid writings, and the name of rhetor is more pleasant to your ear than the name Christian. But we prefer the latter, and all thanks to God! No my dear, do not suffer this any longer; sober up at last, come back into yourself, defend us before the faithful, defend yourself before God and before the mysteries from which you have estranged yourself! And do not serve me captious arguments in the manner of rhetors, saying: 'What then? Was I not a Christian, while I was a rhetor?' No, my dear, you were not! Forgive if I make you sad, it is out of friendship; or if I flare up for your own good, the good of the entire priestly order and, I should add, of all Christians. And since we ought to pray with you or for you, let God assist your weakness, He who brings the dead back to life" (Barrois, pp. 37–8).

> and perfection in self-mastery and social responsibility, of acting before others in the city in such a way as to win their admiration and even their envy.[12]

The significance of the Cappodocians' commitment to learning, to rhetorical beauty, can be best appreciated against the background of the Emperor Julian's policy to prohibit Christians from holding the office of teacher. According to Julian's *Edictum de Professoribus* (June 17, 362), "It is dishonest to think one thing and teach another. No professor, therefore, who does not believe in the gods must expound the ancient writers."[13] Julian argued that a culture cannot be divorced from its religious heritage without being damaged. Constantine had tried to replace the gods with Christianity but that project from Julian's perspective had to fail. Rome could not survive without the gods.

Gregory of Nazianzus rightly understood Julian edict to be a challenge to his rhetorical vocation. Accordingly he gave himself the task of exploring the nature of a Christian alternative to Julian. He, therefore, composed rhetorical texts for the classroom to be used by Christians because he was convinced "of the importance of providing a body of didactic material for Christian training."[14] At the end of his life he sold his books to give the money to the poor, but he also desired that his Letters and Orations be collected because he thought them important for the use of those charged to lead the church.

For Gregory, good Hellenist that he was, rhetoric was intrinsic to the formation of a good society necessary for the training of good people. He held himself accountable for what he said as well as how he said what he had to say. To speak the truth required that the speaker be truthful. Susan Holman observes in the Hellenistic world a leader's moral standing "was judged on the basis of his class, his education, and his consequent ability to verbally express himself with eloquence within a given rhetorical structure. Words in this culture were *spoken* – even when they were (also) written down."[15] Through words and actions, which for Gregory of Nazianzus were the same thing, he sought to build a world that would be an alternative to the world that Julian had tried to reestablish.

The significance of Gregory's Oration, "On Love for the Poor," must be understood against this background. For Gregory is not simply urging those not afflicted by poverty or leprosy to aid those so afflicted. Rather

12 Brian Daley, S.J., "The Cappadocian Fathers and the Rhetoric of Philanthropy," *Journal of Early Christian Studies*, 7(3), 459. Daley argues that Basil's great social and monastic enterprise, the large and complex welfare institution that became known as "Basileias," "represented a new and increasingly intentional drive on the part of these highly cultivated bishops and some of their Christian contemporaries to reconstruct Greek culture and society along Christian lines, in a way that both absorbed its traditional shape and radically reoriented it" (p. 432).

13 McGuckin, p. 117.

14 McGuckin, p. 118.

15 Holman, p. 22.

the rhetorical power of his descriptions of the afflicted seeks to make them unavoidable citizens of the new politics coming to birth called Christian. In "On Love for the Poor" Gregory seeks to make the poor seen, to make the poor part of the community, because unless they are seen to be integral to the community we will fail to see Christ. Gregory, the great Christian rhetor, in the words of Susan Holman,

> expresses moral excellence by his physical style in oral declamation, so he also points his audience to Christ, the word made flesh… The poor and destitute who had no rhetorical voice of their own – the incarnation of the Word takes on meaning by the rhetor's (that is, the bishop's) verbal identification of these poor with the body of Christ. As the Cappadocians use traditional New Testament images to identify the poor with Christ, the body of the poor – in its most literal, mutable sense – gains social meaning. The rhetorical expression of this body gains a language and a voice of its own as it is viewed as the body of the Logos. The theology of the incarnation takes on meaning relative to the culture in which it is defined, and this culture profoundly influences the way the theology is understood.[16]

3. "ON LOVE FOR THE POOR"

Hopefully we are now in a position to appreciate Gregory's argument in his Oration, "On Love for the Poor."[17] The date or the reason for Gregory's Oration cannot be established with certainty. It seems reasonable to associate Gregory's Oration with Basil's building of his hospice for the poor and lepers in Caesarea in response to a famine. McGuckin suggests quite reasonably that "On Love of the Poor" was written in 366 and 367 to raise money for Basil's Leprosarium.[18] That Gregory's Oration was connected to Basil's building for the poor is significant because such a connection makes clear that the building and the Oration should be understood "liturgically."

"Leitourgia" in the ancient world was understood as any "public service performed by private citizens at their own expense."[19] Julian

16 Holman, p. 22.

17 Some might dispute the description "argument" for "On Love for the Poor." For a good defense of Gregory's "method" as argument see Norris, "Introduction," pp. 35–9.

18 McGuckin, pp. 145–6. Holman provides a very good overview of the various arguments for when and why Gregory wrote Oration 14 on pp. 144–6. McGuckin thinks "On Love for the Poor" was "conceived as a general fund raiser, that also served as an important discourse setting out the terms for the Christian imperium's policy of *philanthropia*. As such it is a keynote piece of political oratory, as well as a decisive theological essay in which Gregory sets out his mind on the social altruism that characterizes the inner spirit of the religion of Christ" (p. 147).

19 Holman, p. 21.

had called attention to Christian philanthropy for the poor to shame his pagan priests to do more for the poor than the Christians. Julian argued, without much evidence, that the physical care of the poor – as an act of piety – was required by Hellenic religion. Basil's building and Gregory's Oration were, therefore, a counter politics to that of Julian. Care of the poor constituted the center of the work they understood was necessary for the constitution of the community they were intent on establishing.

Basil's Sermon on behalf of the poor and Gregory's Oration "On Love for the Poor" exemplified Hellenistic leitourgia. The Greeks assumed it was the obligation of well-off citizens to contribute to the well-being of the city. What is different, Holman argues drawing on the work of Evelyne Patlagean, is the rise of a new type of donor. The donor who had been an eminent citizen now renounces the identities of such citizenship – that is, marriage, family, property – "to choose poverty, celibacy, and ascetic generosity."[20] The leitourgia system was a patronage system, but the character of the patron was now transformed.

Gregory, therefore, begins "On Love for the Poor" by making himself one with the poor: "My brothers and fellow paupers – for we are all poor and needy where divine grace is concerned, even though measured by our paltry standards one many may seem to have more than another – give ear to my sermon on loving the poor" (14, 1). Throughout the Oration Gregory emphasizes that those who are better off should never be tempted to think that because they are so they are fundamentally different than the poor and the leper. After all we all share the "affable enemy and scheming friend," that is, the body which has been given to us to remind us of our weakness and true worth (14, 7).

That some are poor and some are rich is but a reminder that we are all subject to fickle fortune. "Our fortunes run in a cyclical pattern that brings changes one after another, frequently within the space of a single day and sometimes even an hour, and one may rather count on the shifting winds, or the wake of a sea-faring ship, or the illusory dreams of night with their brief respite, or the lines that children at play trace in the sand, than on human prosperity. The wise are those who because of their distrust of the present save for themselves the world to come" (14, 19). Gregory asks us to think how abandoned we would be if we were allowed to think our prosperity was permanent. Given how attached we become to what we have, how addicted we are to our possessions, how firmly enthralled by our riches we are, how fortunate it is that misfortune befalls us (14, 20).[21]

20 Holman, p. 17.

21 Gregory says, "Let us not struggle to amass and hoard fortunes while others struggle in poverty, lest from one direction the divine Amos reproach us with these harsh and ominous words, Come now, you who say, 'When will the new moon be over,' that we may sell . . . May we avoid the same fate in our day; may we not be so addicted to luxury as actually to scorn the compassion of a God who condemns this behavior, even though he does not turn his wrath upon sinners at the moment of their transgression or immediately after it" (14, 24). In Oration 17 Gregory observes that "prudent men" declare that it is good to be afflicted. That is why we should

Accordingly Gregory refuses to speculate whether affliction actually comes from God. "Who really knows whether one man is punished for his misdeeds while another is exalted for praiseworthy behavior, or whether the opposite is true: one man is placed on a pedestal because of his wickedness while another is tested because of his goodness, the one raised the higher that he may fall the harder, the other persecuted for no discernible reason in order that any impurity he has, even if scant, may be smelted out?" (14, 30). No one is free of corruption making it impossible to attribute every instance of hardship to moral turpitude or a reprieve from piety (14, 31).

The reason that some are favored and some afflicted is often unintelligible to us and that unintelligibility is itself a gift. For our difficulty of comprehending the reason behind favor or affliction points us to the "reason that transcends all things. For everything that is easily grasped is easily despised, but what is beyond us increases our admiration in proportion to our difficulty in apprehending it; and everything that exceeds our reach whets our desire" (14, 33). That is why we should neither admire health or loathe disease "indiscriminately," but rather we should "both cultivate contempt for the benighted health whose fruit is sin and respect for that disease that bears the badge of saintliness by showing reverence toward those who have triumphed through suffering" (14, 34).

That disease that bears the badge of saintliness Gregory identifies with leprosy, the "sacred disease," that devours flesh and bones and marrow[22] (14, 6). His "respect" for the "disease that bears the badge of saintliness" is witnessed by his profound identification with those that bear the disease. His description of their suffering is devoid of sentimentality. He understands, therefore, that the leper's physical disfigurement is but the outward sign of a deeper disfigurement, namely, they become unrecognizable to themselves. As a result they call out the names of their mothers and fathers in the hope they might be identified from the way they used to look. Yet even the fathers and mothers of those so afflicted drive them away in fear of those they once loved. The mother, this poor woman, "wants to embrace her child's flesh but shrinks from it in hostile fear" (14, 11).

"relinquish neither anxiety in time of happiness nor confidence in time of sorrow. Even in fair weather let us not forget the gale, nor in the storm the pilot; yes, let us not lose heart in the midst of afflictions or become wicked servants who acknowledge their master only when he treats them well and repudiate him when he tries to correct them. Yet there are times when pain is preferable to health, patience to relief, visitation to neglect, punishment to forgiveness. In a word, we must neither let our troubles lay us low nor a glut of good fortune give us airs" (17, 5).

22 Some may think Gregory's focus on leprosy makes his case too easy. Little can be done to cure the leper, but we think much can be done to alleviate poverty. Gregory certainly thought, as we should think, poverty should not exist, but he did not think being poor was the worst thing that could happen to a person. Indeed he thought there might be some distinct advantages to being poor if we are to follow Christ. The rich, not the poor, from Gregory's perspective are the most burdened. Sam Wells recently stated this reality when he remarked, "The rich, if we are Christians, need

The affliction of leprosy is horrid enough, but even worse is the knowledge of those so afflicted that they are hated for their misfortune (14, 9). They are driven away, not only because of the irrational fear that they may infect us, but because we refuse to comprehend their suffering.[23] "So they wander about night and day, helpless, naked, homeless, exposing their sores for all to see, dwelling on their former state, invoking the Creator, leaning on each other's limbs in place of those they have lost, devising songs that tug at the heartstrings, begging for a crust of bread or a bit of food or some tattered rag to hide their shame or provide relief for their wounds" (14, 12). Yet there is no comfort even in their common suffering. "They lie beside one another, a wretched union born of disease, each contributing his own misfortune to the common fund of misery, thus heightening each other's distress; pitiful in their affliction, more so in the sharing of it" (14, 13).

Gregory fears his detailed descriptions of those that suffer from leprosy may alienate his listener's festal spirits. Yet he tells them he speaks with such detail because he seeks to persuade them "that sometimes anguish is of more value than pleasure, sadness than celebration, meritorious tears than unseemly laughter" (14, 13). For whether his hearers like it or not the lepers he describes are formed from the same clay as they are, the lepers are knit together with bones and sinews as they are, and more importantly lepers "have the same portion as the image of God just as we do and who keep it perhaps better, wasted though their bodies may be; whose inner nature has put on the same Christ and who have been entrusted with the same guarantee of the Spirit as we" (14, 14).

It is not the leper, but the well off, who walk by and neglect those so afflicted, who are in greatest peril. Gregory's depiction of the rich is as uncompromising as his portrait of those that suffer from poverty and leprosy. "As for us (he addresses the rich as "us"), we magnificently ensconce ourselves on high and lofty beds amid exquisite and delicate coverlets and are put out of temper if we so much hear the sound of begging. Our floors must be scented with flowers – even out

---

the poor in a manner the poor do not need the rich." My colleague Romand Coles, in a letter responding to this essay, observed the implication of Gregory's Oration is that "truly responding to poverty is to radically transform the world by profoundly questioning the meaning of wealth and poverty and by taking up enduring relationships with those who are poor while recognizing one stands to receive far more than we can give in such relationships."

23 Gregory tells his hearers that they should at least help those suffering from leprosy by offering encouragement and keeping them company. "You will not demean yourself in the process; you will not catch their malady even if the squeamish deceive themselves into believing such nonsense; or rather, this is how they justify their, call it over-cautious or sacrilegious, behavior; in point of fact, they are taking refuge in cowardice as though it were a truly worthwhile and wise course of action. On this score accept the evidence of science as well as of the doctors and nurses who look after these people. Not one of them has ever yet endangered his health through contact with these patients. You, then, servant of Christ, who are devoted to God and your fellow man, let compassion overcome your misgivings, the fear of God your fastidiousness" (14, 27).

of season – and our tables drizzled with perfumes – so that we might coddle ourselves all the more. We eat from a table lavished with meats arranged in a manner to pander to our indecent and ungrateful belly. Wine is rejected and praised in an effort to gain the reputation of being extravagant voluptuaries as if it is shameful not to be considered depraved" (14, 17).

Why, Gregory asks, are we so sick in our souls, a sickness worse than any that affects the body? The body's illness is after all involuntary, but the sickness of wealth is deliberate. Why do the rich revel amid the misfortune of their brothers? Surely it is because we fail to see that we can only "gain our lives by acts of charity."[24] To so give is to imitate the character of God. Gregory reminds his hearers no matter how much they give, "You will never surpass God's generosity even if you hand over your entire substance and yourself in the bargain. Indeed, to receive in the truest sense is to give oneself to God" (14, 22).

Gregory ends "On Love for the Poor" urging his hearers to "appropriate the beatitude" that blesses those who are the merciful (14, 38). He concludes,

> If, then, you place any credence in what I say, servants of Christ and brothers and follow heirs, while we may, let us visit Christ, let us heal Christ, let us feed Christ, let us clothe Christ, let us welcome Christ, let us honor Christ, not with food alone, like some; nor with ointments, like Mary; nor with tomb alone, like Joseph of Arimathea; nor with obsequies, like Nicodemus, who loved Christ in half measure; nor with gold and frankincense and myrrh as the Magi did before these others. Rather, since the Lord of all will have "mercy, and not sacrifice" (Mt. 9:13) and since a kind heart is worth more than myriads "of fat sheep" (Dn. 3:39), this let us offer to him through the poor who are today downtrodden, so that when we depart this world they may receive us into the eternal habitations (Lk. 16:9) in Christ himself, our Lord, to whom be the glory forever. Amen (14, 40).[25]

24 Gregory began "On Love for the Poor" with a description of 20 virtues that might be considered primary, but concludes that charity is the first and greatest of the commandments. For "nothing so serves God as mercy because no other thing is more proper to God, whose mercy and truth go before, and to whom we must demonstrate our capacity for mercy rather than condemnation; and by nothing else more than by showing compassion to our fellow man do we receive compassionate treatment in turn at the hands of him who weighs mercy in his scale and balance and gives just recompense" (14, 5).

25 Holman raises the interesting question whether it matters whether the Christology is Arian or Nicene for Gregory's identification of the poor with Christ. She observes that none of the texts by Basil, Nyssa, or Nazianzus on the poor are theological treatises, but she says their "elevated view of the poor as they relate to transcendent and incarnate deity in the Cappadocian texts is different from implications that logically attend Eunomius's Arian view of Christ, at least as the Cappadocians understood that view, as one in which the Son differed from the Father in hypotasis

4. A UNIVERSITY OF THE POOR

Gregory's "On Love for the Poor" was a liturgical action in which the poor and the leper, through the power of beautiful words, were made the center of a city ruled by Christ. Lepers are not recipients of charity, but rather they are God's charity for a community formed by as well as to be charity. Gregory "entitles" the poor, but, as Holman observes "the power of the poor depends on their place of primary honor in the kingdom of God. It depends on their revisionist identity as kin. The rights of these poor depend on their constructed religious role: as patrons, engaging in civic gift exchanges by receiving alms and effecting redemption."[26] Gregory's great gift, a gift made possible by his classical education, was to make his words work. Norris beautifully describes the way Gregory's words work this way:

> When Gregory looked outside his own life to the lives of others, he found it easier to describe how any Christian ought to look at the poor and the lepers by speaking of the situations in picturesque language. He focused the attention of the Constantinopolitan community on such problems by rhetorically connecting the death of Christ for human sins and the Christian treatment of those economically less fortunate or those so pitifully diseased. He made his appeals through strong rhetorical arguments, images that convinced. Here, as a contemplative who painted the ugliness of poverty and leprosy contrasted with the beautiful life created by Christ, he empowered his congregation to recognize that the saved, sinners nursed to health, should assist those whose condition was so grave. Contemplation was good but so was action. He described the afflicted in poignant terms. Those with no voice, no breath, no hands and no feet gave thanks that they had no eyes to see their ravaged bodies. Not even the misery of human life in itself could be detailed without the use of images and carefully crafted phrases. Ugliness would have to be presented with the same attention to detail that the contemplation of beauty demanded for

and substance precisely because of the Son's generate nature. A Eunomian identification of the poor with Christ would most logically, in theory at least, maintain a certain unbroachable divide between generate (be it Christ or the poor) and transcendent. None of the three Cappadocians recognizes any such barrier. The religious power of the poor in fact rests on the belief that they hold a direct line of access to the highest realm of deity; their generate nature in no way limits this access and is in fact one of its most characteristic features" (Holman, p. 181).

Gregory's rhetoric, as this quote makes clear, is suffused with biblical allusions. I have obviously not done justice to his use of scripture as integral to the rhetorical power of his argument.

26 Holman, p. 151.

> speaking of magnificence. The contrast would only be properly strong if the same approach were employed in discussing each.[27]

Gregory had been born rich, but he had learned to live as one born poor. Gregory had received the best education available, but that education had not alienated him from the poor. Yet that is exactly what happens to most that receive university education in our time. At best the modern university produces people, even some who may have come to the university from poverty, who after being at the university want to "do something for the poor." The university is not able to produce people, as Gregory was able, to see and describe the poor as beautiful. He was able to see the beauty of the poor because schooled by Christ he had no reason to deny or wish they did not exist. His descriptions of those who suffered from leprosy were loving because he had learned to love Christ and, therefore, he could not help but love the afflicted, even those afflicted with leprosy.

Yet love of the poor and the leper is a profound challenge for those schooled by the presumptions of the modern university. In her extraordinary book, *Politics of Piety: The Islamic Revival and the Feminist Subject*, Saba Mahmood observes that the scholarship surrounding the poor and oppressed sponsored by the modern university robs them of agency. Mahmood's subject is Islamic women determined to learn to live lives of submissive modesty through prayer and the veil. Mahmood observes that such women are usually described in scholarly studies as deprived of the ability to enact the ethics of freedom "founded on their capacity to distinguish their own (true) desires from (external) religious and cultural demands."[28] Yet Mahmood observes,

> If we recognize that the desire for freedom from, or subversion of, norms is not an innate desire that motivates all beings at all times, but is also profoundly mediated by cultural and historical conditions, then the question arises: how do we analyze operations of power that construct different kinds of bodies, knowledges, and subjectivities whose trajectories do not follow the entelechy of liberatory politics.[29]

[27] Frederick Norris, "Gregory Contemplating the Beautiful: Knowing Human Misery and Divine Mystery Through and Being Persuaded By Images," in *Gregory Nazianzus: Images and Reflections*, edited by Jostein Bortnes and Tomas Hagg (Copenhagen: Museum Tusculanum Press, 2006), pp. 19–35. I am using a manuscript in which the above quote came from p. 11.

[28] Saba Mahmood, *Politics of Piety: The Islamic Revival and the Feminist Subject* (Princeton: University of Princeton Press, 2005), p. 148.

[29] Saba Mahmood, *Politics of Piety*, p. 14. Mahmood observes that even subaltern studies that are intent to show that the oppressed are not without agency through subversion or resistance nonetheless continue to presume that a category of actions exists shaped by the universal desire for freedom. In contrast Mahmood notes that

Mahmood notes that there is a politics assumed and legitimated by the scholarship that describes Islamic women as devoid of agency. It is politics of secular liberalism that assumes the task is to privatize religious convictions in the interest of a progressive realization of freedom.[30] The university has been a crucial legitimating institution for such a politics by underwriting the state as the agent of liberation. Claims of and for rights, goods, and services made on the basis of identities shaped by liberal understandings of agency fall on the state as the source of their fulfillment. As a result all aspects of human life such as those associated with the family, education, worship, welfare, commercial transactions, birth and death, are now "brought under the regulatory apparatus of the state."[31]

The privileged place of the sciences, particularly the sciences associated with medicine, in the modern university reflects this ethos of freedom and subsequent legitimation of the state. The sciences are often justified as having special status because allegedly scientific knowledge is less arbitrary than the knowledges associated with the humanities. However, the prestige of science in the contemporary university has less to do with its assumed epistic status than the assumption that science promises to give us the power to be freed from the limits of the body. Accordingly science enjoys governmental support because governments in modernity legitimate themselves by promising to save us from illness and death.

In such a world Gregory's Oration, "On Love for the Poor," is unintelligible. Indeed "On Love for the Poor" challenges the deepest presuppositions of the politics of our day that gains its legitimacy by promising to eliminate suffering. Christians would be fortunate if the political challenge to Gregory was a Julian, but our problem is more

---

even though her study focuses "on the practices of the mosque participants, this does not mean that their activities and operations they perform on themselves are products of their independent wills; rather my argument is that these activities are the products of authoritative discursive traditions whose logic and power far exceed the consciousness of the subjects they enable. The kind of agency I am exploring here does not belong to the women themselves, but is a product of the historically discursive traditions in which they are located" (p. 32). That, I believe, is almost an exact description of what Gregory's Oration "On Love for the Poor" performs for lepers.

30 I am hesitant to use the descriptor "liberalism," but Mahmood uses that term to describe "the belief that all human beings have an innate desire for freedom, that we all somehow seek to assert our autonomy when allowed to do so, that human agency primarily consists of acts that challenge social norms and not those that uphold them" (p. 5). This view, which she also identifies as secular, is not simply a view of the state, though it is that, but rather she identifies it as a "form of life" (p. 191). I think she quite reasonably calls this position "liberal."

31 Mahmood, p. 193. It is important, however, to note that to the credit of the modern university someone like Mahmood has been produced. The liberal formation of knowledges characteristic of the university as we know it is capable of self-correction. That it is so indicates that Christians cannot nor should we want to disparage the work of the liberal university. There is no "going back," but we must go forward in the world as we find it.

complex. We are now the enemy unable to sustain educational alternatives capable of producing people like Gregory who through the gift of speech create community in which the loneliness of suffering is overwhelmed. Shaped by the rhetorical habits of the modern university, Christian and non-Christian alike cannot help but read Gregory's "On Love for the Poor" as reactionary.

Of course it may well be asked why Christians need universities at all if they are institutions that are antithetical to Gregory's call for us to love the poor. The answer to such a challenge is that Christians need places of study where works like that of Gregory's "On Love for the Poor" will continue to be studied and hopefully imitated.[32] Like Gregory Christians must continue to learn from Hellenism, which will no doubt come in surprising forms, if we are to say for ourselves and the world why eloquence, an eloquence learned from patient endurance, is crucial if we are to love and be loved by the poor.[33]

Crucial for such an enterprise is that people like Gregory of Nazianzus exist. "No monks, no Christianity" is, I think, a generalization that is true for the very existence of the church. But I also think any university that would be about the formation of people who can love the poor will need those who have learned to live as the poor by living with the poor. It may well be, for example, that universities that desire to have what they teach be disciplined by the Gospel have at the center of their work a L'Arche home or a Catholic Worker house.[34]

Gregory drew on Hellenism to learn to be a rhetor, but he would not have been able to write an Oration like "On Love for the Poor" without

32 Harry Huebner argues that the church needs to challenge the university to place on its agenda the claim that a people's faith can be sustained only when its people are trained to negotiate economics, politics, science, sociology, and philosophy of the biblical faith in a world of competing claims. "The church needs an educated people to present more complexified views of human nature – of violence, sin, peace, and love – than most people have, given their somewhat distorted view of things learned from popular culture. The church needs an educated people to present alternative answers to questions of justice, international relations, and power to present alternative models for how people can live together in ways that liberate and heal brokenness. The church needs an educated people to promote structures that foster the art of welcoming the stranger in a culture of protectionism; to promote that truth is not a possession but a gift in a age of capitalism; to promote that forgiveness is a viable strategy of social reconstruction in a culture of fear" ("Learning Made Strange: Can a University be Christian?" in *God, Truth, and Witness: Engaging Stanley Hauerwas*, edited by Greg Jones, Reinhard Hutter, and Rosalee Velloso Ewell (Grand Rapids: Brazos Press, 2005), p. 303). Bruce Kaye, however, reminds me that the study of Gregory could take place in the church if necessary.

33 Mahmood has an extraordinary account of the virtue "sabr" which is akin to Christian patience, but means "to persevere in the face of difficulty without complaint" (p. 171). Mahmood notes that the justification of sabr is not the ability to reduce suffering or to help one achieve self-directed choices, but rather how such a virtue makes one subservient to God (p. 173).

34 Moreover it should not be forgotten that the Catholic Worker movement, and Dorothy Day and Peter Maurin, were formed and formed ways of understanding the world that came from universities. See, for example, Mark and Louise Zwick,

being baptized into Christ. To produce Gregorys in our day we will need the gifts of the university, but we will equally need people who do not need to attend the university to live faithful to their baptism. For Gregory knew, great rhetor that he was, that a people must exist with ears trained by the worship of the true God if the beauty of words like those he used in "On Love for the Poor" could persuade. Our task as Christians, and in particular those of us privileged to serve in the university, is to be as well as to train a people capable of reading and receiving a Gregory. Fred Norris has spent his life trying to help us listen to Gregory, which is why it is so appropriate we honor him on this occasion.[35]

The Catholic Worker Movement: Intellectual and Spiritual Origins (New York: Paulist Press, 2005). Jean Vanier, the founder of L'Arche, wrote his dissertation about Aristotle on friendship. His book, *Made for Happiness: Discovering the Meaning of Life with Aristotle* (London: DLT, 2001) is a wonderful exemplification of his ability to transform Aristotle's understanding of happiness and friendship through what he has learned through L'Arche. Drawing on the work of Ernst Bloch, Romand Coles argues that the hunger of the belly and the hunger of the mind cannot be separated. The intellectual task will fall short, Coles suggests, if it seeks to proceed without engaging the questions of hunger with the hungry. See his "Hunger, Ethics, and the University: A Radical Democratic Good in Ten Pieces."

35 I am indebted to Sheila McCarthy for pressing me to try to articulate the relation between the university and the poor.

Appendix A

Duke University: The Good of This Place

In his eloquent goodbye to Yale entitled *The Good of This Place*,[1] Richard Brodhead has the courage to ask, "What is a school like Yale for?" It takes courage to ask that question because it is by no means clear we have even the beginnings of an answer. There are two questions you cannot ask in the contemporary university, namely, "what is it for?" and "whom does it serve?" I want to suggest in these brief remarks one of the reasons we do not welcome such questions is because they presume something we do not know i.e., whether the contemporary university is a "place."

This is not a new problem, but I think we find ourselves in a time in which the problem has taken new forms. The very name "university" suggests that the universities have ambitions to transcend whatever place they occupy. At one time the ambition to be a university was a correlative of the presumption that whatever truth might be discovered through the inquiry constitutive of the university, the concept of truth, as Alasdair MacIntyre maintains, is "timeless."[2] A "timeless" truth is also a truth that seems "placeless" even if it is true that truth as such is a truth of a concrete particular. So universities have been the place where the desire to know what is true is in tension with the necessity to be somewhere rather than anywhere.

In another one of his Freshman Addresses Dick Brodhead tells the freshman that the university to which they have come is and does a thousand things. But he suggests that two ideas hold the university together:

> First this community is unified by the sense of the beauty of excellence in its many forms and the pleasure of striving to attain it. Second, the university is a community of inquiry: that is, a community founded on the premise that nothing is

1 Richard H. Brodhead, *The Good of This Place: Values and Challenges in College Education* (New Haven: Yale University Press, 2004).

2 Alasdair MacIntyre, *Whose Justice? Which Rationality?* (Notre Dame: University of Notre Dame Press, 1988), p. 363.

> yet the whole of the truth. In saying this the university does not mean nothing is true, or that there is no such thing as the truth. Rather it means that no human understanding has or could contain the whole of the truth – that nothing is so true that it is not susceptible to expansion, challenge, revision, and deeper realization.[3]

This is a lovely statement of what is known as the unity of the transcendentals, that is, the inseparability of beauty, truth, and the good. That unity, or perhaps better, the intimations of such unity that require ongoing investigation is why there will always be a tension between the purpose of the university and the way such a purpose must be enacted upon. Roses cannot be beautiful, but a rose can be.

In this time often called modern, however, a different kind of universal haunts the halls of the university – one that can be confused with the desire to know and even say what it true. Under the conditions of the market, a university dare not be too different, that is, dare to be a place. The American people continue to think spending money to buy time for the young to be at a university or college is a good idea. As a result, those who teach and those who administer the universities cannot let any emphasis on a school's history or place make it impossible to attract students who think every university is like every other university except that some are more excellent than others. Never forget, capitalism is the most egalitarian movement the world has ever known. Unfortunately, we are all counted equal by our ability to make money, and students come to the university hoping that the university will help them become more equal than their neighbor. The market, therefore, makes it very hard for the university to be a place. Distinctiveness can be emphasized only as a strategy to get our market shares.

The modern university also has difficulty being a place because of the domination of science as the standard of knowledge. Please do not misunderstand. I am not a theological Luddite who regrets the development of modern science (though I share Wendell Berry's view that the Luddites are sorely misrepresented). Rather I am calling attention to how the heart of modern science – that is, the reproducible experiment – requires that science insofar as possible be transferable. Every lab should be like every other lab that is concerned with this or that research agenda. I think the actual practice of science is often more complicated than this account suggests. But it is hard to deny that at least as an ideal (dare I say ideology) of science, this standard makes a large contribution to the "placelessness" of the current university. Such placelessness, moreover, contributes to the constant flow of faculty from one institution to another in the hope that they will "get a better deal."

That universities have difficulty being places, I believe, in turn contributes to the inability of the contemporary university to figure

3 Brodhead, *The Good of This Place*, p. 18.

out the role of the humanities. The issue is not whether Shakespeare or Dante should be read, but how they should be read in relation to other literatures. Literature and art are traditioned disciplines (which I also think is true of the sciences) even if the tradition, as good traditions must be, is controvertible. Why controversy is at the heart of learning to read is often a lesson those of us in the humanities have trouble articulating for our friends in the university who think whatever is true should be obvious. Dante's truth is a truth that is true for anyone, but to understand Dante it helps to know something about the particular place called Florence.

This brings me to now speak about the particular "place" called Duke. Duke is a place because Duke is in Durham and Durham is in the South. Duke lacks the eloquence of Florence, but since we are Southern we arrogantly believe we are at least as sinful as Dante's Florentines. That Duke is marked by its being a place of the South means that Duke can never forget slavery flourished here and racism remains a present reality. This is a memory and reality that cannot and should not want to be lost in the "mists of history." In particular, we should never forget that Christians owned slaves. In other words, Duke cannot be Duke unless we are dedicated to the truthful telling and retelling of the story of slavery and racism.

To be in the South, moreover, means we can never forget our life is determined by the red clay we, that is, those bred in the South, pretentiously call soil. And the soil we are raised upon at Duke also raises the trees that make Duke Duke. Accordingly, I think that no unit of the university may be more important than the School of the Environment. I am a good friend of Bill Schlesinger, the Dean of the School of the Environment, and I no doubt think the School is so important because of what Bill has taught me. I make no apology, however, that our friendship has so influenced my views about the importance of Duke Forest because friendship is one of the most crucial ways we learn to love the place in which we find ourselves.

In his "President's Welcome" published in the *Blue Devil Advocate* (August, 2004), President Brodhead observes, "Each part of Duke has a local character, but the parts add up to a coherent whole." I hope he is right, but I must confess that the current departmentalization of the contemporary university makes it very hard to see that "coherent whole." I am convinced, however, that friendship is key to making that "whole" visible. Hopefully we will continue to discover such friendships through the common engagements in our disciplines which are necessary to discover what it means to be a friend of creation, and particularly what it means to be friends to that particular part of creation which makes up the foundation for this university.

Finally, Duke could not be Duke without the Chapel – a glorious building that certainly anchors us to this place. I realize Duke is not quite sure what to do with this building. I once heard it described as a "symbol of the spiritual dimension of all knowledge." I wrote to the person who used that description and observed that I thought the Chapel was for the worship of God. Yet for many in our culture God is thought to be the ultimate universal, which usually means that you have got to believe something had to start it all. However, I think the problem with God, at least the God that this Chapel praises, is that God is so damned particular, so placed, made known through the particular people called Jews. You do not get more particular than that. Duke will not serve our students or the world well if we do not take advantage of the place this Chapel is.

So, Dick Brodhead, welcome to this place. In *The Good of This Place*, you describe yourself as a person of "strong attachments and powerful devotions" who wants to do nothing more then use your energy for the good of the universities. We rejoice that you are ready to attach yourself, to burden yourself, with this God-haunted Southern university. In a lovely paragraph near the close of your book you observe:

> Music is always a game played with time, in which time's shapeless successions are refashioned into something measured and composed. But if music defeats time by inscribing it in human order, it is still a thing of time, filling the moment with its beauty without escaping the law of evanescence.[4]

I hope Duke University will be for you such music.

[4] Brodhead, *The Good of This Place*, p. 215.

Appendix B

Seminaries are in Trouble: Chastened Reflections on the Centennial of Bethany Theological Seminary

Seminaries are in trouble. Seminaries are in trouble because churches in America are in trouble. Freestanding seminaries – that is, seminaries free of university ties – are particularly in trouble. Mainstream Protestant seminaries are in even more trouble. It is not for me to say whether Bethany Theological Seminary exemplifies or does not exemplify the trouble seminaries are in. Indeed it may seem ill advised for me to use this celebratory occasion to "unload" my worries about seminaries, but if I know anything about the Brethren it is they think you ought to tell the truth even if the truth is unpleasant. I do not necessarily believe that the truth will make us free, but I am convinced we will be less than faithful to God if we try to go on as if we know what we are doing in seminaries today.

Seminaries are allegedly for training people for the ministry of the church of Jesus Christ. However, given the ambiguous character of the modern ministry, it is unclear what it means to train people not only to survive but also to flourish in the ministry. Nowhere is this more readily apparent than in the alleged gulf that is said to exist between the more academic courses in seminaries and those courses called practical or ministerial. The former are too often derided by those in the ministry as of little use for preparing people for the actual challenges of the ministry. Thus the slogan is heard far too often: "They (meaning the congregation) do not care what you know. They want to know that you care."

As a result there has developed a deep anti-intellectual culture among the students who come to seminaries. Indeed the strangest possible coalition develops in some seminaries between Protestant pietists, fundamentalists, liberationists, and feminists who – each for quite different reasons – question the more academic courses in the curriculum. Few developments could be more disastrous for the church than acquiescence to the demand to "dumb down" the curriculum to make seminaries more responsive to pastoral care. The challenges confronting the church in a consumer society demand more not less formation in the intellectual skills the church calls theology.

I noted above that freestanding seminaries seem to me to be particularly susceptible to the demand to turn out more "caring" pastors. They are so because they are too close to their constituency. University-related seminaries have their own pathologies, but at least being in the university means the faculties in those institutions can give reasons why theology should remain an intellectually demanding enterprise. That those to be tenured in such institutions have to meet the standards of the university at least is a check against the tendency to make theology "understandable" to those who would prefer never to hear who Karl Barth was, much less read a volume of the *Church Dogmatics*.

Of course, contributing to this problem is the lack of preparation students bring to their work in the seminary. Seminaries can no longer afford to turn down anyone who wants to "study" for the ministry. Moreover, the best and the brightest are not necessarily going into the ministry. The ministry is not exactly a status profession. The problem with many of our students, however, is not that they are ill prepared, but that they are just lazy. They have felt "called" to the ministry because they often like "to work with people" but it has never occurred to them that the work they are to do with people in the name of Jesus Christ means more than being a nice person. Indeed I suspect the reason why so many leave the ministry or find themselves in such compromised positions in the ministry is due to the unrelieved boredom of facing a life-time of being "nice."

Some years ago I was advising a first-year student in an effort to help him select his courses. He had gone to the University of Texas where he had majored in business administration. After graduating he had worked for several years before he discovered he wanted to be a minister. I asked him if he had taken any courses in the humanities during his undergraduate years. He said he had a few courses in the humanities, so I asked if he had ever taken any philosophy. He said, "I am not sure." I thought that was either the smartest or dumbest answer I had ever heard. To find out which it was, I asked him if he had ever read Plato. He responded, "Who?"

I would be the last person to argue that you need to know who Plato is to worship Jesus Christ. But if you are to be a minister trained to lead a congregation through the wilderness of this society called America, I certainly think you not only need to know who Plato was but why Plato was such an important figure for Origen and Augustine. Of course the "ordinary Christian" probably does not care whether their minister does or does not know Plato or Augustine, but it is my contention that anyone serving in the ministry today who lacks the resources Augustine provides risks abandoning their congregation to the omnivorous desires of the market. Who, more than Augustine, can teach us what it means to be possessed by that which we think we desire by our own free will?

The problem is not just the lack of clarity about what the ministry should be about in our day or the kind of students that come to seminaries, but the problem is also the disciplinary divisions that constitute the modern seminary. That the study of scripture has become in most seminaries a "historical discipline" is a major problem. Too often it is assumed that scripture is dealt with in Old Testament (which unfortunately should be really taught as Hebrew Bible) and New Testament courses, which means those who teach systematic theology and ethics are freed from making scripture constitutive of their work. Even if those who teach theology and ethics would like to be more scriptural, we lack (given the character of our graduate education) the skills necessary for exemplifying for our students theological exegesis. As a result, too often students think what they learned in their scripture courses is more certain than theology because the latter is largely a matter of "opinion."

I am well aware that many will find my account of why seminaries are in trouble to be exaggerated. Many seminaries are forming future ministers in quite admirable ways. They are able to do so, however, because they have become quite candid about the challenges facing the churches and the seminaries today. Those seminaries that are doing well, and I am happy to say that I think Duke Divinity School is doing very well, are able to do so because they have become very intentional about the kind of faculty they hire. When all is said and done, people matter. Which means churches, individual congregations, not only need to hold themselves accountable for sending people into the seminary who have the talent and energy to meet the high demands of their calling, they must also be ready to receive them back.

It would be presumptive of me to say how what I have said may or may not have implications for Bethany Theological Seminary. I was honored some years ago to lecture at Bethany, but I cannot pretend I know the Seminary well. I do think, however, that the Brethren Church has some real advantages as you look to the future. The first advantage is your lack of numbers. The Brethren Church has never been part of the American Protestant establishment. You have nothing to lose, so you might as well be faithful to your heritage to the extent that heritage has been faithful to the Gospel. That means you do not have to imitate the seminaries of the Protestant mainstream, but rather your task is to be a church that understands if Jesus has not been raised from the dead then all that you are is unintelligible.

Moreover, the Church of the Brethren is committed to nonviolence. It may seem odd to call attention to nonviolence for consideration of seminary education, but the theological work required to make nonviolence intelligible as well as for shaping the pastoral ministry of the church is the kind of imaginative challenge so desperately needed if we are to overcome the false division between academic and pastoral courses in the seminary curriculums. So may Bethany Theological Seminary flourish as the seminary of the Church of the Brethren and in so flourishing may she help us all faithfully to serve God.

Appendix C
Ordinary Time: A Tribute to Rowan Williams

"The hardest thing in the world is to be where we are" observes Rowan Williams in his Lent book, *Christ on Trial: How the Gospel Unsettles Our Judgment*. Enigmatic though it may be I think the Archbishop's remark, "The hardest thing in the world is to be where we are," is one worth pondering if we are to negotiate faithfully the current challenges before church and world. By asking you to reflect with me on this remark I hope to show why we are fortunate at this time to have Rowan Williams as our Archbishop of Canterbury. He is an extraordinary theologian whose work is an invaluable resource for helping the church "to be where we are." Accordingly I want to use this occasion to honor Rowan by suggesting how his understanding of time can help us be the church God has called us to be.

The anthropologist David Scott has described our time as damaged. By damaged he means we live in a time in which the once familiar characterizations of time no longer seem compelling. According to Scott, "inerasable residues from the past stick to the hinges of the temporality we have come to rely on to secure our way, and consequently time is not quite as yielding as we have grown to expect it to be." The persistence of racism and war name the "inerasable residues from the past" that make the time in which we live seem damaged. We live after civil rights and after the cold war but nothing it seems has fundamentally changed. In fact the problems of race and war seem even more intractable because the past now seems useless for helping us discern any hope for the future.

In a damaged time we might expect – or at least hope – the church would be a beacon of hope, but instead we find ourselves consumed by debates about sexual conduct. That we are captivated by issues surrounding something called "sexuality" is an indication of the captivity of the church to money, class, and liberal political arrangements. Nothing makes such captivity more apparent than the relegation of the church to the "private." Sex becomes *the* issue before the church because sex constitutes the realm of the "private." Watching Christians tear themselves apart over sexual conduct not only must entertain the secular powers, but also assure them that they will face no challenge from

Christians. If we live in a damaged time we fear the church is part of the wreckage.

Yet I believe that living in damaged times and in a damaged church is where God would have us be. “The hardest thing in the world is to be where we are” is Rowan Williams’s way to remind us that the time we have been given, our confusing and damaged time, is all the time we need to attend patiently to what seems to be the intractable and contingent problems that beset us. The name for that time, a name that has always been at the heart of Williams’s work, is ordinary time. Animating Williams’s work and ministry has been the conviction that through cross and resurrection we have been given the time, in a world that believes it has no time, to participate patiently in the conversation necessary for the discovery that we swim in the sea of God’s love.

To learn to live well in ordinary time requires the recognition that time, and the speech that constitutes time, is a gift. In *Lost Icons* Williams observes that we have been given speech so that we might learn to honor God through the recognition of our dependency on the “unchosen truths about the universe, and ultimately with the most comprehensive ‘fact’ of all, the *dependent* condition of the universe and everything in it.” Look at the birds of the air and consider the lilies of the field and see the love that moves the sun and the stars. Only such a love makes it possible to live where we are recognizing that today’s trouble is enough for today.

By calling attention to sheer gratuity of speech Williams is trying to help us recognize the miraculous character of ordinary time. For to live well in ordinary time is no easy achievement because we are tempted to the dramatic in the desperate attempt to make our lives significant if not heroic. We are the church of the martyrs, who Williams observes in *Christ on Trial*, overcame the imperatives of violence by paying the most dramatic cost imaginable. Compared to the martyrs Williams asks how can our lives, our ordinary lives, lives that will never have to face the violence the martyrs faced, express the truth that violence has been overwhelmed and silenced by Christ?

Williams argues that we cannot and should not try to make our lives more authentic by dramatic gestures. Rather we must learn to engage in everyday tasks as common as learning to speak the truth and, perhaps even more demanding, to hear the truth through the time-consuming work of conversation. For when we are no longer able to speak and hear the truth, language decays making it impossible to trust ourselves or our neighbor. We lose the ability, as Wendell Berry puts it, to “stand by our words.” But “if there is no presence in words,” Williams reminds us in *Lost Icons*, then there will be “no presence in speakers. If you can’t trust the contract between word and world, speech and what it’s trying to respond to, you can’t trust what you may think you perceive ‘within’ either.”

That we no longer trust ourselves or our language is the breeding ground of violence. Which means learning to speak the truth, learning to hear the truth, is the work of peace. It is hard and slow work requiring the overwhelming of the distrust of ourselves and one another. To be in conversation requires that we see ourselves with the eyes of others in a manner that our stance toward the world is put into question. It requires that "I have to face, and face down, my boredom, my expectation that the world will always give me satisfying roles to play. To put it more positively. I have to make an art of ordinary living."

The art of ordinary living, according to Williams, requires that we learn to live without fear of the complexity of everyday life. Learning to live with the complexity of everyday life means the church cannot fear having the conflicts necessary for peace. Moreover if the church is capable of such conflict the church cannot help but be deeply threatening to the world's systems of power based as they are on the fear of the other. A church constituted by peace, moreover, far from withdrawing from the world rather reveals that the world is the realm of the private. Therefore in contrast to the oft made suggestion that a commitment to nonviolence means the church must be apolitical, Williams argues in *The Truce of God*, it is the cloister which abandons the privacy of the world for "a solitude which forces people to confront their fear and evasiveness and so equips them for involvement by a stripping-down of the will."

The art of ordinary living as the art of learning to live with complexity obviously has implications for learning to live with the complexity of a confused and confusing church. In *Christ on Trial* Williams reports, having returned to England after working in the Anglican Church in South Africa for some months, he found he was overwhelmed by a nostalgia for the church he had left. In South Africa the central questions seemed clear. In South Africa you knew where you should stand because the choices seemed dramatically clear. Returning to Britain meant facing a context in which the central questions were not clear nor did one know what kind of "resistance" was possible or constructive. He was painfully aware that it was no easy task to translate what he had learned in South Africa into the "more confused and weary environment" of England.

Williams confesses that he longs for a church more true to itself. Such a church would be one more determined to oppose war, a church capable of offering hospitality to resident aliens who may be gay, a church that can challenge the economic practices that perpetuate poverty. Williams believes his desire for such a church is Godly yet he believes he

> must also learn to live in and attend to the reality of the Church *as it is*, to do the prosaic things that can be and must be done now and to work at my relations now with the people who will not listen to me or those like me – because what God asks of me is not to live in the future but to live with honesty and attentiveness in the present, i.e., to be at home. We constantly try to start from somewhere other than where we are. Truthful living involves being at home with

> ourselves, not complacently but patiently, recognizing that what we are today, at this moment, is sufficiently loved and valued by God to be the material with which he will work, and that the longed-for transformation will not come by refusing the love and the value that is simply *there* in the present moment. Living in the truth involves the same sober attention to what is there – to the body, the chair, the floor, the voice we hear, the face we see – with all the unsatisfactoriness that this brings. Yet this is what it means to live in the kingdom where Jesus rules, the kingdom that has no frontiers to be defended (*Christ on Trial*, pp. 85–6).

I suspect that some of you are beginning to think – this cannot be Stanley Hauerwas saying this. Is Hauerwas, who spent a life criticizing the complacent church, becoming mellow in his old age? Has becoming an Anglican given him the delusion that he is now part of the establishment? Is he going to do the unimaginable, that is, say something nice about liberals? Let me assure you I do not think I am becoming mellow, I have always been part of the establishment but I have tried not to justify that placement, and I am certainly not going to say anything nice about liberals. Yet it is my conviction that Archbishop Williams's understanding of the time in which we must live as Christians, of how we must live in the world as we find it, shares much with what I learned first from John Howard Yoder.

An Anabaptist and the Archbishop of Canterbury are, to be sure, an odd couple, but confusing times can help us discover friends we did not know we had. At the heart of Yoder's work has been the attempt to teach us the difficult task of living where we are. Yoder's defense of Christian nonviolence depends on an account of time very similar to that of Rowan Williams. For Christian pacifism does not promise to give us a warless world, but rather Christian pacifism depends on the presumption that in a world of war a people exist who have the time to engage in the slow and painful work of living in peace with one another.

They have the time to do such work because they have learned to sing:

> "You are worthy to take the scroll and to open its seals,
> for you were slaughtered and by your blood you ransomed for God
> saints from every tribe and language and people and nation,
> you have made them to be a
> kingdom and priests
> serving our God,
> and they will reign on earth."
>
> Revelation 5:9–10 (NRSV)

Yoder observes to "rule the world" in fellowship with the Lamb "will sometimes mean humbly building a grassroots culture, with Jeremiah.

Sometimes (as with Joseph and Daniel) it will mean helping the pagan king solve one problem at a time. Sometimes (again with Daniel and his friends) it will mean disobeying the king's imperative of idolatry, refusing to be bamboozled by the claims made for the emperor's new robe or his fiery furnace." We are able to live so in the time "where we are" because we believe to so live is the shape of the work of Christ.

Yoder points out that when Jesus washed the feet of his disciples he did not make a lasting contribution to the hygiene of Palestine. "Similarly, when Christians devote themselves to the care of the seriously ill, of the mentally retarded, of the unproductive aged, the fruitfulness of this service cannot be measured by any statistical index of economic efficacy." Rather the meaning of the deed is what it signifies, namely, in a damaged time and in a damaged church we have learned to live "where we are" because that is the way of peace. In short, we have been given all we need to endure.

Recently two of my friends were discussing the decision of one of them to make an "ecclesial transition" to another church. The friend who was arguing against making such a move pointed out that there are many rooms in God's kingdom. This elicited the response that while that is certainly true some of the rooms are better furnished than others. I think we are extremely fortunate to live in a church that is well furnished. We have all we need to live where we are. At the very least we have an Archbishop who exemplifies what it means to live patiently in time by refusing to let us isolate ourselves from one another. The name we give to that refusal is "communion."

The patience exemplified in the work and ministry of our Archbishop will also be required of you. You are going to spend most of your life dealing with the ordinary work of caring for the sick and dying, disputes between people who should know better, the failure of marriages, the child or youth who has done something really stupid, the celebration of a life of someone you do not like, questions of whether you still need an eight o'clock service for those who will not let go of Rite One. In short, you are going to live in ordinary time, undramatic time, in which your life will seem to dribble out one grain of sand at a time. But you will know where you are. You are in the time God has made possible, kingdom time, and the work you do is the peace of God. Be patient, practice word care, keep the conversation going, and may God help you even learn to love our damaged church which is the only hope we have if we are to endure this damaged time.

Index